Thesis Writer's Guide
Making an Argument in the Humanities and Social Sciences

人文与社会科学
学术论文写作指南

（汉英对照）

〔美〕迈克尔·E.查普曼 著　〔美〕桑凯丽 译

北京大学出版社
PEKING UNIVERSITY PRESS

著作权合同登记号　图字：01-2012-0598

图书在版编目(CIP)数据

人文与社会科学学术论文写作指南/(美)迈克尔·E.查普曼著；(美)桑凯丽译．—北京：北京大学出版社，2012.12
ISBN 978-7-301-21176-2

Ⅰ.①人… Ⅱ.①查…②桑… Ⅲ.①人文科学－论文－写作②社会科学－论文－写作　Ⅳ.①H052

中国版本图书馆 CIP 数据核字(2012)第 210366 号

Copyright Acknowledgments
Copyright © Michael E. Chapman 2011
All rights reserved. Photocopying, electronic storage or transmittal, or any other form of duplication of material covered by copyright requires written permission from the publisher.
Published in the People's Republic of China by Peking University Press.

书　　　　名：	人文与社会科学学术论文写作指南
著作责任者：	〔美〕迈克尔·E.查普曼　著　〔美〕桑凯丽　译
策划编辑：	赵学敏
责任编辑：	赵学敏
标准书号：	ISBN 978-7-301-21176-2/C·0797
出版发行：	北京大学出版社
地　　　址：	北京市海淀区成府路 205 号　100871
网　　　址：	http://www.pup.cn　新浪官方微博：@北京大学出版社
电子邮箱：	编辑部 zyjy@pup.cn　总编室 zpup@pup.cn
电　　　话：	邮购部 010-62752015　发行部 010-62750672　编辑部 010-62754934
印　刷　者：	三河市博文印刷有限公司
经　销　者：	新华书店
	650 毫米×980 毫米　16 开本　13.25 印张　180 千字
	2012 年 12 月第 1 版　2023 年 11 月第 7 次印刷
定　　　价：	35.00 元

未经许可，不得以任何方式复制或抄袭本书之部分或全部内容。
版权所有，侵权必究
举报电话：010-62752024　电子邮箱：fd@pup.cn

谨以此书献给我尊重的中国读者

Sincerely dedicated to my Chinese readers

目录

推荐序	8
译者序	12
引言	16
中文格式注意事项	20

通过头脑风暴形成一个论点 — 1

案例研究方法 — 2
- 选择一个主题 — 2
- 寻找—速读—二手资料 — 6
- 浏览档案 — 8

提出假说 — 8
- 确定论题，提出问题，尝试作答 — 10
- 建立概念论证 — 12
- 设计论文题目 — 12

开题报告的撰写 — 14
- 主题与论点 — 14
- 文献综述的三个用途 — 14
- 资料、方法论、大纲 — 16

搜集论据 — 19

资料 — 20
- 在线数据库 — 20
- 口述历史采访 — 22
- 影音资料和文物资料 — 24

闪击档案馆 — 26
- 出发之前 — 26
- 入馆之日 — 28
- 入馆之后 — 28
- 复印、拍照、遥控 — 30

侦查 — 34
- 跟着线索走 — 34
- 缺失的原始资料 — 34
- 核对事实 — 36

办公活动 — 36
- 文书工作 — 36
- 数字资料 — 38
- 电子表格 — 38

写作 — 43

文本置入 — 44
- 引言 — 46
- 引文 — 56
- 插入人物 — 62
- 驱逐被动语态 — 64

结构的精练 — 66
- 以段落为工作单位 — 66

CONTENTS

Preface	9
Translators' Foreword	13
Introduction	17
Note on Chinese Style	21
Brainstorming a Thesis	**1**
Case-Study Approach	**3**
Choose a Topic	3
Pull—and Speed-Read—Secondary Sources	7
Scan the Archives	9
Hypothesize	**9**
Identify a Problem, Ask a Question, Pose an Answer	11
Establish Proof of Concept	13
Design the Title	13
Writing a Proposal	**15**
Topic and Thesis	15
Historiography: Three Uses	15
Sources, Methodology, Outline	17
Gathering the Evidence	**19**
Sources	**21**
Online Databases	21
Oral History Interviews	23
Film and Material Culture	25
Blitzing an Archive	**27**
Before You Leave	27
On the Day	29
Once Inside	29
Photocopying, Photographing, Remote Control	31
Detection	**35**
Following Leads	35
What's Missing	35
Fact Checking	37
Office Work	**37**
Paperwork	37
Digital Material	39
Spreadsheets	39
Writing a Paper or Dissertation	**43**
Textual Immersion	**45**
Quotations	47
Citations	55
Plug in the Actors	61
Banish the Passive Voice	63
Structured Précis	**65**
Paragraphs as Work Units	65

脉络图	68
练习精练的技艺	70
润色的行文	**70**
学术写作风格	72
建构论证	80
打印—编辑—复查的循环	84
完成项目	**86**
反思	88
最后几个步骤	88

出版或发表	**93**
审稿时的同行评审	**94**
投稿	94
评审报告	96
修改和准备出版	98
专业道德	**100**
水分和抄袭	102
语法及格式的基本知识	**105**
十种最常见的写作方面的问题	**106**
句首的开场白	106
标准结构	108
逗号	108
破折号、空格	110
日期、数字	112
独立分词（动名词）从句	112
That/Which的用法	112
不完整的英文表达	114
代词的不搭配	114
称呼的首字母小写	114
大写字体和格式——美国视角下的示例	116
魔咒性的单词和短语	116
美式英文 vs. 英式英文	118
对东亚作者的写作建议	**120**
定冠词	120
MS-Word 2010 设置	**122**
修辞结构	**126**
有用——但经常弄错的词汇	**130**
参考文献	**138**
缩写词	**140**
案例	**142**
中文的引用和引证	**172**
如何进行历史研究	**178**
词汇表	**180**

Road Maps	67
Practice the Fine Art of Précis	69
Polished Prose	**71**
Scholarly Style	71
Building the Argument	81
Print–Edit–Review Cycle	85
Completing the Project	**87**
Introspection	87
Concluding Steps	89
Publishing an Article or Monograph	**93**
Peer Review Process	**95**
Submission	95
Reviewers' Reports	97
Revision and Pre-Press	99
Professional Ethics	**101**
Padding and Plagiarism	103
Grammar and Style Essentials	**105**
Ten Most Common Stylistic Problems	107
Opening Gambits	107
Standard Constructions	109
Commas	109
Dashes, Spacing	111
Dates, Numbers	113
Orphaned Participle (Gerund) Clauses	113
That/Which Usage	113
Fractured English	115
Pronoun Disagreement	115
Down-Style, Naming	115
Capitalization and Style—Examples from a U.S. Perspective	117
Anathemous Words and Phrases	117
American vs. British English	119
Tips for East Asian Writers	**119**
Definite Article	121
MS-Word 2010 Settings	**123**
Rhetorical Constructs	**127**
Useful—and Misused—Words	**131**
Bibliography	**139**
Abbreviations	**141**
Examples	**143**
Quoting and Citing in Chinese	**173**
Doing History	**179**
Glossary	**181**

推荐序

改革开放以来，中国各大学都越来越注重学术研究和学术论文的发表，一些学校还立志要在学术水准上赶超世界一流大学。这方面的进步是明显的。以本人所在的北京大学为例，从2001年到2010年的十年间，被SCI（Science Citation Index）收录的论文（以理、工、医论文为主），数量从2001年的1700余篇增加到了2010年的4700余篇，质量若以影响指数（Impact Factor）计算，则从不足1.0提升到了2.97。与此相对应，学科质量也有了明显提高。如果按照国际上22个学科的划分标准和评价指标（Essential Science Indicators），十年前北大只有4个学科能够进入全球最好的1%，而如今已经达到了17个，排名顺序也在快速前移。但是，研究北大我们也发现，在北大具有传统优势的人文社科的论文发表，特别是在国际学术界的影响力，其进步好像不如理、工、医学科明显。这是为什么呢？迈克尔·E.查普曼的这本《人文与社会科学学术论文写作指南》或许已经给出了答案。

迈克尔·E.查普曼目前在北京大学任教。正如他所观察到的：亚洲国家的论文更倾向于堆砌资料而非解释性分析，而一篇论文应该是有关一个论题的探讨。他说："论文作者在学术意义上等同于辩护律师。换句话说，一篇论文，无论是博士学位论文还是期刊文章，如果没有明确的论点就不值得被授予学位或得到出版的机会。"

学术论文是学术研究物质化、社会化的载体，它使知识得以跨越时空广泛传播，穿越古今而源远流长，是科研的重要组成部分，集创造、传播、传承、应用于一体。作为严肃的研究性写作，学术论文因学科领域不同而拥有各自独特的写作规范和评定标准。学术论文的写作标准与国际接轨，不仅可以通过比照，自省学业训练的得失，反思国际人才培养经验的优势与不足，而且有利于将自身的学术研究成果推向国际，使更多成果得以在国际期刊上发表，让更多学术精英能够在世界舞台之上一展风采。

迈克尔·E.查普曼先生是历史系副教授，国际关系史专家。他生于英国，在美国接受了历史学的学科训练，对于英式英语和美式英语，以及英国和美国的学术规范都有着切身的体验。现已出版几部专著和许多期刊论文，包括他最新的 *Arguing Americanism: Franco Lobbyists, Roosevelt's Foreign Policy, and the Spanish Civil War*（《再论美国主义：弗朗哥政府游说者，罗斯福的外

PREFACE

Since China's 1978 opening and reform, Chinese universities have placed increasing value on scholastic research and publication; some institutions even aspire to surpass the global best universities in the realm of academic standards. Progress has been obvious. Taking my own institution Peking University as an example, in the decade from 2001 to 2010, the annual number of local publications recorded in the Science Citation Index (SCI) (which centers on science, technology, and medical works) has increased from 1700 in 2001 to 4700 in 2010; furthermore, the impact factor of these works has also increased from less than 1.0 to 2.97. Correspondingly, the quality of our academic departments has also clearly risen. If we limit our argument to twenty-two Essential Science Indicators, internationally recognized indices for standardizing and critiquing academic endeavors, ten years ago only four of Peking University's departments could have been considered among the top one percent in the world, while today this number has risen to seventeen, with rapid progress in ranking order. Nevertheless, upon investigating Peking University's case, we also discover that even our traditionally excellent humanities and social science departments have made less than ideal progress toward increasing the influence of their publications on global academia; their growth seems to be less clear than that of the science, engineering, and medical departments. Why is this? Perhaps Michael E. Chapman's *Thesis Writer's Guide* has provided an answer.

Michael Chapman is currently a professor at Peking University. Just as he has observed, the academic papers of Asian countries tend toward repositories of data rather than interpretive analyses. But a paper should be a deep discussion of an argumentative thesis. He says: "Thesis writers are the scholarly equivalent of trial lawyers. To put it another way, a thesis, dissertation, or journal article that does not make an argument is unworthy of a degree or publication."

Academic papers are the materialized and socialized vehicles of scholastic inquiry; as such, they allow knowledge to broadcast widely across time and link the ancient with the current. They are a most important component of academia, bringing together the processes of creating, transmitting, and preserving knowledge into one material object. As the formal products of research, academic papers, owing to the differences among various disciplines, possess a variety of rules and standards of review. The alignment of these standards with international practices not only enables the introspective training of professional academic writers and honest review of the strengths and weaknesses of their cultivation as international scholars, but it also benefits the submission of academic results to the world, making more of our country's scholarship worth publishing and enabling more of our academic elites to stand atop the global stage.

交政策和西班牙内战》);其有关"九一八"事变的论文 *Fidgeting Over Foreign Policy: Henry L. Stimson and the Shenyang Incident, 1931*(《外交政策上的焦躁:亨利·L.斯廷森和"九一八"事变》)亦即将在美国顶级期刊 *Diplomatic History*(《外交史》)上发表。

  由他执笔的该书可以作为人文学科和社会科学领域论文写作的入门教材。该书的实用性和可读性都很强。全文涉及了从提出问题、寻找线索、搜集资料、明确论点、正式写作到文本编辑等学术论文从构思成文到出版或发表的各个环节;逻辑清晰,简明扼要,深入浅出,并附有大量生动的语汇和作者自身的研究案例。我相信,对本书的精确理解和系统应用将大大提高人文学科和社会科学领域的研究者向国际一流期刊投稿的命中几率,也是有意出版研究专著,尤其是英语研究专著的研究者的必备工具读物。在此特向大家郑重推荐。

  学术规范乃学科安身立命之本,厚积薄发之基,希望本书能够像《新华字典》之于初识文断字的小学生一般,成为有志于学术的文科同学的案头必备,得以随时翻阅;更希望各位能善用本书,严守学术规范,维护学术尊严,严明学术纪律,勇攀学术高峰。

周其凤
北京大学校长,2012年

Michael Chapman is an associate professor of history and scholar of international relations. Born in England and trained as a historian in the United States, he has firsthand experience with the linguistic and the academic practices of both countries. He has published several books and monographs, including his latest *Arguing Americanism: Franco Lobbyists, Roosevelt's Foreign Policy, and the Spanish Civil War*, as well as several articles, including his latest "Fidgeting Over Foreign Policy: Henry L. Stimson and the Shenyang Incident, 1931" on the September 18 Shenyang incident, to be published in the leading American journal *Diplomatic History*.

His book *Thesis Writer's Guide* is a fundamental source of study for students in the humanities and social sciences. It offers highly applicable and readable advice on every step of preparing and producing an academic paper, from developing a research question, searching for evidentiary leads, and collecting data, to clarifying a thesis, formally composing an argument, and finally editing your work. Its logic is clear and its style concise, with heady concepts explained in simple terms, using rich vocabulary and an abundance of personal anecdotes throughout. I believe that the precise understanding and systematic implementation of this system will greatly enhance the international standing of researchers in the humanities and social sciences, as well as increase the viability of their works before international publications. The book is a must-read for anyone who wishes to publish his or her research in English, and I earnestly recommend it to everyone.

Academic standards are the lifeblood of a discipline and the foundation of a solid education; therefore, I hope this book may become as fundamental a resource among students as the Xinhua Dictionary is to elementary school students learning to read, with a copy in the hand of every scholar with aspirations in the humanities to be browsed at will. I especially hope that everyone is able to apply this book to the fullest, respecting academic standards, protecting academic dignity, firmly and fairly upholding academic law, and bravely paving the way for new academic breakthroughs.

ZHOU QIFENG, PRESIDENT, PEKING UNIVERSITY, 2012

译者序

　　入乡随俗。

　　在翻译《人文与社会科学学术论文写作指南》的过程中，一直体现着这句中国俗话的意义。随着我和本书编辑者对这个任务的努力，我们越来越远离于美式英语读者的文化领域，而走向一个居住着十多亿中文读者的"村庄"。为了得到这些读者的信任并吸引他们的兴趣，我们就需要学会这里的习俗——就是说，学会用谈话性的方式，清楚地、地地道道地表达自己——尽管这样做就需要我们把作者的一部分初衷抛弃在"村庄"门外。

　　但是这个初衷——就是传播本书作者所认为的经过时间考验的、值得推广的研究、争论和陈述的方法与中国读者的语言和写作风格习惯之间的不同，甚至矛盾，正是我们企图进入这个"村庄"的根本理由。本书作者在前言中坦承，中国学术界好像缺乏一种创作严肃学术作品所需要的充满自信、直截了当、简练的争论方式，这个现象成为他创作《人文与社会科学学术论文写作指南》中文版的一部分动力。可能中国学者确实不习惯于本书英文版在各种层面所体现的直接而且简练的陈述形式，即直率的简介、直接的命令，还有单词的节省使用。中国读者或许更习惯于以第三人称虚心地提供其看法、以常见的"请"字来装饰命令性的句子，并且往往以"比如说"这个短语来作为证据内容开头。怎么解决这个问题呢？

　　我们的答案是，找到遵循中国"村庄"的习俗和传播美式英语传统之间的中间方法。这个平衡是通过与我的同事邹皓丹的不断积极讨论才得到的——我，努力维持对原文的忠诚，而邹皓丹则尽力使其符合中文阅读习惯。在此，感谢邹皓丹对本书的翻译工作给予的巨大帮助。我们希望对彼此作品的无数次重写和更改能产生一本体现作者的原意但又不显得完全奇怪的书籍。为此，在我们偶尔决定违反一些中文习惯并也许令中国读者有点不舒服的时候，该决定确实是经过了谦虚的犹豫后作出的。例如，我们选择保持原文的脚注页码格式"p.42"而没有改成中文的标准格式"第42页"，因为p.和pp.的用法就是本书着意说明的观点。我们也尽量减少"请"这个词在直接命令中的使用，因为本书反复提到简练写作方式的重要性。其他的与中文传统的差别还很多，大部分会在《中文格式注意事项》中明确谈到。

TRANSLATORS' FOREWORD

When entering a village, follow its customs.

This Chinese proverb's implications have never been far from the translation of *Thesis Writer's Guide*. As the editors and I strove to render Michael E. Chapman's book in a different language, we left the cultural territory of American English readers and stepped into a village of more than a billion Chinese ones, whose trust we needed to gain and interest we needed to attract. Imperative in this endeavor was learning to follow the customs of the village—or expressing ourselves as conversationally, clearly, and natively as possible—even at the cost of leaving behind some of Chapman's original intent at the gates.

But the difference, even antagonism, between this original intent—namely, to pass on a method of research, argumentation, and exposition that Chapman deems time-tested and worthy of dissemination—and the linguistic and stylistic customs of our Chinese readers, is precisely the reason that we attempted to gain access to the village in the first place. Chapman explains in his introduction that he decided, in part, to write a Chinese edition of *Thesis Writer's Guide* after observing a lack of confidence, directness, and concise argumentation in Chinese scholarship, which he feels are essential today. But if Chinese academics are indeed unused to the frank and parsimonious exposition exemplified on so many levels in the book's English edition, with its plainly stated judgments, direct commands, and economy of words, then how were we to render it in Chinese without offending the sensibilities of readers accustomed to scholars who humbly offer their thoughts in the third person, decorate imperative sentences with the frequent *please*, and rarely fail to precede evidence with the often superfluous words *for example*?

Our answer was to cultivate a middle ground between following the customs of the Chinese village and proselytizing the traditions of our own, a balance that we struck by constant and lively dialogue between the book's two translators—I striving for loyalty to the author's original messages and my colleague Zou Haodan, whose editing efforts deserve special mention and thanks, stressing comfort of use by Chinese readers. Only through scores of rewrites and reconfigurations of each other's work have we created a product that, we hope, embodies Chapman's lessons without sounding alien to our readers. To this end, when we did choose to break from custom at the risk of discomforting our Chinese audience, it was not without humble reluctance and always for good reason. We chose to keep the original footnote pagination format (p. 42) rather than changing it to the standard Chinese format (第42页) because the use of p. and pp. is a point specifically discussed in the guide. We strove to minimize the use of *please* in direct commands because the importance of concise style is also emphasized throughout the book. Other deviations from Chinese tradition abound, most of which the Note on Chinese Style addresses.

Still, the final balance we achieved is imperfect. Some readers will com-

虽然如此，我们最终所得到的平衡无疑仍不完美。有的读者会抱怨，本书中文版没有充分地体现作者所提倡的写作风格，而有的读者则会埋怨它离学术性中文写作的习惯太远。欢迎对这些或其他方面不满的读者把评论、建议和疑问发给我们（swanberg@post.harvard.edu）。我们带着开放的心态，进入这个"村庄"来了，在传播自己的传统的同时，也做好了向中国习俗学习的准备。

桑凯丽
2012年

plain that the Chinese inadequately exemplifies the style Chapman advocates, while others will judge it to be uncomfortably distant from convention. Readers dissatisfied by these or other aspects of the work are welcome to send their comments, suggestions, and questions to swanberg@post.harvard.edu. After all, it is not without open ears and open minds that we have entered your village, ready to learn from its customs even while passing on our own.

Kelley Swanberg, 2012

引　言

如果你希望撰写出一篇符合国际公认标准的、高品质的、具有突破性的、有深度的本科论文、硕士学位论文、博士学位论文或者期刊论文，无论是以中文、英文还是其他语言来撰写，我皆保证本指南将适用于你。我的视角是从一个历史学研究者的眼光出发，所以我所列举的案例自然皆来源于我进行历史研究的经验，而并非来源于诸如哲学等其他领域。不过，我所论述的这套方法也同样适用于与历史学有关的学科领域，例如民族志学、国际关系学或文学，还适用于从政治学到社会学这些会使用其他引用方式的社会科学领域。尽管我于1954年生于英国，但于2002—2006年在美国求学并受到专业训练。之所以提到这一点，是因为从20世纪90年代开始，在改良以引语段、被动态和轻浅的立论著称的欧洲模式的基础上形成的这套美式方法，其论证过程更加主动、文本分析更加深入、立论更加有说服力。此外，比起在欧洲、印度和亚洲的学校所教授的英式英语，美式英语因其在连贯性与精确性方面具有优势，目前正成为最具权威的国际学术期刊和出版社的标准语言。

我在中国的同事越来越感到亚洲国家的论文更倾向于堆砌资料而不是作解释性分析，故而促请我出版这本指南以纠错。事实上，我深有同感。最近在北京大学研究生的讨论班里，我问学生们："什么是论文呢？"其中一个回答："我的论题。"另一个补充说："我的研究工作。"当他们发现字典中关于"论文"的解释是"一篇论文是以论证的形式提出的论点"时，感到很惊讶。确实，一篇论文是有关一个论题的探讨，并且呈现了作者的研究，但它同时也解读研究资料，以便把事实当做论据。论文作者在学术意义上等同于辩护律师。换句话说，一篇论文，无论是博士学位论文还是期刊文章，如果没有明确的论点就不值得被授予学位或得到出版的机会。

考虑到本指南的易用性和对于非英语国家读者的可读性，我把本书分为通过头脑风暴形成一个论点、搜集论据、写作和出版四个部分，每一部分再细分任务，然后再细分，直到差不多能够用一段来表述一个关键问题的程度。我感到抱歉的是，如此划分产生内容重复将无可避免，但是很多关键性的观点是值得被反复强调的。我的阅读建议是：先略读本指南，然后根据自身研究的项目、研究方法和研究进度，反过来再进行有选择的各部分的精读。在研究过程中，每年最好都要重读一遍本指南，因为实践可能会使得以前不懂的内容越来越清楚明晰。

INTRODUCTION

If you intend to produce a high-quality, groundbreaking senior research paper, graduation thesis, MA thesis, PhD dissertation, or journal article, whether in English, Chinese, or any other language, and in conformity with internationally-recognized standards, then this guide is for you. My perspective happens to be that of a historian, so naturally I will draw examples from my experience of doing history rather than, say, philosophy. Yet the system I describe applies just as well to related disciplines like ethnography, international relations, or literary studies, as well as to most social sciences fields from political science to sociology that may use alternative styles of citation. While I was born in Britain in 1954, I trained most recently in the United States during 2002—2006; I mention this because since the 1990s American historiography has improved on the European model characterized by multi-sentence quotations, passive voice, and understated argumentation to create expositions that are more textually immersive, actor driven, and argumentative. As distinct from the British English taught in European, Indian, and Asian schools, American English furthermore offers benefits of flow and precision, and is now normative at leading journals and publishing houses worldwide.

Colleagues in China urged me to publish this guide from a concern that Asian theses had become repositories of information rather than interpretive analyses. Indeed, at a recent graduate seminar at Peking University's history department, I asked my PhD students, "What is a thesis?" to which one replied, "My topic," and another added, "My research." They were surprised to hear the standard dictionary definition: "A thesis is *a proposition advanced as an argument*." Yes, a thesis is about a topic, and, for sure, it does present research, but it interprets that research as evidence to build a case. Thesis writers are the scholarly equivalent of trial lawyers. To put it another way, a thesis, dissertation, or journal article that does not make an argument is unworthy of a degree or publication.

For ease of use, as well as readability by non-native English speakers, I have divided the process of brainstorming, gathering the evidence, writing, and publishing a thesis into four chapters, each of which I subdivide into tasks, and subdivide again virtually at the paragraph level into important points I wish to make. All this dividing has inevitably created duplication, for which I apologize, although the more crucial points bear restatement. I recommend skimming this guide at the outset, then returning to it in detail, a section here, a section there, as your project—and expertise—progresses. Re-read the guide each year of your program because concepts that might not make sense now will soon become clear.

请允许我给欧洲和北美以外的研究者一个建议。在亚洲和南美的社会科学研究领域，只有为数不多的毕业生用英文发表他们的成果。我希望本指南将给予你们用英文写作的信心，因为如此一来你会进入一个更广阔的学术领域，并在自己的同道中出类拔萃。随着研究质量的提高，你的研究将得到与之相应的国际认可，你所在的研究机构将会声名鹊起，从而提高你的学位的含金量。不过，我在中国大学的两年教学经验使我意识到了其中所面临的困难，并使我意识到其实我的一些建议，尤其是有关图书馆手续和档案查询的建议，在当前是不可行的。但是假使有足够的学生和教师有志于改进，我相信并期待，在本指南出版后的几年时间里，通过馆际互借得到一本书或者一个缩微胶卷，将不再需要支付一笔很高的费用；浏览开架书库和政府档案或者查阅丰富的网络在线资料，将不需要再进行付费。

学者在使用专业术语时未必十分严格，比如可能会交替使用"引证"、"引用"和"脚注"。请翻阅本书附注的词汇表，以免混淆以上专业术语。为了避免正文中遍布着零碎的案例，我将全书中用以说明关键概念和方法的案例汇总为独立的案例部分；其中许多案例都来源于我自己的写作成果，之所以如此，并非由于我骄矜自满，而是为了避免知识产权的纠纷。

假如你对本指南将来的第二次印刷有任何问题或看法，或者你发现我之前并未注意到的错误，敬请致函 m4chapman@verizon.net 予以告知。

我要对以下人士表示衷心感谢：我充满悟性的学生，评论这本书最初版本的人，特别是罗伯特·尼布尔（Robert Niebuhr）、钟逸明、桑凯丽（Kelley M. Swanberg）和邹皓丹，以及买到此指南的你。亲爱的读者——我希望它能够对你有所帮助。

迈克尔·E. 查普曼

北京大学副教授

2012年

A note, if I may, for researchers and writers outside Europe and North America. Few social sciences graduates in Asia and South America present their work in English. I hope this guide gives you the confidence to do so because you will then be able to reach a far larger scholarly universe, while distinguishing yourself from other graduates. As the quality of your work improves and it receives the international recognition it deserves, so the prestige of your institution will rise, thereby increasing the value of your degree. Still, having spent the last two years teaching at a Chinese university, I am well aware of the bureaucratic hurdles and institutional inertia you face, and that some of my recommendations, particularly regarding library procedures and archival accessibility, are inappropriate. But providing sufficient students and faculty lobby for improvements, I am optimistic that within a few years of this guide's publication, it will be possible to request a book or roll of microfilm from interlibrary loan without paying a hefty fee, or browse through open stacks of books and government documents, or quickly access a rich array of online databases without a charge.

Academics are not always rigorous in their use of professional terms, interchanging, say, *citation*, *reference*, and *footnote*, so to avoid confusion please consult the glossary at the end of the guide. Rather than fill the main chapters with clutter, I have included samples of work that illustrate key concepts and styles in a separate Examples section; several of the samples are my own work, not from egotism but to simplify copyright issues.

If you have questions or suggestions for enhancements to the second printing, or if you spot errors that have slipped my attention then please email: m4chapman@verizon.net.

My sincerest thanks to my students for your insights; to those who provided feedback on early drafts, particularly Robert Niebuhr, Cheng Yimeng, Kelley Swanberg and Zou Haodan; and to you, dear reader, for buying this guide—I hope you find it useful.

MICHAEL E. CHAPMAN,
ASSOCIATE PROFESSOR,
PEKING UNIVERSITY, 2012

中文格式注意事项

在19世纪，学者为补充中文标点句号"。"和顿号"、"的不足而增加了引号和其他符号的时候，不但借用了英式符号，而且保留了一些必需的本土传统。例如，英式符号以斜体字表达概念的方法虽然很容易在罗马字体环境下得到应用、在中文字体的环境下却显得不切实际，因此没有采纳斜体字形式，而是保留了中文传统。正如英式和美式标点体系的差别导致了环大西洋地区的符号混乱一样，中文使用地区由于标点发展而引起的不同格式习惯也导致了环太平洋地区的格式混乱，这种情况无论是在本科一年级论文的写作还是出版学术作品方面都有所体现。在谈到英语的标点用法时，本书遵照的是《芝加哥论文格式手册》所倡导的美式英语格式系统，即人文学科和社会科学领域撰写正式英语文章的实际国际通用标准。按照《芝加哥论文格式手册》的要求，本指南强调在中文写作时标点格式简化和一致化的必要性，不过却没有遵照香港的普遍趋势，即在写作时使用英文句号"."而不用中文的"。"，或者使用英文的逗号","而不是中文的顿号"、"。

在本指南的中文文本中有以下几点需要说明。

- 书名号标注的斜体字标示任何出版作品名称，包括电影片名。[1] 例如：
  我将探讨王岱的《雅典共和国》。
  I will discuss *The Athenian Republic*, by Wang Dai.[2]
- 书名号标示英语书写时以斜体字、罗马字体显示的内容。例如：
  我将探讨王岱的《柏拉图〈理想国〉的历史》。
  I will discuss *The History of Plato's* Republic, by Wang Dai.
- 所有逗号和句号都被置于引号中，无论它们是否是原文的一部分（只有在添加冒号、分号或者问号时，才要把这些符号放在引号外）。[3] 例如：

  [原文] 亨利·戴维·梭罗（1849年）："直到国家认可个体的更高层级的、独立的力量，并意识到个体力量是国家权力和权威的来源，并且给予个体相应的待遇，否则，它永远不会成为一个自由并开明的国家。"
  [隐含性引言] 梭罗相信一个进步着的社会取决于国家是否认可"个

---

1. 根据中文惯例，本书中文部分的书名号也用于未出版作品名称，但美国正式英语规范中仅用于已出版作品。——编者注
2. 为了简化，假设本书中作为案例所提到的作品同时存在英语和中文两种版本。
3. 根据中文惯例，本书中文正文部分的逗号和句号将根据需要调整，并非都置于引号中。英语惯例请遵循英语部分的表述。——编者注

NOTE ON CHINESE STYLE

During the nineteenth century, when scholars added quotation and other marks to supplement the Chinese period "。" and comma "、" they adopted British-style punctuation, along with homegrown conventions to express concepts such as italicization, which is easy to implement with Romanized script but impractical with Chinese characters. Just as disparate British and American punctuation systems have created a stylistic muddle across the Atlantic, so the different conventions that evolved in greater China have created confusion around the Pacific, whether in freshman essays or published scholarly works. For English usage, this guide adheres to the American-English system advocated by the *Chicago Manual of Style*, the de-facto global standard for writing formal English in the humanities and social sciences. In line with *Chicago*, the Chinese text in this guide emphasizes the necessity for both simplicity and consistency of style, although it stops short of the trend in Hong Kong of using the English period "." instead of the Chinese one "。", or the English comma "," instead of the Chinese enumeration mark "、" for items in a list.

In the Chinese text throughout this guide:
- double angle-brackets enclose italicized text for any published work, including film titles:
  我将探讨《雅典共和国》，王岱。
  I will discuss *The Athenian Republic*, by Wang Dai.[1]
- single angle-brackets nest roman within italicized script:
  我将探讨《柏拉图〈理想国〉的历史》，王岱。
  I will discuss *The History of Plato's* Republic, by Wang Dai.
- all commas and periods go inside quotation marks, irrespective of whether they were part of the original quote (on the rare occasion when the author adds a colon, semicolon, or question mark these go outside the quotation marks).
  [original text] Henry David Thoreau (1849): "There will never be a really free and enlightened State, until the State comes to recognize the individual as a higher and independent power, from which all its own power and authority are derived, and treats him accordingly."
  [embedded quotation] Thoreau believed that a progressive society depended on the state recognizing "the individual as a higher and independent power."
- two of these —— designate an em-dash rather than a single iteration of this symbol —.
- these square bracket symbols ［文明的冲突］ enclose changes to quota-

---

1. For the sake of simplicity with these examples, I am assuming that the books exist as published works in both English and Chinese editions.

体更高层级的、独立的力量。"
- 用"——"表示破折号，而非这个符号"—"。
- 美国正式英语中用方括号［文明的冲突］，而非【文明的冲突】，标示着引言或者翻译标题的更改。[1]
- 为求行文明确，在中文译文中，外国人名以"·"形式被分隔开来。

---

[1] 根据中文惯例，本书中文部分用引号或单独成段等方式标示引言，用括号里加书名号的方式标示翻译标题的更改。——编者注

tions or translated titles, instead of 【文明的冲突】.
- for clarity, this middle dot symbol · separates personal names translated into Chinese.

通过头脑风暴形成一个论点
BRAINSTORMING A THESIS

2 通过头脑风暴形成一个论点

学生经常问这样一个问题:"我甚至连研究都没开始,怎么可能形成一个论点?"确实,你的论点是你研究的产物,但花六个月时间钻研档案再花一年写论文,最后才意识到你的论文没有可以证明的论点,将是浪费时间的悲剧。所谓的"头脑风暴"的方法,将指导你形成一个实验性的论点或者科学用语上所谓的"有可操作性的假设",从而形成开题报告的中心思想,为初始阶段的研究提供方向,并且成为你的最终论证,尽管很可能随着研究的深入,你将抛弃它,转而提出更具说服力的论点。但是我必须强调:一篇没有论点陈述的硕士或者博士学位论文的开题报告就不算开题报告;不要在没有论点之前就仓促开始研究。本章首先将概要地论述你研究中所需要运用的案例研究的方法,然后解释怎样确认你的论文所要回答的问题,怎样达到工程师所谓的"概念论证",最后提供一篇在研究初级阶段所需要的开题报告的模板。

案例研究方法

一篇理想的研究性文章——无论是一篇30页的期刊文章还是一篇300页的博士学位论文——都需运用案例研究的方法。尽管整篇文章都是关于一个给定的主题,但是围绕主题论述大量的细节从而使得非专业人士也能够了解上下文内容是论文必须做到的。当然,论文的大部分内容是在整理、检验、分析该主题的一系列分论题。在此过程中,需要通过论证一个案例来支持一个狭义的、微调的、有创意的论点。同时,该论点还将提供一个广义的总体论证平台。因此,你的论文将呈现一个聚焦并且充满细节的研究,它以第一手资料为基础,但也暗含着更为广阔的考量。

选择一个主题

很有可能你会被动进入而非主动选择一个主题。也很有可能该主题来源于你先前从事研究过程中得到的结果。虽然主题的选择与一篇论文的质量或者论点不甚相关,但是鉴于所选主题的可行性,以下相关的四项是在选择过程中一定要考量的,即兴趣、资料来源、奖学金和职业前景。第一,你会花费几年的时间完成你的研究,所以你最好对它感兴趣;因为没有指导就不可能完成研究,所以你的主题也最好能引起你的导师和读者的兴趣。第二,如果你有掌握乃至翻译第二外语或者第三外语的能力,那么你的研究主题或许可以基于一些国外档案馆的馆藏。同样的,位于你所在大学或者家乡附近的档案馆馆藏也可能会因其便利而引起你的注意。第

"How can I possibly have a thesis when I have not even started my research," students often ask. For sure, your thesis will be a product of your research, but it would be a tragic waste of time to spend six months in the archives and a year writing a dissertation only to realize that you had not made an argument, let alone proven one. Through a process of what I call *brainstorming*, you will be able to formulate a tentative argument, or *working hypothesis* in scientific parlance, which will form the centerpiece of your proposal, guide your initial research, and develop into your final argument, although it may be that you will discard it in favor of a stronger thesis once your research is underway. But I must stress: an MA or PhD proposal without a thesis statement is not a proposal; do not begin to work in earnest until you have one. This chapter first outlines the case-study approach that your research will take, it then explains how to identify a question that your thesis will answer, and how to arrive at what engineers refer to as a *proof of concept*, and it finishes by providing a template for the essential preliminary step of writing a proposal.

CASE-STUDY APPROACH

An ideal research paper—from a thirty-page journal article to a 300-page dissertation—takes a case-study approach. While it will be about a given topic or theme, which of necessity you will need to detail sufficiently for a non-specialist reader to grasp the context, what the bulk of the paper will actually do is to document, examine, and analyze a subset of that topic. In the process, it will argue a case that supports a narrow, finely tuned, and original thesis, but, at the same time, your thesis should address a much larger, overarching argument. Your paper, then, should present a focused, detailed account of your research, based on primary-source documents, yet one that speaks to a big-picture concern.

Choose a Topic

It is more likely that you will have fallen into rather than chosen a topic. It is probable, too, that it will be an outgrowth from a previous project, in the course of which you acquired expertise. Although the topic has little bearing on a paper's quality or argument, it is advisable to consider the practical implications of your choice, on the four related grounds of interest, sources, grants, and career. First, you will devote several years to the project so it should interest you, and because you cannot complete it without guidance, it should also interest your advisor and readers. Second, if you have acquired translation proficiency in a second or third language then your topic may be contingent on research in particular foreign archives. Similarly, archival sources located conveniently close to your university or hometown may have

三,你或许需要一笔奖学金或补助金,而且一些特定的主题,例如和平研究、环境研究、国家建设等,更容易使你获得金额更高的资金。第四,你的研究主题很可能决定你的职业前景,但是,事先预知热门领域是不容易的,除非你拥有一个具有魔力的水晶球。"9·11"以后,刚入行的伊斯兰历史研究者具有广泛的需求,但是他们十多年前选择研究阿拉伯语时并不能预知十年后的情景。

你的研究主题无疑关系到或者起源于你所选择的研究领域或方法论。这个选择一定基于你的个人背景;许多军事史研究者曾经是士兵、许多非裔美国人史研究者为黑种人、许多妇女史研究者为女性,还有许多劳工史研究者为社会主义者的存在,证明了这个现象。也许可以说,如果身为白种人的研究者研究非裔奴隶史,身为蒙古人种的研究者研究拉美史,信奉天主教徒的研究者研究同性恋,在研讨会发表论文时或者申请教授职位时其研究可信度会被打了折扣。但是,难道与本人背景相悖的研究主题就不具有实践价值吗?优秀的历史学研究总是呈现事实客观性。批评家就不会轻易谴责日本学者对爱尔兰移民的研究、俄罗斯学者对非洲人口外流的研究具有个人偏见。而且,优秀的历史学研究皆基于独创的论点,与研究对象保持适当的学术距离可能会使得你更容易发掘这样的论点。总之,尽管你所选择的研究主题是部分地基于现实的考量,请不要对此有太多利害得失的判断——省下这些脑力加强理论才是正道。

请允许我强调比较研究、跨国研究,还有方法论、意识形态,甚至心理学在确定主题中的重要作用。研究机构——确切地说,其中的论文导师和学术委员们——为自身的历史研究套上了死板的枷锁,使其具有国家和时代的局限性,比如说宋代的中国或者殖民地时代的美国。虽然这种分门别类的研究无疑有助于学术专门化的发展,但它却妨碍了,或者至少复杂化了,有意义而且有意思的比较性研究。即使在一个既定的范畴内,要么通过方法论的应用、思想意识的变化,要么通过对中心人物之间因果关系的不同解释,即通过横向多样化都可以拓宽研究的范围。比如对宋代徽宗皇帝的研究可以以奢侈和消费主义为切入点;对殖民时代美国的研究可以以贵格会教徒的分立为切入点;研究第二次世界大战时期加拿大的外交政策,可以以首相威廉·莱昂·麦肯齐·金的心理活动为切入点,以便研究首相与灵异世界的沟通是如何影响其决策的。

brought a topic to your attention. Third, you may well need a scholarship or a grant, and certain topics—peace research, environmental studies, state building—attract deeper pockets. Fourth, your topic will define your career path, but predicting hot-button fields years in advance requires a crystal ball. Newly minted scholars of Islamic history were in high demand after 9/11, but they could not have foreseen this situation a decade earlier when they elected to study Arabic.

Your topic will no doubt mesh with or derive from your chosen field or methodology, to which you have gravitated on personal grounds; so many scholars of military history were once soldiers, of African American history are Black, of women's history are female, or of labor history are socialists to suggest otherwise. It may be that white historians of African slavery, or Mongolian historians of Latin America, or Catholic historians of homosexuality suffer a credibility gap when they present conference papers or apply for faculty positions. And yet, consider whether a counter-field topic would have practical merit. Good history, after all, posits objectivism. Critics would think twice before charging a Japanese scholar of Irish immigration or a Russian scholar of the African diaspora with personal bias. Good history, furthermore, depends on an original argument, and you are more likely to find one if you can keep your academic distance. So while your choice of topic does have practical considerations, do not obsess about it—save your mental energy for developing the argument.

A plea, if I may, for comparative and transnational approaches, as well as methodology, ideology, and even psychology as topic determinants. Institutions—thesis advisors and hiring committees, more to the point—cling to rigid boxes in which to study history, constructed around national boundaries and chronological eras, such as Song China or colonial America. While this pigeonholing doubtless creates specialized scholarship, it tends to preclude, or at least complicate, what are often valuable and interesting comparative studies. But even within a given box, there should be scope for lateral diversification, whether through the methods you employ, the ideologies you investigate, or the causation you attribute to your actors' agency. A study of Song China's Emperor Huizong could hinge on the topic of luxury and consumption; a study of colonial America might have for its topic the Quaker schism; a study of World War II-era Canadian foreign relations might take the psychology of Prime Minister William Lyon Mackenzie King as its topic to analyze how King's communing with the spirit world through séances affected his policymaking.

6 通过头脑风暴形成一个论点

寻找—速读—二手资料

二手资料可以为你的研究提供切入点和关于档案馆藏的认识。正如有关浮游生物活动性的科学研究是建立在过去海洋生物学一系列研究的基础上一样,你的文章将建立在其他历史学者研究的基础上,并将丰富历史学研究。即使确认了与你的研究计划最相关的一系列前人成果,但还需要去图书馆。如果是一个好的图书馆,就会有开架书库。在抽出一本特定的书之前,先用几分钟浏览下周围的书架,特别注意那些崭新的、没有磨损书脊的书,因为那表明此书属于最新的研究成果。这样一来,你会发现比你预期目标更有价值的书籍,它可能是你在在线目录中通过关键词搜索所无法找到的。速读,包含了两种基本技巧,将帮助你评价所找到书籍的价值。

要在两个半钟头内读完一本大概有280页的常见学术专著,就要从前言和致谢读起,因为它们会提示你作者的个人背景、学术导师、经济资助来源和其他与本书视角相关的因素。一般来讲,读引言的时候,特别注意论点陈述,然后读其结语。对于每一章,先读引言部分,然后读主体部分各段落的首句,只有在该段看起来特别重要或者吸引你的情况下,才继续阅读该段落主要内容。阅读时,要做笔记或者眉批,或者既做笔记又做眉批。我的习惯是,简单地用铅笔在正文的外边缘画垂线用于眉批,用双线标注关键,用星号标注概念。速读最好在上午,而不是刚吃了饭以后,可以喝一点含有咖啡因的饮料,并保持专注。这是一个痛苦但有效的过程;如果开始后半个钟头你的前额还没有发热,就证明你不够专注。但是通过速读也许你会意识到,这样做所吸收到的书本中的内容比你花费一周时间慢慢阅读更有效。速读法的升级版即扫读法适合浏览书架,它的技巧是把视线集中在每一页的中心,从上往下。这种方法或许听起来很奇怪,但是经过一点练习,它就可以使你在5到10分钟内掌握一本书的主旨。书评对于速读很有助益,但要首先速读过文本以形成对文本的属于自己的判断,再去查看书评。利用JSTOR或Project Muse等数据库搜索书评,同时下载综述了三到六本书的评述文章,它们不但综述了当前的研究成果,而且指明了未来的学术发展方向。

一旦读了一本书,就要翻到它的参考书目,记录下体现前几十年该领域研究成果的基础著作和体现作者方法论的其他领域中的著作。另外,即使一本重要的书不在你所在学校的图书馆藏之列,你也没有借口忽略它的存在;

Pull—and Speed-Read—Secondary Sources

Let secondary sources provide your point of departure as well as insights into archival collections. Just as in the sciences, where a study of zooplankton motility, say, will rest on a pyramid of prior studies in marine biology, so your paper will both build on and add to the work of other historians. Having identified a dozen of the studies most relevant to your project, go to the library, which, if it is a good one, will have open stacks. Before pulling a title, be sure to spend a few minutes browsing the nearby shelves, looking in particular for books with new, unworn spines, indicating the latest scholarship. Invariably, you will spot a work that is more useful than your intended target, and which you would not have found using a keyword search of the online catalogue. Speed-reading, of which there are two basic techniques, will help you evaluate a title's worth.

To speed-read a typical 280-page monograph in about two-and-a-half hours, begin with the foreword and credits, for these can alert you to the author's personal background, intellectual mentors, economic sponsorship, and other factors suggestive of the book's viewpoint. Read most of the introduction, looking in particular for the thesis statement, then the conclusion. For each chapter, read the introductory section, then skim the body paragraphs by reading the first sentence and only continuing if the paragraph seems particularly important or interesting. As you read, take notes or annotate or both; I use a simple vertical pencil line in the outside margin, doubling the line for key points, with an asterisk for concepts. Drink caffeinated beverages and stay focused; speed-read in the morning, and never after a meal. Speed-reading is a painful process—if your forehead is not hot after half-an-hour then you are insufficiently intense—but so effective can it be that you may well realize you have absorbed the book's points far better than had you dragged it out over a week. A turbo-charged variation ideally suited for browsing stacks is to cast your eye down the center of each page; bizarre though it sounds, with a little practice this method allows you to pick up the gist of a book in five or ten minutes. Book reviews are useful adjuncts to speed-reading, although be sure to tackle them after finishing the book so you form your own judgment first. While checking for reviews in databases such as JSTOR or Project Muse, do make a point of downloading relevant review articles—those that evaluate from three to six titles simultaneously—for these both summarize the field and point the way for future scholarship.

Once you have assessed the book, turn to its bibliography. Make a note of foundational works from prior decades that you should pull later, as well as works from other fields that informed the author's methodology. Simply because an important book is not on your library's shelf is no excuse for ig-

要充分利用所在大学的馆际互借业务（在一些国家，很遗憾，馆际互借是要个人缴纳高额费用的；其实，这种业务应该总是免费的）。头脑风暴阶段最有直接意义的作用是使你获得有关原始文献资料的出处——档案馆藏、政府档案、日记和回忆录、报纸和杂志——这些信息都隐藏在参考书目和更为详细的脚注当中。

浏览档案

不久，你就会进入对研究计划的实现至关重要的原始档案探索阶段。除非你足够幸运，这些确认有用的档案在微缩胶卷或者所在大学的特藏中，否则，旅行则是必要的。不过，有的时候，不亲自去档案馆而是用所谓"遥控"的方式获得特定档案夹中的特定影印本，也是可行的，具体操作我将在下一章进行解释。为了避免重复作业，认真记录笔记和档案中的引文，但请浏览而不精读它。本阶段你所需的，仅仅是对于原始档案的搜集并对此获得一个大概印象，而且，如果运气好的话，可以获得一两个确凿证据，或一些关键文本，它们或许有潜力成为以后证明论点的有力论据。

提出假说

思考的时刻到了。沐浴、慢跑、爬山，做一切有助于思考的事情，并在这些过程中冥思苦想。拓宽思考，跳出你接收智慧的条条框框。下面举个例子来描述形成论点过程中的这一关键阶段。汉娜进入波士顿学院就读于爱尔兰裔美国史专业，她选择爱尔兰移民史作为博士学位论文的选题，并进一步把其缩短至马铃薯饥荒时期。但是在浏览过了波士顿图书馆三架二手资料后，她竟然发现了四本新的关于饥荒时期的专著，这使她压力倍增。还有什么余地可以供她发挥呢？于是，她致力于向地方政府档案馆的网上检索工具寻求答案。几个小时之后，她注意到波士顿城市档案馆存有一盒关于1847年鹿岛隔离医院的信件、日记和报告的档案资料。于是她发送邮件给档案馆工作人员询问具体情况，得到回复竟然说从来没有学者索取过那盒档案。带着兴奋之情，汉娜登上了开往档案馆的汽车，实地勘察了那些文件夹。一份鹿岛医生提到的有关报纸上热烈争论的信件吸引了汉娜的眼球，于是第二天她走访了波士顿公立图书馆，查看了1848年前几个月的 *Boston Daily Advertiser*（《波士顿广告日报》）。

noring its existence; make full use of your university's interlibrary loan (ILL) service. (In some countries there is an expensive charge for each ILL request, which is regrettable because it should always be a free service.) Of most immediate use when you are at the brainstorming stage will be references to primary sources—archival collections, government documents, diaries and memoirs, newspapers and magazines—both in the bibliography and more specifically in the footnotes.

Scan the Archives

You will soon reach the point when you need to explore the primary archive or archives that you have identified as crucial to your project's viability. Unless you are lucky enough to have your intended sources on microfilm or in your university's special collections, travel will be necessary, though it is sometimes practical to order photocopies of specific folders without visiting the archive, through what I call *remote control*, as described in the next chapter. To avoid duplication of effort, be diligent with note taking and citations, but scan rather than pore over the documents. All you need at this stage is a sense of what is there and, with luck, one or two smoking guns, a couple of key texts, that is, with the potential to provide evidence for an argument.

HYPOTHESIZE

It is now time to think. Think deeply, while showering, jogging, hiking a mountain, whatever helps. Think laterally—step outside the box of your received wisdom. To illustrate this critical stage in brainstorming a thesis, Hannah has enrolled at Boston College, where her field is Irish-American history, and for her doctoral dissertation has chosen to study Irish immigration, which she has further narrowed down to the Potato Famine period. But after leafing through three shelves of secondary sources in Boston College's library, and noticing four new monographs on the Famine, she felt overwhelmed. How could there possibly be anything left to say? She started, nevertheless, to work through the online finding aids of local government archives. Several hours later, she noticed a tranche of letters, diaries, and reports pertaining to an 1847 quarantine hospital on Deer Island and located in a box at the Boston City Archives. Hannah emailed the archivist, who noted in his reply that no researcher had yet requested the box. Excited, Hannah took a bus to the archive and skimmed through the folders. A letter from the island's doctor mentioning a heated debate in the newspapers caught Hannah's eye, so next day she visited the Boston Public Library to check microfilm of the *Boston Daily Advertiser* for a couple of months in early 1848.

确定论题，提出问题，尝试作答

作为头脑风暴的辅助，把一张纸水平放置（三折），并在其左侧记录下速读二手资料和略读档案资料时所意识到的问题，尤其注意其中的矛盾、讽刺、悖论，或运用现代语言风格的"不符之处"。是什么卡住你的思路使你觉得行文古怪呢？什么是你觉得叙述中所缺失的呢？在汉娜的案例中，她不仅惊讶于《波士顿广告日报》上刊登的有关隔离设施所引起的激烈的公共论争，而且惊讶于波士顿爱尔兰精英界存在的这个意见分歧。他们中一部分人希望医院中的病人能够被遣送回爱尔兰，因为这些病人对公共卫生造成了明显的危害，而且一旦他们出院，就会成为福利系统的负担。另一些人则认为病人们作为共和兄弟会的一员，应该被致以热烈的欢迎，觉得波士顿本来就是一座闪耀着慈善之光的山城。列出论题后，在纸的中部把它们以问题的形式呈现出来。汉娜写道："为什么本身作为新进移民的爱尔兰波士顿人竟然产生如此分歧，以至于达到想要遣返最近一拨自身移民的程度？"

选出其中最重要或令人困惑的问题。绞尽脑汁去继续头脑风暴。基于你在阅读二手资料时对该领域的理解，在纸的右侧大概记下所有可能的答案，其中最具说服力的那个答案就成为了你的研究假说。理想状态上，它将是一个能够尽可能统合不符之处的总体论点。当然，你的假说会存在至少一个反面观点，这也是你需要讨论的内容。一个完整的头脑风暴图表仿佛一个沙漏。最后，写下你的论文论点陈述。汉娜是这样写的："本篇博士学位论文要论证的是，有隔离设施的公共辩论造成了波士顿爱尔兰人的分裂，因为它激起了新进爱尔兰人的民族主义情绪，促使一部分爱尔兰人开始认同老派美国本土人的主张。"至此，汉娜已意识到，她有关隔离医院所进行的案例分析属于全国范围的一无所知党运动的一部分，叫做"本土主义运动"。她满怀信心地写道："这场公开辩论加剧了原本有一定容忍度的美国北方精英们的种族歧视意识。通过列举爱尔兰裔美国政客们支持'一无所知党'的例子，对该辩论的研究将改变对反爱尔兰人这一本土主义历史的当代解读。"[1]

注意，如果你无法确认一个或更多的反面观点，那么你的论点则不可以被称之为论点，只能被称之为观察描述。不过，有的时候存在另外一种可能性，也就是说，即使你所思考的问题仅仅是观察所得，但是通过与其他观察进行对比，它可能会成为一个强有力的论点。举个例子。假设我观察

---

1. "一无所知党"是存在于1849—1860年间的美国多个秘密的、政治性政党的总称。——译者注

Identify a Problem, Ask a Question, Pose an Answer

As an aid to brainstorming, down the left side of a horizontal sheet of paper, list the problems that you noticed while speed-reading the secondary sources and scanning the archival materials; think especially about contradictions, ironies, paradoxes, or *disconnects*, to use a modern idiom. What struck you as odd? What have you realized is missing from the story? In Hannah's case, she was surprised to see not only the high level of public debate over the quarantine facility, as evidenced in the *Advertiser*, but also that even Irish Bostonian elites held such divided opinions. Some wanted to send the hospital's patients back to Ireland, for they posed a genuine risk to public health, and once released would be a burden on the welfare rolls. Others wanted to welcome them as republican brothers, for Boston should be like a shining city on a hill. In a central column, write out each problem in the form of a question. Hannah wrote, "Why did Irish Bostonians, who themselves were recent immigrants, have such divided opinions, to the extent that some wanted to repatriate the new arrivals?"

Select the most pressing or troubling question. Brainstorm some more. Based on your understanding of the field from readings in the secondary literature, on the right side of the page jot down a shortlist of answers, the most plausible of which will be your working hypothesis. Ideally, it will be the single overarching argument that best ties together as many disconnects as possible. Your hypothesis, of course, will have at least one counter-argument, which you should also plan to address. A completed brainstorming chart resembles a funnel. Finally, write out your thesis statement. Hannah's was, "This dissertation will argue that public debate over the quarantine facility split Boston's Irish because it intensified their newfound Irish-American nationalism, prompting some Irish to identify with old stock Yankees." By this time, Hannah had realized that her case study of public reactions to the quarantine hospital was a subset of the much larger Nativist movement embodied in the nation-wide Know-Nothing Party. Confident about her project, she wrote, "A study of this public debate, moreover, which exacerbated racism among previously tolerant Yankee elites, will modify prevailing historiography on anti-Irish Nativism, by giving examples of Irish-American politicians who backed the Know-Nothing platform."

Note that if you cannot identify one or more counter-arguments then you do not have an argument, rather, you have an observation. Sometimes, though, it is possible to take what you thought was merely an observation and, by identifying a contrasting observation, turn it into a strong argument. Suppose I observe that Beijing's sidewalks, subways, hospitals, and other facilities are congested and overcrowded. "China has too many people," I say,

到了北京的人行道、地铁、医院以及其他设施都人满为患。"中国人太多了，"我说。这就意味着政府明智的计划生育政策在限制人口增长方面是绝对必要的。我的朋友杨玉则反驳我的观点，他认为，狭窄的人行道上充斥着街头摊点和违章停靠车辆；尽管又新增了几条线路，但是北京的地铁还是无法满足一个拥有2000万人口的城市的出行需求，而且医院和其他公共设施都太少了。他提出："北京的症结在于劣质的城市规划、松散的执法和基础设施投资的缺乏。"这就意味着政府官员把中国的人口基数作为推卸其拙劣政策的借口。至此，原本简单的观察竟然成为了复杂的、极具争议性的论点。正如该案例论点陈述所表明的那样：通过对六个主要首都城市作比较分析后发现，北京历史上所存在的拥挤不堪现象并非是中国巨大人口基数下形成的不可避免的结果，而是源于缺乏远见的规划政策、对于法规和交通规则的松散执法，以及必要基础设施的投资不足所致。

建立概念论证

除非形成了一个建构的概念论证体系，即拥有足以证明假说（就是指在论题陈述时列出的假说）的可行性的证据，否则请不要为你的研究计划进一步耗费任何精力，当然也不要浪费时间考虑开题报告。虽然汉娜仅仅翻阅了一些档案并翻查了一份报纸的十几个版面，但是她得到了她需要的概念论证。在波士顿学院学术委员会通过了她的开题报告之后，她利用整个夏天辛勤地埋首于其他三份报纸和期刊中，查阅州议会的记录，利用补助金飞到爱尔兰都柏林查阅那些病患寄回家里的信件。这一切的目的都是为了搜集到具有说服力的论据以使得其他学者很难对她的原始观点提出质疑。当然，就像一个工程师只有在把设计原型投入生产的过程中才有可能发现意料之外的问题一样，汉娜也有可能找到一些报纸社论使得她不得不修正自己的论点，但是可能还不至于使她放弃整个研究计划，再从头开始。

设计论文题目

在进入开题报告书写之前，有时作为头脑风暴过程的有益补充，设计一个暂定标题是十分重要的。一种观点认为，最有效的标题仅仅由一个简单词组构成，例如 *Trade and Diplomacy on the China Coast*（《中国海岸的贸易和外交》），而另一种观点则主张，学术性标题需要一个副标题以形成一个完整的描述，例如 *Cherishing Men from Afar: Qing Guest Ritual and the Macartney Embassy of 1793*（《怀柔远人：马嘎尔尼使华的中英礼仪冲突》）。同时要

implying that the government's wise one-child policy is essential to limit population growth. My friend Yang Yu then counters that narrow sidewalks are choked with street vendors' stalls and illegally parked vehicles; despite several new lines, the subway system is still inadequate for a city of twenty million people; and there are too few hospitals and other public facilities. "Beijing suffers from poor urban planning, lax enforcement of regulations, and a lack of investment in infrastructure," he says, implying that government officials have used China's population as an excuse to deflect criticism from unwise policies. Now the once-simple observation becomes a complex and controversial argument, as this sample thesis statement indicates: Through a comparative analysis of data from six major capital cities, this study argues that Beijing's historic overcrowding has not been an unavoidable consequence of China's vast population, but rather has resulted from shortsighted planning policies, lax enforcement of municipal codes and traffic regulations, and inadequate capital investment in essential infrastructure.

Establish Proof of Concept

Do not commit any further resources to your project, and certainly do not waste time on a proposal, until you have an established proof of concept, meaning you have sufficient evidence to indicate the feasibility of your hypothesis, as outlined in your thesis statement. Hannah had only flipped through a few folders and checked a dozen editions of a single newspaper, yet she had a proof of concept. After Boston College's dissertation committee approved her proposal, she spent all summer diligently working through three other newspapers and a range of journals, she examined records at the State House, and, with the aid of a research grant, traveled to Dublin to read letters the hospital patients sent home. But the purpose of all that work was to accumulate such a preponderant body of evidence that scholars would find it hard to challenge her original contention. Of course, just as an engineer might have discovered an unforeseen snag while putting a prototype into production, so Hannah might have found newspaper editorials that forced a modification of her argument, although it was unlikely she would have needed to abandon the project and start anew.

Design the Title

Before continuing to the proposal, and sometimes as a useful adjunct to the brainstorming process, it is important to design a working title. One school of thought maintains that the most effective titles are but a single phrase, like *Trade and Diplomacy on the China Coast*, while another holds that the title of a scholarly work needs a subtitle to provide a full description,

注意：数字化搜索以关键词为准，而你又希望推广你的作品使其拥有尽可能广泛的读者群。一般来说，主标题是一则与论点相关的通俗短语，副标题则要表明研究的主题和时期。经过一段时间之后，汉娜为她的博士学位论文选择了一则较长的标题"Shining-City Nativism: Debating the Repatriation of Irish Immigrants at Boston's Deer Island Quarantine Facility, 1847—1848"（《闪耀慈善光芒之城的本土主义：有关身处波士顿鹿岛隔离设施中的爱尔兰移民之遣送问题的辩论，1847—1848年》），而她的导师则建议，如果到了要吸引出版社的阶段时，应该使其变得简短一些。

开题报告的撰写

最好计划用几个星期的时间写作、润色和证明你的开题报告，因为它不仅是你说服学术委员会相信你有能力前进所必备的文件，也是你申请补助金的敲门砖，并将为你构建论文提供基本框架。你应该准备三种不同版本的开题报告。标准版要采用全文、双倍行距的格式，形成大约12—13页（3000—3300个单词）的文章容量，其中设立6至7个副标题。概略版适用于补助金的申请，要由精练的1000个单词、大约3页纸构成，不需要副标题。缩减版适用于向会议提交研究计划，它要由300个单词、1页纸构成。

主题与论点

在题为**概述**的标题下，你要明确地阐明并描述论文的主题。一定要说明它在历史中的重要意义和研究价值。你还可以在第一段中通过引用论文中一位人物语录的方式为自己的论文增添些许文艺色彩，这样可以吸引读者的阅读兴趣。有效的开题报告，是在段落开篇就点明论点，或者陈述一个复杂论点，并将论述过程在本段中以700—1000个单词左右的容量呈现出来。然后，在题为**论点以及其意义**的标题下，陈述问题——或者说是疑问——并尝试性地以明确的论点陈述形式回答该问题。为保持行文紧凑，即使为了明确性和强调性的需要而值得一再重复，亦请把此部分的几个段落限制在500个单词以内。

文献综述的三个用途

在名为**文献综述**的标题下，列出与你的研究计划相关的历史研究，并解释你的论文是如何建构并超越过往研究的。一份理想的研究计划既要填补既存文献的空白，又要向主流学术提出挑战。以下是文献综述的三种主要作用。

such as *Cherishing Men from Afar: Qing Guest Ritual and the Macartney Embassy of 1793*. Bear in mind, too, that digital searches locate keywords, and you want to promote your work to the widest possible readership. Typically, the main title will be a catchy phrase suggestive of the thesis, while the subtitle will indicate the topic and period of study. After thinking about it for some time, Hannah chose a long title for her dissertation, which her advisor suggested ought to be shorter when it came time to attract a publisher. "Shining-City Nativism: Debating the Repatriation of Irish Immigrants at Boston's Deer Island Quarantine Facility, 1847—1848."

WRITING A PROPOSAL

Plan to spend several weeks developing, polishing, and proofing your proposal, for it will not only be the document that convinces your committee you are ready to move forward but it will also be your calling card when you apply for grants, and provide a framework when you begin to construct the paper. You should produce three variations of your proposal. In its standard, full-length form, it will be about twelve or thirteen double-spaced pages (3,000–3,300 words), structured with six or seven subheads. In its overview form, suitable for grant applications, it will be three pages of exactly 1,000 words, with no subheads. And in its abstract form, which will be useful for promoting your project at conferences, it will be 300 words that fit on a single page.

Topic and Thesis

Beneath an **Overview** subhead, begin by clearly identifying and describing your topic. Be sure to explain its historical significance, and say why it is worth studying. You may decide to pique your reader's interest while providing a flavor of your sources by including in the first paragraph a pithy quotation from one of your actors. Effective proposals, particularly those that lay out the thesis early on, or have a complex argument, may devote 700–1,000 words to this section. Next, under a **Thesis and Its Significance** subhead, state the problem—or question—that you intend to address, and provide your tentative answer in the form of an explicit thesis statement. For greater impact, keep this section to a couple of paragraphs of less than 500 words, although your thesis will bear restating or recasting for clarity and emphasis.

Historiography: Three Uses

Beneath a **Historiography** subhead, locate your project in the relevant historiography, explaining how it will both build on and transcend that body of historical work. An ideal project fills a gap in existing literature, just as it challenges prevailing scholarship. There are three broad uses of historiography.

第一，为论文的成立构建合法性并寻求（理论）支持。你所确立的研究领域和主题中的大量与之相关的期刊论文、专著和综合性著作都需要进行权威性的探讨。记住：到你进行论文答辩的那一刻，你就是该领域的领军学者——很可能是世界级的领军学者——其他学者皆在翘首以待你去发表该领域的专家建议，所以阅读主流著作相当重要，对该领域的最新出版状况和博士学位论文了如指掌也很重要。你的研究计划要建立在知识的金字塔上，但同时，还要发现并填补其中的一个空白。此部分的行文容量大约为600—1000个单词。

第二，借鉴你所需要的方法论。假设你是一位现实主义学派的外交史研究者，而你怀疑论文中的主角自身所患的残障影响了他的政治判断，但你对心理学却一窍不通，那么就需要找到其他三部通识著作和一个案例研究来解决关于这位主角的病理行为的疑难问题。

第三，瞄准"稻草人"。"稻草人"的字面含义是士兵为全力冲刺练习刺刀拼杀所准备的一个装满谷壳的麻袋。你会发现在你论点的反面观点中挑选出一本著作作为假想敌是很有建设性的。但也要注意，这可能使你在现实生活中真正树敌，所以最保险的做法是去攻击那些业已退休或去世的学者们的观点。但同时也要注意：打破陈规的方法也可能隐含着你的研究方法可能有事实上的缺陷。

资料、方法论、大纲

在名为**资料**的标题下，列出所需的包括档案文献和出版文献的这些第一手资料，说明档案和出版物的所在地并描述其中的内容。而专门的**方法论**标题下的内容则是有选择性的，尤其要对影像资料、出土文物研究，或者依靠口述历史采访、内容分析、计量史学的研究计划进行说明。在名为**大纲**的标题下，简洁、尝试性地列出论文可能的书写内容。对于一份研究报告来说，有可能是只要列出副标题就足够了，但若是博士学位论文，则需要列出每章大纲或者目录，或者二者皆有，并要大概列出从目前角度所预期作品的结果。开题报告要以一份简洁的**研究计划进度**作为结尾，其中指出不同阶段的研究和写作计划以及预计完成的时间。

在开题报告的定稿过程中，不但要向目前的导师、读者和同学们征求意见，也要向过往求学过程中对你的研究感兴趣的教授和教师们请教；他们无疑会很乐意接收到你的去信并能够提供有用的建议。在向那些决定你研究计划命运的学术委员会成员提交开题报告之前，请先把业已完成的开题报告搁置几天。

First, to establish legitimacy and build support. There will be a corpus of journal articles, monographs, and synthetic works relevant to your field and to your topic, all of which you should be able to discuss with authority. Remember: by the time you defend your thesis, you will be a leading expert—maybe the world's expert—on your topic, and other scholars will expect you to be capable of demonstrating that expertise, so it is vital not merely to read the prevailing works but also to keep abreast of new publications and dissertations. Your project will stand on a pyramid of knowledge, yet, at the same time, it will identify a lacuna and then fill that void. Allocate 600–1,000 words to this section.

Second, to borrow methodology that informs your approach. Suppose you are a diplomatic historian of the realist school, but your primary actor suffered from a disability that you suspect affected his judgment. As you have only a rudimentary grounding in psychology, you have identified three general works and a case study that addresses your actor's pathology.

Third, to charge at straw men. A literal straw man is a burlap bag stuffed with chaff at which soldiers run full tilt to practice bayonet thrusts. You will find it constructive to single out a work that serves as a model enemy by taking the opposite line from your argument. But be careful here, as you may make a real enemy, which is why it is prudent to attack the interpretations of retired or even deceased scholars; iconoclasm, too, can suggest that your approach is actually destructive.

Sources, Methodology, Outline

Beneath a **Sources** subhead, identify your primary sources, both archival and published; give the location of the archives or published collections and describe what they contain. A dedicated **Methodology** section is optional, typically for film or material culture studies as well as projects that rely on oral history interviews, content analysis, or cliometrics. Beneath an **Outline** subhead, include a brief, tentative outline of the written work that will result. For a research paper, perhaps an indication of the sub-sections may suffice, while for a dissertation provide a chapter outline or table of contents or both, giving a sense of the structure of the planned work as currently envisaged. Finish your proposal with a brief **Work Schedule**, indicating when you will conduct the various stages of research and writing, along with a target date for completion.

In finalizing the proposal, solicit input not only from your advisor, readers, and fellow students but also from instructors and mentors at a prior institution who took interest in your work; they will no doubt be pleased to hear from you and may have useful tips. Sit on the completed proposal for a couple of days before submitting it to the faculty committee members who will decide whether you are ready to begin your project.

搜集论据
GATHERING THE EVIDENCE

在学术委员会通过了你的开题报告之后，漫长并往往枯燥的论据搜集征程就以你的开题报告为模板开始了。在20世纪90年代文化热潮回归的影响下，出于对自下而上的社会历史和非政治历史人物的重视，类似于博士学位论文这样大一些的研究项目越来越倾向于运用更多来源进行资料搜集，包括从口述采访到影音资料，这样做能够使得论文行文更加生动有趣，尽管不一定会使得行文更加连贯。不过，传统档案依然是可能为你提供大量论据的最佳资料来源，所以掌握切实有效的整理文件的方法将会最大程度上节约你的旅行预算。本章在强调发掘资料工作的价值同时，也将探讨可靠的档案管理系统和数据处理方法的必要作用。

资料

从论文提出到最终完成，资料会一直伴你左右。就像维系友情，它们一样需要你费心对待。只有你对它们表示忠诚之心，它们才能服务于你。你对它们的感情将逐渐变得爱恨交织。但是，如果没有资料，你的论点将会变得毫无意义，所以请尽你所能与它们培养感情。

在线数据库

一则研究者的福音是：全世界的档案管理者都正在对文本进行有条不紊的数据化存档，而且最新的视觉图像文字识别（Optical Character Recognition，OCR）软件的性能正不断增强。例如，就美国早期共和国时期波士顿和中国贸易问题研究而言，输入关键词就可以检索从缅因州至罗得岛州发行过的两百余份报纸和杂志，并可以把相关文章打印出来或者采用PDF文件格式存储下来。几分钟之内，拥有庞大数据库的在线搜索引擎将追索到甚至几年的人工查询都无法发现的资料。即便如此，数字化搜索也仅仅是搜集资料的一种工具，就像锤子或螺丝刀一样，千万别把它当做能治百病的灵丹妙药，也千万别把它视为蜗居在舒适公寓中逃避实地考察的借口。要同时了解数字化搜索的益处和局限性。数据输入人员往往不屑扫描那些损坏的、不完整的、对比度低的文件，正如文件污损、古语字体，还有过时的拼写仍然成为OCR软件的隐患一样。例如以"Congressional Session"（国会会期）或"Woodmass and Offley"（伍德马斯和奥夫利）为关键词进行搜索，将会所获甚微，因为该关键词可能与原始文本有所差距，如果原始文本中该词被拼写为"Congrefsional Fefsion"或"Woodmafs & Offley"。[1]记

---

1. Congressional Session 和 Woodmass and Offley（运输公司名称）为现代的拼写方式，而 Congrefsional Fefsion 和 Woodmafs & Offley 则是过去的拼写方式。——译者注

With your proposal as a template and a green light from your faculty committee, it is time to begin the long and often tedious business of evidence gathering. In part as a response to the cultural turn of the 1990s with its stress on bottom-up social history and the role of non-state actors, larger projects such as PhD dissertations increasingly tend to employ a range of sources, from oral interviews to film, which can make for a more interesting if not necessarily more cohesive narrative. Still, traditional archives are likely to supply the bulk of your evidence, so methods to facilitate the efficient processing of documents will stretch your travel budget. This chapter also emphasizes the value of detective work, and discusses the need for reliable filing systems and data handling.

SOURCES

Over the period it will take to bring your project to completion, sources will be your constant companion. As with any friendship, they will often be high maintenance. They will only work for you if you are faithful to them. You will grow to hate them as well as love them. Yet without sources, your thesis would be meaningless, so do all you can to cultivate the relationship.

Online Databases

A boon for the researcher is that archivists around the world are systematically digitizing texts, while the performance of the latest Optical Character Recognition (OCR) software is constantly improving. For a project on Boston's China trade during the Early Republic, say, it is now possible to run a keyword search across some two hundred newspapers and magazines published in towns from Maine to Rhode Island, then print or save to disk Portable Document Format (PDF) images of relevant articles. In minutes, online searches of vast databases retrieve sources that years of manual searching would not have discovered. That said, treat digitization as a tool rather than a panacea, and never as a substitute for leaving your cozy apartment. Like a hammer or a screwdriver, understand digitization's limitations as well as its usefulness. Operatives will not bother to scan damaged, incomplete, or low-contrast documents, just as blemishes, archaic typefaces, or anachronistic spelling are still the bane of OCR programs. Searching for "Congressional Session" or "Woodmass and Offley" will result in few hits if the original texts say "Congrefsional Fefsion" or "Woodmafs & Offley." Remember, too, that unless you can image full pages for an entire edition, you have to rely on the operative who entered the edition's dates and page numbers, which is why it is good practice to mention in the footnote your use of a digitized source.

住，如果你无法在电脑上看到所查文章整版的所有页码的整个页面，就要依靠数据输入人员的记录来查询其发表日期和页码，所以在脚注中标明所使用的是数据资料这一做法是一种良好的习惯。

口述历史采访

对当代历史学者来说，口述历史采访将不仅为你的研究提供丰富多彩的背景资料，而且会成为研究中重要的论据来源。事实上，在制度禁止或限制公众查阅关键档案的情况下——例如天主教托莱多总教区对于20世纪30年代历史的态度，或者沃特迪斯尼公司对于20世纪70年代历史的态度——口述历史也许会成为仅存的一手资料和目击信息来源。除了业已以数字化形式或者文本形式记录并转录在案的逐渐增多的口述史资料，例如美国工程进度管理署20世纪30年代编辑的奴隶叙事或罗纳德·弗雷泽所著的 *Blood of Spain: An Oral History of the Spanish Civil War*（《西班牙之血：西班牙内战的口述史》）之外，进行自己的口述史采访也具有相当大的价值。一些学者轻视口述采访的作用，但是只要你以对待文本一样的、具有建设性的怀疑态度处理采访内容，它们就能变得比日记或者书信更具史料价值。毕竟，独自坐在书桌一畔提供了当事人足够的悠闲空间来编造一个故事，而面对录音机的嗡嗡运转和采访者咄咄逼人的问题，那种临场感就好像使得当事人置身于法庭，而不容易说谎。总之，将你平日里严谨的学术态度应用于可以接受的口述史学方法论上，将使你避免潜在的批评。

进行口述采访之前，请首先学习一下权威性的口述史学理论著作，例如唐纳德·A. 里奇的 *Doing Oral History: A Practical Guide*（《口述历史研究实务指南》）。请注意：如果你的论点是建立在口述采访的基础上，例如一份典型的人类学研究，那么最好在拥有五到六位能够独立证明相同观点的采访者基础上才把采访对象扩大到其他的组群中。一对一的采访是比较常规的方式，但是如果能够邀请到受访者的一位伙伴共同参与的话也是不无益处。卸下羞怯感，受访者会逐渐忘记录音机的运转，而他的朋友亦能帮助其回溯记忆并监督其评价的真实性。在你事先准备提问问题时，一定要准备一段确认受访者身份的开场白，包括访问的地点、日期和时间，以及征询受访者同意接受采访和出版的对白。录音音质很重要，所以最好从正规厂商那里购买录音设备，例如索尼或奥林巴斯，并在家试验以获得其动态音频的亲身感觉。最理想的状态是把录音设备放到你和受访者之间的咖啡桌上，并拉上窗帘以减轻回音。在条件允许的情况下，最好在离开访问

Oral History Interviews

For historians of the contemporary period, oral interviews can provide not merely colorful background but also an important source of evidence. Indeed, in situations where institutional policy denies or restricts public access to crucial archives—the Archdiocese of Toledo for the 1930s, or the Walt Disney Corporation for the 1970s—oral histories may be the only source of first-hand or eyewitness information. In addition to a growing body of recorded and transcribed interviews in digital as well as book form, such as the slave narratives produced in the 1930s by the Works Progress Administration or *Blood of Spain: An Oral History of the Spanish Civil War* by Ronald Fraser, there is great value in conducting your own interviews. Some academics discount oral interviews, but providing you handle them with the same constructive skepticism with which you should approach any textual source, they can be more valuable than a letter or diary. After all, when seated alone at a desk, a writer has ample leisure to spin a tale, whereas with a recorder running and an interviewer firing questions, there is a tension akin to a courtroom's. Head off potential criticism by applying your usual academic rigor to accepted methodology.

Begin with an authority such as Donald A. Ritchie's *Doing Oral History: A Practical Guide*. Note that when your argument rests on interviews, as in a typical ethnographic study, it is best to have five or six interviewees make the same point independently before extrapolating from your subjects to a larger group. Single-subject interviews are the normal format, although there can be benefits to having one of your subject's friends participate. Being less shy, the subject forgets about the recorder sooner, while the friend serves as an aid to memory and a check on fanciful remarks. When you pre-prepare your questions, be sure to include opening comments to identify those present, give the place, date, and time, and ask for your subjects' consent to the interview and its publication. Sound quality is important, so buy a digital recorder from a manufacturer such as Sony or Olympus, and test it at home to gain a sense of its audio dynamics. Placing the recorder on a coffee table between yourself and the interviewee is usually ideal, as is drawing curtains to soften echoic harshness. Whenever possible, upload the sound file to your laptop before you leave. Jot down proper nouns during the interview, then ask your subject to check the spellings and provide additional information at the end.

地点之前就把音频文件上传到你的笔记本电脑中。随手记下访问中的专有名词，然后在采访的结尾向受访者确认其拼写，并请其提供更多的额外信息。无论是哪种转录方法，从小范围编辑到逐字记录，都是既费时又枯燥的；所以请为每个采访留下一整天的时间用以整理记录。我注重呈现细节以体现采访的完整性，于是记录下每一个"哦"、"啊"的语气助词，并在括号中呈现出诸如"笑声"或"强忍住眼泪"这种神态描写。

要了解，尤其在美国，研究者要尊重采访对象应得的权利，你无法承担将自身或自身的研究机构卷入法律诉讼中的后果。一份书面同意书，至少详细地记录下得到受访者的允许来引用其采访内容，并伴有受访者的签名，从来都是避免纠纷的不二选择。注意，和你的院系确认一下你是否需要研究综述公告（IRB）或独立伦理委员会（IEC）的服务。在为了保护受访者，论文写作中必须应用其化名的情况下，应在脚注中标明："我在非公开情况下进行了本次采访，双方一致决议隐去受访者的真实姓名。"

影音资料和文物资料

自从 D.W. 格里菲斯所著的 *The Birth of a Nation*（《一个国家的诞生》）于1915年获得一千万美元的票房收入以来，故事片反映并开始影响公众舆论和社会风俗的风向，所以其也具有作为论据资料的重要作用，尤其反映在受教育程度低的群体的研究方面。就像口述采访一样，以严谨的研究方法致力于影音资料的使用，其效果会给那些认为电影对于学术来说过于粗俗的学者留下好印象。在语境中进行的分析，请尝试借鉴使用詹美思·查普曼于 *Cinemas of the World: Film and Society, from 1895 to the Present*（《世界电影院：影片与社会，从1895到现在》）中运用的理论方法。以追求真实性和准确性的态度把影音资料当做文本资料一样对待。直接从影片角色的对话中转录所需要引用的部分，而不是取材于剧本或者电影字幕，只有演员的对话才是观众当时最直观聆听到的内容。同时，确认你所使用的影音版本是否与其原发行版本内容一致，针对此，影片的运行时间是个有用的指标。我建议阐述影片内容时最好不要像传统的方法一样使用现在时态。过去时态的使用会保持叙述的一致性，避免使用会引发歧义的短语，而在以一个当代学者的身份解读影片时才使用现在时态，可以使得读者能够更好地区分影音资料的本意和当代学者的文意。

文物资料研究正由艺术史研究领域逐渐扩展到并丰富着主流的史学。有两本论文集提供了有关此方面的方法论背景，即大卫·金格里的 *Learning from Things: Method and Theory of Material Culture Studies*（《向事物学习：物质文化学的

Methods of transcription, from minor editing to verbatim, vary, but all are time consuming and tedious; allow a full day for every hour of interview. I err on the side of completeness, writing out every "ooh" and "um," and I include comments such as [laughs] or [fighting back tears] in square brackets.

Be aware, particularly in the United States, that human subjects have rights, which researchers must respect, and you cannot afford to embroil yourself or your institution in a lawsuit. A written consent form, detailing, at minimum, permission to cite the interview and signed by your interviewee, is always a good precaution. Check with your department if you will need the services of an institutional review board (IRB) or independent ethics committee (IEC). When protecting the identity of an interviewee with a pseudonym, mention in a footnote that, "I conducted this interview in confidentiality and have withheld the name of the interviewee by mutual consent."

Film and Material Culture

Ever since D.W. Griffith's *The Birth of a Nation* grossed $10 million at the box office in 1915, feature films have reflected as well as affected public opinion and social mores, hence their importance as sources of evidence, particularly for studies of groups with low rates of literacy. As with oral interviews, a rigorous approach should impress those who still feel that cinema is too lowbrow for academia. To put your analysis in context, try James Chapman's *Cinemas of the World: Film and Society, from 1895 to the Present*. Treat a film as you would any textual source, with faithfulness and accuracy. Transcribe your quotations directly from the actors' dialogue rather than from a screenplay or subtitles, for that is what the audience would have heard. Similarly, verify that the version you are watching has the same footage as the original release, the runtime of the film being a good indicator. I advise breaking away from the tradition of interpreting film in the present tense. Past tense will ensure your narrative's consistency, obviate awkward phrasing, and allow you to reserve present tense for distinguishing the voice of a contemporary scholar.

Material culture studies are moving out of the art history field and enriching mainstream historiography. Two edited collections provide methodological grounding: W. David Kingery's *Learning from Things: Method and Theory of Material Culture Studies*, and Thomas J. Schlereth's *Material Culture Studies in America*; consult, too, Peter Burke's *Eyewitnessing*. When you are

方法和理论》），以及托马斯·J.施勒雷特的 *Material Culture Studies in America*（《物质文化学在美国》）。另外，彼得·伯克的 *Eyewitnessing*（《目击者》）一书亦值得参考。当你需要博物馆内的文物资料作为论据时，请不要盲目借鉴博物馆提供的打印资料内容，最好去和该馆负责该方面的主管聊一聊。

闪击档案馆

之所以大量研究报告所需的资料一直是由传统档案馆提供，仅仅是因为在此还保存着大量的尚待利用的资料。只要每家每户持续保存其家庭文件，社会名流和企业持续注意其遗产归属，大学持续扩大其特藏书库，这种状况就可能得到改变。就算你有幸能够暂居邻近档案馆的朋友的公寓，而且所查阅的档案馆不限制阅览时间，出于自身的利益考量，还是要做到我所谓的闪击档案馆，即以有效的速度、尽职的勤勉和绝对的专注工作，从而使你在查阅过程中不太有可能造成失误或者漏掉重要的线索。在我看来，即使你获得的奖学金允许你整学期或整个夏天都待在国外，而且还可以留宿在学校提供的宿舍里，闪击亦是一样的重要。抛下自由散漫的心态，代之以设定完成写作或研究一两章的目标，你将发现你的成果是如此丰富——奇迹一般——使你在完成任务之后还能余下足够多的时间来观光和访友。

出发之前

为了熟悉档案馆的收藏，要先阅读在线检索工具和档案管理员所提供的档案概览。一定要向目的地档案馆发送电子邮件以确认其开放时间和确认你是否需要携带特殊身份证明，并询问有关复印和拍照的具体规定。借机向其介绍你本人和你的研究兴趣。档案管理员通常业务繁忙，但他们同时又是谙熟收藏文献的专家。在了解了你的需求之后，他们将很乐意为你提供帮助，可能会向你介绍与该文献相关，但你却可能未曾留意的其他文件。档案馆越来越倾向于把日积月累的文献资料堆积到其他地方，所以可能需要你花费几个钟头甚至几天的时间等其取回，故而一定要询问其馆藏情况，如果有必要的话，还要事先向该馆进行预约。

宾馆在周末时入住率最高，所以在你预订之前，先在网上查询是否提供平日特价，再给目标宾馆发封电子邮件询问是否提供学生或者社团会员（例如美国汽车协会）更多的优惠。学校的邮递名录服务器和允许张贴租房广告的在线论坛是你身在异国查询打折住宿的理想场所。整理你的查阅装备，其中要包括空白纸张、两支质量好的削尖的铅笔以及备用的铅笔

working with museum pieces, do not take an exhibit's printed description at face value, and make a point of chatting with a subject curator.

BLITZING AN ARCHIVE

Conventional archives continue to provide the bulk of a research project's sources, if only because they contain so much untapped material. As long as households preserve family papers, celebrities and corporations have an eye for their legacy, and universities seek to expand their special collections, that situation is unlikely to change. Even if you have the luxury of staying in a friend's apartment while visiting a facility that does not restrict its hours, it is still in your best interest to blitz, as I call it, to work with efficient speed, due diligence, and above all intensity, for then you are less likely to make an error or miss an important lead. Blitzing is just as important, I suggest, when you have a grant to research abroad for an entire semester or summer, and are staying in university accommodation. Instead of relaxing carefree, set yourself a target of writing a chapter or two as well as researching. You will discover that your resulting productive attitude has created—as if by magic—more than enough time for sightseeing and socializing.

Before You Leave

Become familiar with the collection by reading the online finding aid and any overviews provided by the archivist. Always email to verify opening hours, check if you need to take special identification, and ask about policies for photocopying and photography. Use the opportunity to introduce yourself and your research interests. Archivists are busy people but they are also professionals who care deeply about their collections. After learning your needs, they will be happy to offer advice, perhaps suggesting documents in related collections that you had not thought to examine. Archives increasingly store boxes of their growing collections offsite, for which retrieval can take anywhere from a few hours to several days, so be sure to ask about this and submit an advance order if necessary.

Hotels have their highest occupancies at weekends, so search the internet for midweek specials, and, before you book, email to ask about further special pricing for students or holders of a card like the American Automobile Association's. Academic listservs and online forums that allow you to post room-wanted advertisements are an ideal way to track down cut-price accommodation in foreign countries. Gather your equipment, which should include blank paper, two quality mechanical pencils with spare leads, laptop with power supply, memory stick (flash drive) for backup plus a DVD-R disc for peace of mind, camera and ancillary items (if permissible), and a water

芯、笔记本电脑和电源、备份记忆棒（U盘）、一张空白DVD-R光盘以保持心平气和，相机及其配件（如果允许的话），还有水杯和零食。带够用以在档案馆支付复印费用的现金，因为档案馆通常不提供信用卡支付服务。去国外查阅资料的时候，要事先确认是否需要一个电源变压器，检查自己的电子产品是否能够适用于当地的电压。大部分的可携电子产品的电源都具有自动感知双电压（110/240V）以及自动循环（50/60Hz）功能，也可携带价位不贵又适用于多个国家的万能变压器套装，但如果目的地是英国，一定要带上那种特殊的、接头又大又扁的三相插座。

入馆之日

尽量利用你与资料接触的宝贵时间：第一名去排队，最后一名离开。如果这是你首次入馆，入馆工作是必不可少的，所以要更早到达以避开高峰时间。注意：不同类型，尤其是不同国家的档案馆，其入馆规章和程序是不同的，即使你提前对此有所了解，也同样有可能违反规定。例如，爱尔兰国家图书馆要求来访者提前办理研究者卡，所以我带着两张照片，并事先预留出我认为足够的时间办手续，但当我从机场到图书馆之后，才发现那里的保安办公室由于午饭休息而暂停接待，两个小时后才重新办公，而等我办好了研究者卡，下午就几乎没剩多少时间去特定藏室寻找档案了。办完入馆手续之后，你需要把所有随身物品锁到一个柜子里，只携带纸张、铅笔、笔记本电脑、照相机和其他辅助电子产品入馆。小心——你承担不起犯错误的代价，而且你正置身于一个未知的领地之内。在美国国家档案馆的一天清晨，我在其开馆之时昂首阔步地来到其安全检查服务台，被那里的保安要求审查我的笔记本电脑。当我把笔记本电脑放到抛光的花岗石服务台上的时候，它突然倾斜落下，千钧一发之际我伸手抓住了，生生避免了它摔落在石板地上的惨剧。当我的心跳因突发事故的解决而渐趋平稳之后，才意识到原来一个看门人在几分钟之前才把硅酮光泽剂喷在了花岗岩服务台之上，而我对作为第一位入馆客人的渴望使我差点成为了此项行为的蒙在鼓里的受害者。

入馆之后

把你的笔记本电脑放到离复印机很近的书桌上占座，然后直奔服务台。假如你已经明确自己的首要需求，立即填写申请索求在规定范围内最多的档案盒或档案夹；大部分档案馆一张申请单只能索求一份档案。而且档案到达你手中的时间可能是两分钟也可能是两个钟头，所以利用等待的

bottle and light snack. Take sufficient cash to cover photocopying at the archive, where the desk staff are unlikely to accept a credit card. When traveling to another country, check if you will need a power outlet adapter, and whether your electronic equipment will work on a different voltage. Most power supplies for portable electronics are now self-sensing for dual-voltage (110/240V) and cycles (50/60Hz); adapter kits for multiple countries are inexpensive, although for a trip to Britain, make sure your kit includes the special three-prong adapter with large, flat pins.

On the Day

Maximize your precious time with the sources; be first in line and the last to leave. If it is your initial visit then there will inevitably be paperwork, so arrive especially early to beat the rush. Note that policies and procedures vary, particularly from country to country, and even when you inquire in advance, you may still fall foul of the system. Visiting the National Library of Ireland requires obtaining a researcher's card, for which I had brought two photographs and allowed what I thought would be ample time, but I arrived from the airport to discover that the security office had closed early for a two-hour lunch break; by the time I had my ID card, there was little time to pull folders for what was left of the afternoon. With the paperwork complete, you will need to put your things into a locker, taking only paper, pencil, laptop, and camera plus ancillary electronics with you. Do be careful—you cannot afford to make any mistakes, and you are in unfamiliar territory. At the U.S. National Archives one morning, I strode through the doors as they opened and over to the security desk, where the guard asked to see inside my laptop. As I put it down on the polished granite counter, it suddenly slid away from me, and I only just had time to slap a hand on it before it crashed to the stone floor. When my heart had settled down a few beats, I realized a janitor had sprayed silicone polish on the granite minutes earlier, and my eagerness to be first had cast me as the unsuspecting victim.

Once Inside

Snag desk space close to the photocopier, marking it with your laptop, then head directly to the counter. Providing you have already identified your first requests, immediately fill out call slips for as many boxes or folders as the limit allows; most archives require one slip per request. It may take anywhere from two minutes to two hours for the materials to arrive, so use the intervening time for setup. Check you have plugged your laptop into a receptacle that works, open up the document containing your notes, and remind yourself of the day's objectives. Once your materials arrive, you may be able to submit a second batch of requests, which means they will be waiting when

时间来为查阅档案做好准备——确认你笔记本电脑的电源已经插在了合适的插座上，打开记录笔记的文档来阅读，并反复提醒自己本日的工作目标。一旦你所需的资料到手，你就可以再提交所需的第二批档案申请单，这意味着你在结束查阅第一批档案之后就能立即看到第二批。迅速而彻底地投入工作中。首先查询档案盒说明，并确认档案资料。依次从盒中一个一个地拿出档案夹，并在取出档案的所在位置用标签进行标记。仔细对待其中的文件，尤其当翻阅到泛黄或者泛褐的文件时，因为这意味着文件纸张呈酸性，易于损坏。在全程抄写过程中，准确性是基本的。把资料抄写在纸张上的时候，字迹要清晰可辨，并要审核每一页的抄写，以确保不存在语法错误和标点错误；同样，当把资料输入到 MS-Word 文档的时候，打字时切忌匆忙，每输入一页后都要花时间对照原文核实内容，然后再继续输入。以上工作基于如下基本原则，即你可能再也看不到所查阅的原始文献了，所以包括其位置所在信息和内容都要完全精确，否则你无法把它运用到以后的论文写作中去。

除了去洗手间以外，不要停下工作的进程。偶尔用饮水器，或者去你的橱柜里拿自备的水瓶补充水分满足身体所需，必要时吃些零食。即使当档案馆午休关门，建议你也不要吃正式的午饭，因为用餐后所带来的疲倦会消磨你的整个下午。利用午休时间处理资料或者准备下午的工作。多日入馆的情况下，在当日最后索求档案到手之后再填写一张新的档案申请单，这样一来第二日早晨你将可以立即获得所需的档案。闭馆回家之前，记得要与档案管理员或该馆的你研究领域的有关专家谈一谈。在听取了你的研究情况之后，有可能热心的管理员会通过翻阅记录为你发掘他们组织代办的某些报告；或者会提供你一个研究津贴或者演讲机会。一定要记住，在你论文的致谢部分写下为你提供帮助的档案管理员的姓名，因为他们的职业往往较少引起足够的回报。偷窃癖患者要谨记的是：偷窃一份文档是会起到反作用的，因为你怎么可能引用一份档案馆没有备案的资料呢？

复印、拍照、遥控

有的档案馆依然不允许以任何形式复制资料，或坚持只有他们内部的复印部门才能复制资料，从而全面否定了复制资料的好处。不过条件允许的情况下，一定要复印或者复制资料。复印是最有效的保存文件的方法，因为这样一来，你就可以拥有一份可随身携带的、高对比度的实物文本，虽然有时高达0.2美元一页的开销将花掉你很多的预算。以档案盒"b."和档案夹"f."的方式标记每张复印页面的来源信息是很关键的。没有遵循此

you finish the first pull. Work quickly yet thoroughly. Begin by noting the document box description, then verify the folders. Remove one folder at a time, inserting a marker into the box to identify its location. Treat the documents with care, particularly if yellowing or browning indicates fragile, acidic paper. Accuracy is essential for all transcriptions. When transcribing to paper, print legibly and check each page, not just for spelling errors but also for precise punctuation; similarly, when transcribing to an MS-Word file, do not rush your typing and take the time to verify each page against the original text before moving on. Work on the basis that you will neither see the original again, nor can use the source unless its location information and transcription is exact.

Other than for essential bathroom breaks, do not stop. An occasional swig from a water fountain or, failing that, from the water bottle in your locker will keep you going, along with a snack if you must. Even when an archive closes for lunch, forswear a meal because food-induced drowsiness will waste your afternoon; use the time to process materials or prepare for the coming session. For multi-day research, fill out call slips before the last pull of the day so that you have a new batch of materials waiting for you the following morning. Before returning home, make a point to chat with the archivist or subject specialist. After hearing about your work, thoughtful curators will dig through files for reports their organization commissioned, or perhaps offer a study grant or the opportunity to give a lecture. Acknowledge, by name, the help they have provided in the credits section of your dissertation, for theirs can be a thankless vocation. A cautionary note for kleptomaniacs: stealing a document is counterproductive—how can you reference it in your work if it is not sitting in an archive?

Photocopying, Photographing, Remote Control

Some archives still do not permit copying in any form, or insist their reprographic department handles the job, which can negate the advantages. But when you can photocopy or photograph, do so. Nothing beats photocopying because then you have a high-contrast hard copy to take with you, although at much above 20¢ per page it soon becomes costly. It is crucial to mark every page with the document's box [b.] and folder [f.] information. Failure to follow this elementary step renders the exercise useless, for how can you cite a document unless you know its precise location? When photocopying a series of pages, do number them, saving the problem of reordering them

一基本步骤很可能使你的工作前功尽弃。试问，如果你不了解文档的精确位置，那怎么能引用它呢？当影印很多页文本的时候，一定要标注页码，这样一来，如果你把文档弄掉的话，也可以很容易重新排序。

无需额外每页花费但却有其自身局限性的数码拍照复制文档的方式变得越来越实用，尤其是从伦敦国家档案馆到布达佩斯公共社会档案馆，很多档案馆都安装了高度可调的相机支架。在花费500美元购买一台能与你的笔记本电脑适配的数码相机之前，你就该意识到这500美元其实买到的是几千张的影印品，而且你有照相机的话往往可以在档案馆更加迅速地工作；但是，事后阅读拍摄下来的图像文本并非那么方便，而且想边读边注释的话需要额外进行编辑或者打印。注意，除非你应用 Adobe Photoshop 这样的图像处理软件来提高对比度和明亮度以去掉背景颜色，否则灰色的背景将在打印过程中迅速地消耗掉打印机中的硒鼓。应付偶尔的拍照工作，袖珍式的傻瓜相机就可以胜任，但是当你把相机设置调到流水线模式一般不停地拍照时，你会发现你的背部比预期的更容易疲累酸痛，而且一块没电的电池也很可能使你当天的计划搁浅。所以，要投资一部高档微型数码相机（诸如佳能 PowerShot G-10），它可以与你的笔记本电脑连接，价位低于一部单反相机，并且其重量很轻不至于使得桌面三脚架失衡。同时，还要投资一个充电器以避免受到电池没电的困扰；另外，别忘了携带一个小型的电源插线和一个适用于国外插座的变压器。在相机稳定于三脚架之上的情况下，对拍照来说，均匀照明比明亮度来得更重要。对于拍照复制文档来说，可靠的图像识别是必需的，在此需要两个基本技巧。第一，你可以在原文档上附一条标记着档案盒和档案夹信息的便签；第二，当你通过笔记本电脑控制照相机的时候，可以把所拍摄到的 JPG 文件直接归之于硬盘的某一文件夹中，该文件夹已得到事先的命名，标示了文档的来源资料。第二种方法在标记一些顺序性的记录，例如标记航海日志或者分类账簿的时候更加适用。

在你所需档案有限并且档案馆提供复印服务的情况下，有时通过所谓的"远程遥控"的方式订购档案夹中的档案资料复制品而不亲自跑一趟档案馆是明智的选择。尽管每一页复印文件也许要花费高达0.5美分，而且你势必会花费多余的文件复印费，因为不了解哪一部分是自己真正需要的。但是即使加上邮费，三到四份文件夹，75美元的花销也比飞去离你2000英里外的档案所在地便宜得多。远程遥控来获取资料的研究方法尤其适用于开题报告时需要建立一个概念论证的时候。

correctly if you happen to drop the sheaf.

Digital photography, at no cost per page yet with its own share of disadvantages, is increasingly practical, particularly now that facilities from London's National Archives to Budapest's Open Society Archive have installed height-adjustable camera stands. Before shelling out on a camera capable of interfacing with your laptop, understand that $500 buys several thousand photocopies, and while you can typically work quicker in the archive, reading the images later is far less convenient, and annotation requires the extra steps of processing and printing. Note, that unless you use a program like Adobe Photoshop to boost the contrast and brightness thereby washing out the background, all that grey will soon empty your toner cartridge. Pocket-sized point-and-shoot cameras work fine for occasional imaging, but in production-line mode, your back will ache faster than you expected, and a dead battery will leave you stranded. Instead, invest in a high-end subcompact model (like the Canon PowerShot G-10), which has the technology to interface with your laptop but is less expensive than an SLR, while its light weight will not overbalance a desktop tripod. Invest, too, in a transformer pack so you no longer have to worry about the battery, although remember to take a small power-strip as well as an adapter for foreign receptacles. Providing the camera is steady in a tripod, brightness is less important than even illumination. Photography necessitates reliable image identification, of which there are two basic methods: first, you can place a strip of paper on the original document, giving its box and folder. Alternatively, when operating the camera from your laptop, you can dump the JPG file directly into a folder on your hard drive that you have pre-named to match the document's location; this second method is ideal for sequential records, such as a ship's logbook or a probate ledger.

When your interest is limited to a specific range of folders and the archive offers a copying service, it is sometimes worthwhile to order a duplicate of the folders' contents without visiting the archive, by what I call *remote control*. Each copy may cost as much as 50¢, and you will pay for copies of superfluous documents, but even after adding the postage, $75 for three or four folders is far cheaper than flying to a facility two thousand miles away. Researching by remote control is especially appropriate when you are trying to establish a proof of concept.

侦查

  有效率的研究者仿若优秀的侦探。诸如谋杀等犯罪，在现场很少会遗留尚存子弹烟雾的手枪或者行凶者、受害者以外的目击证人——一个自然不愿意开口作证，而另外一个已无法再开口作证了。故而，侦探，还有律师和法官，他们承认，正确确认和认定谋杀犯均是基于把破碎的证据粘合起来建构成的事实，这些单独的破碎的证据可能价值甚微，但是组合起来却能够打消陪审团的合理疑问。成功的侦探要遵循每一条线索，虽然对这些线索的追寻可能多陷于徒劳；他们思考更多的并非是案发现场呈现的事实而是其中所缺失的部分，他们在把案件做成报告提交给法庭经受考验之前，需要核对大量的事实。

跟着线索走

  当你的研究开始时，可能只存在零星的、探索性质的线索，诸如引人深思的掌故、其他历史学者的只言片语，或者一些历史人物的背景资料。你可能对如何才能找到足够的事实资料来建构事实产生疑虑。但当你开始调查每一条线索的时候，那些分散的证据开始集中，你会发现更新的线索，它们或许会指引你深入研究的新范围。事实上，不久后你就会面临一个更加严峻的问题，即一大堆相关信息的处理问题。筛选资料，但不要轻率地把那些不直接相关的线索弃之不理。把它们存放在名为"待定"的文件夹中，这样一来，如果事后你发现其重要性时还可以找得到它们。读本科的时候，我曾经在佐治亚镇大学的 *America*（《美国》）杂志档案馆研读一份报纸，其中，在与一位住在马萨诸塞州皮兹菲尔德市的作家的通信中，我注意到一些事项。而当我思寻博士学位论文的主题之时，正是这些事项指引着我从皮兹菲尔德去到附近莱恩斯伯勒，从而在一个旧马棚的屋檐下发现了20世纪30年代的长达18000页的原始文档资料。

缺失的原始资料

  这个标题初看可能好像有点愚蠢，但这种思维方式却经常被事实证明为出色完成侦探任务时最重要的因素。档案研究发掘了大量既引人入胜又使人困惑的原始资料。人类的本性决定了你必然会探索和撰写未知世界，也许到鬼迷心窍的程度。所以，很可能你的思绪将完全沉浸于此无法跳脱出来，从而导致只见树木、不见森林。要学会暂停，渐次反省，别仅仅思索所建构事实的状态，更要思索建构过程中的缺失。什么人、什么事是犯罪现场中所必需的，但却缺失了呢？为什么会造成这种缺失呢？确认缺失与记录

DETECTION

Effective researchers are like good detectives. For a crime such as murder, there is rarely a still-smoking gun or eyewitnesses other than the perpetrator and victim, one of whom will be unwilling to talk while the other is unable to speak. Detectives, along with lawyers and judges, therefore accept that correctly identifying and then convicting the murderer depends on building a case from pieces of circumstantial evidence, which individually mean little but collectively leave no reasonable doubt in jurors' minds. Successful detectives follow every lead however fruitless the endeavor may prove to be, think about what is missing from the scene rather than what is simply present, and check their facts carefully before filing a report that will have to withstand scrutiny in a court of law.

Following Leads

At the outset of your research, you will only have a few tentative leads, such as suggestive anecdotes, tips from other historians, and background on some actors. You may wonder how you will ever find sufficient facts to make your case. As you begin to investigate each lead, and the loose strands of evidence start to coalesce, you will uncover fresh leads with the potential for taking you into new areas of research. Indeed, it will not be long before you are facing an even more daunting problem: processing a massive amount of pertinent information. Be selective, although avoid hastily consigning leads to the trash if they are not directly relevant. Move them instead to a Pending folder, where they will be handy in the event that you later discover their importance. As an undergraduate, I had been researching a paper in the *America* magazine archive at Georgetown University, and noticed several items of correspondence with a writer whose address was in Pittsfield, Massachusetts; when I was casting around for a doctoral dissertation topic, I followed this lead, through Pittsfield to another address in nearby Lanesboro, thereby discovering 18,000 document pages of material from the 1930s in the roof of an old horse barn.

What's Missing

This point may seem foolish at first, yet it often proves to be the most vital element of successful detection. Archival research uncovers piles of material that can be as fascinating as it is beguiling. Human nature dictates that you will pore through it and write about it, perhaps obsessively. So deeply will you immerse yourself in it that you risk losing sight of the forest for the trees. Learn to stop, take a step back, and think not about what is there but about what is missing. Who, or what, is absent from the scene of the crime, and hence why? Absence, of course, is as difficult to identify as it is to docu-

缺失一样艰难，对此，你要拥有创造性的思维方式。举个例子：我曾在富兰克林·D.罗斯福图书馆研究罗斯福对西班牙内战的观感。在第二天黄昏开车回宾馆的路上，我开始思索罗斯福备忘录和信件中相关记载的简明性以及总体研究中相关资料的缺乏问题。这种情况正常吗？我思索着。第二天早晨，我向档案管理员索要中国方面而非西班牙方面的档案资料，使得他大吃一惊。中国方面的档案中蕴涵着大量往来书信，其中竟包含着被学界誉为不立文字的总统罗斯福亲笔书写的多页信函。通过两套档案的对比，再回顾自己的研究，我可以得出这样的结论：与充满颓废色彩的旧大陆西班牙相比，充满异域色彩的亚洲中国吸引了罗斯福更多的关注。

核对事实

除了明显的错误，没什么能比粗疏所造成的不精确更能快速降低你的研究价值和你的学术声誉了。另外，错误会蚕食学科领域的知识金字塔，因为其他研究者会在假设你的研究确实正确的基础上借鉴它。核对事实——在研究进程中核对所有事实——不要等到研究的尾声，核对任务变得过于艰巨而难以掌控时才开始着手。不能简单地只核对日期、地点、人物和事件，也要核对拼写。虽然像维基百科那样的资源唾手可得而且方便应用，但是却要依据业已出版、经同行评论的参考著作进行核实，另外对那些关键性事实和前后不符之处，要咨询第二方或第三方的意见。特别要提醒大家：当你运用在你经受学科训练初期所依据的著作时，要慎之又慎，因为可能那时，你所受到的学科训练不够严格，贸然使用可能会有所疏漏。

办公活动

在研究结束前的很长一段时间里，你所积累的资料会变得混乱不堪。为了避免使自己陷入困扰的泥淖，你需要像一位富有效率的办公室经理那样，在研究开始时抽出时间建立可靠的系统来管理和储存信息。

文书工作

纸板档案盒和带有标签的档案夹是一种既有效又廉价的管理文书的方法。根据需求，为研究对象中的人物和档案资料、二手资料、媒体资料等建立各种归档档案夹，以字母顺序排列。用铅笔在附带的标签上注明主题有利于档案夹的二次整理和重复使用。可能的情况下，用双面打印的方式打印文章和其他材料以节省存储空间。整理多页文档和文章时尽量少用订书钉，以避免档案夹不平衡地凸起而移出文档后又凹陷以致无法复原。

ment, calling for a creative approach. By way of example, I was at the Franklin D. Roosevelt Library researching Roosevelt's interest in the Spanish Civil War. At the end of the second day while driving back to my hotel, I began to think about the terseness of Roosevelt's memoranda and letters, and then about the paucity of material in general. How normal was this, I wondered. Next morning, I surprised the archivist by asking not for folders on Spain but on China, which, it soon became apparent, bulged with correspondence, including many multi-page letters from a president known for brevity. With the contrast between the two sets of files as my point of departure, I was able to build a case that Roosevelt was far more interested in exotic Asian China than he ever was in decadent Old World Spain.

Fact Checking

Nothing will devalue your project's worth, along with your scholarly credibility, faster than sloppy inaccuracies, let alone outright errors. Errors, moreover, undermine the pyramid of knowledge on which academic disciplines rest, for other researchers will draw on your work presuming it to be factually correct. Check facts—all facts—as you go, not at the end of the project when the task will be too daunting to tackle. Do not simply check dates, places, names, and events—check spellings too. Although a resource at your fingertips like Wikipedia has the merit of convenience, rely on published, peer-reviewed reference works, and, for mission-critical facts or where there is any discrepancy, corroborate with a second or third opinion. Be particularly assiduous when relying on work you conducted at an earlier stage in your training, when your self-discipline may have been lax.

OFFICE WORK

Long before a project's completion, the materials you have accumulated will become confounding. Instead of miring yourself in chaos and confusion, take the time at the outset to implement reliable systems for organizing and storing information, just as if you were an efficient office manager.

Paperwork

Cardboard archive (banker's) boxes and tabbed file folders provide an efficient, low-cost system for organizing paperwork. Set up series of folders, arranged alphabetically, for actors and archival collections, secondary-source topics, media sources, and so on, as required. Writing on the tabs in pencil allows for rearrangement or reuse. When possible, print articles and other materials double sided to save storage space. Minimize staples for multi-page documents and articles, as these will cause the folders to bulge unevenly and eventually sag.

数字资料

如何管理电脑中存储的文件和文件夹会依据个人的喜好和所研究的内容而形式各异，但是下面的管理策略却是通用的。为一项研究专门创建一个文件夹，然后在其下建立名为文章、资料、备忘录、人物和期刊的子文件夹。在名为人物的子文件夹下，为每一位主要人物创建一个子文件夹，在此你可以存储该人物的传记性文档并下载与该人物有关的期刊文章。除了主要文档及其相关资料，我的主要文件夹中皆包含了以下几种MS-Word文档：**年表**，其中至少包含一般事件和特殊事件两项列表；**想法**，为以后深度研究随意记下一些想法；**主控书目**，罗列出所有相关资料来源；**资料**，详细记录图书馆、档案馆藏、联系方式及期刊信息；"**稻草人**"**标靶**，记录其他历史学者或支持或反对的史学观点，在这个文档中，我记录下引文并对此进行二次核查，却没有附加引号，仅在脚注中完整记载下引用来源，如此一来，我就可以把它们方便地剪切并粘贴到关键文档中去；**该做未做之事**，包括需要查阅或者在馆际互借上借阅的图书资料、需要下载的文章、需要追求的线索以及需要修改的方面。

一定要定期将你的文件备份到其他媒介上，也要保存文件的旧版本以避免新版本在保存过程中被存为错误文件。为以防万一，没有什么比打印文档资料形成影印本更好的方式了。记住，除非你的笔记本电脑内置有一个固态硬盘，否则电脑的摔坏会损毁所有的文件。至少，每天都更新U盘的备份，每周都把电脑中的信息备份到另外一个地方例如朋友的电脑中、电子邮件的服务器中，每个月要存备份到一张CD硬盘中。如果你使用的是台式电脑，请再为它投资一个备用电池。对于MS-Word使用者来说，要注意这些操作：选项——高级——保存——{☑始终创建备份副本}——{☑允许后台保存}；选项——保存——{☑保存自动恢复信息时间间隔：10分钟}。不要陷入假想的安全感中，因为Word软件并非每十分钟把你的更新备份到一个独立的文件中，而仅是把更新备份到损毁恢复文件中，所以键要养成定时点击菜单中软盘保存图标的习惯（或者定时按下Ctrl+S键）。

电子表格

除了问卷调查、计量史学统计或定量分析外，很可惜，很少有历史学者把Excel电子表格的应用作为一种常规管理资料的方法，但它确实很实用，尤其适用于数据分类和交叉比对。它对于报纸发行量数据、组织及其成员名单，或请愿书签字者，很适用；而且对于有关州或省、政治倾向、

Digital Material

Arrangements for folders and files on your computer will vary according to personal preference and the nature of the project, but this schema is typical. Within a folder for the project, create subfolders for Articles, Data, Memos, People, and Periodicals. Within the People subfolder, create further subfolders for each major actor, where you can store a biographical file and downloaded journal articles. In addition to the master document and its backup, my main folder usually contains these MS-Word files: **Chronology**, with at least two listings for general and specific events. **Ideas**, for jotting down thoughts for later development. **Master Bibliography,** for listings of all the relevant sources. **Resources**, for details about libraries, archival collections, contacts, and journals. **Straw Men**, for arguments, pro and con, by other historians; I include quotations, double-checked for accuracy, without additional quotation marks, and footnoted with full citations so that I can conveniently cut-and-paste into my master document. **To Do**, for books to pull or request from Interlibrary Loan, articles to download, leads to follow, and corrections to make.

Be sure to backup all your files routinely to a variety of media, and retain old copies to safeguard against replacing a good file with a corrupted one. For peace of mind, nothing beats printing hardcopies. Remember, unless your laptop has a solid-state hard drive, dropping it will kill your files. At minimum, back up daily to a memory stick, weekly to a computer at a different location such as a friend's laptop or an email server, and monthly to a CD-Rom. If you are using a desktop computer then invest in a battery backup. For MS-Word users: Options—Advanced—Save—{☑ Always create backup copy}—{☑ Allow background saves. Options—Save—{☑ Save AutoRecover information every: 10 minutes}. Do not fall into a false sense of security, for Word does not back up your work every ten minutes to a separate file, merely to a disaster recovery file, so adopt the habit of periodically clicking the floppy disk icon on the menu bar (or <Ctrl> <S>).

Spreadsheets

Other than for surveys, cliometrics, or quantitative content analyses, few historians use MS-Excel spreadsheets as a matter of routine, which is a shame for they provide utility, particularly for data that needs sorting or cross-referencing. Newspaper circulation figures, organizations and their lists of members, or signatories to a petition would all be worthwhile candidates; extra columns for *Who's Who* background on state or province, politics, religion, and so forth

宗教信仰等类似于 *Who's Who*（《世界人名录》）的人物身份背景信息、创建单列更利于勾勒出人物形象。分析身为不同集团成员的大量人物时，可以在电子表格中制作多重工作表（柱状图或三维图）以分析其共同特点。我曾经研究过一份500页的美国联邦调查局（FBI）档案，其中记载了80位工作人员在5年时间内访问过200名证人的内容。利用电子表格，我把证人和工作人员的相关数据分别制成两份独立的工作表，表头分别包括日期、访问编号、驻外办公室、家乡、所属组织等，这确实是需要花费几个小时才能完成的工作，但是却一目了然，便于以后分类和评估一些例如姓名、日期、地点、政治派系等基准。简单的电子表格，再配合你设置的其他可靠的、使用得当的办公系统，会有利于你在写作过程中索取证据。写作中最令人沮丧的莫过于你知道自己曾经读到过一条当时觉得无关紧要的引文，现在却发觉至关重要，但是你却记不清在哪里看到它了。为了节省后期像疯子一样疯狂彻查你所搜集的所有资料而消耗的精力，请在名为"想法"的文档下，持续记录下一些随意的研读点滴心得——包括记录下必不可少的来源引文——并把它们以有逻辑、有条理的方式存档。

would then allow for convenient profiling. For actors with memberships across several organizations, say, create multiple worksheets (stacked, or three-dimensional sheets) to analyze common denominators. I had an FBI dossier of some five hundred reports, filed by eighty agents who had interviewed two hundred witnesses over a five-year period. Entering the data into separate worksheets for witnesses and agents, along with column headings for date, report number, field office, home town, organization, and so forth, admittedly took a few hours, but then it was a snap to sort and evaluate the data based on criteria such as name, date, place, or political affiliation. Simple spreadsheets, along with the other reliable office systems you have put in place, will facilitate evidence acquisition once you start the business of writing. There is nothing more frustrating than knowing you have read a quotation that at the time seemed tangential but now is vital, and yet you cannot remember where you saw it. Save yourself the aggravation of rummaging through piles of papers like a crazy person by always jotting down random observations—including the all-important reference—in your Ideas file, and storing your evidence in a logical, organized fashion.

写 作
WRITING A PAPER OR DISSERTATION

本章讨论的主题是撰写一篇杰出的，既流畅又有说服力，并有能力获奖的论文所需要的方法和形式。你可能在开始时信心满满，但却要做好心理准备——尤其是对于博士学位论文来说——其写作过程会逐渐变得枯燥甚至煎熬，到时你或许会痴痴盯着空白的电脑屏幕，或许会在室内焦躁踱步，满心疑虑，不知自己是否有能力完成甚至一个章节的写作，更别提整项研究工作了。大部分博士学位论文作者从他们自己认为的核心章节开始动笔，把此章作为一篇会议论文的基础并期望发展成为期刊论文。然后，他们可能撰写内容多为强调某一种方法论或研究领域现状的一至两个章节，例如电影或性别。虽然这种流程具有实用价值，甚至可以说是不可避免的，但是它也往往导致整篇论文章节的不连贯和叙述的不统一。我在以后的论述中会探讨到如何建构论文章节，并把它们统合为一个无懈可击的整体。但首先，在讨论结构的精练和以段落为写作单位这些概念之前，我将从语句层面着手论述，探讨如何以有效的、现代的方法进行论据呈现，此方法我称之为"文本置入"。

文本置入

在人文学科领域的学术训练中，两种涉及呈现和解读论据的方法是十分有益的。这两种方法皆曾受到拥护但现在皆早已过时，并且它们远没有所谓的文本置入的方法那么有效率。第一种是，遵循英国写作传统的作者倾向于多句引用，更有甚者，倾向于引用段落（其引用方式是直接引用很长的节选、格式为缩进排列、不用引号标注）。我最近评论了一篇依此学术规范而写成的权威性力作，其中呈现了两个世纪的、巨幅的档案研究成果，但是行文中普遍存在着长篇引用段落和引语段，它们有时竟然占据了一页的所有空间，只有三四行的空间属于作者的正式写作，导致整篇行文没有留下很多余地用于解读文本。如此一来，此书与其说是一部分析性的历史学著作，不如说是一篇第一手资料的编辑整理著作。第二种是，一些作者在写作中遵循以人类学家克利福德·格尔茨为先驱进而使用的"深描"的方法。细节描述是令人钦佩的，况且格尔茨的确以扣人心弦的细节把巴厘岛的斗鸡过程描绘得栩栩如生，但是行文中，他没有进行任何引用，即没有呈现任何能够支持他所持主张的论据。即使他在无引文的 *The Interpretation of Culture* （《文化的解读》）一书第423页声明其斗鸡传统"曾被记载在棕榈叶上"，却并没有引用它们。他指出，没有一个巴厘人曾经质疑过裁判的判决或者控诉过获胜方以不公平的方式获胜，但是他却没有提出任何文本论据，例如口述采访的摘录。文本置入是在此两种极端方法中持中间立场的一种浓厚描述方式，方法是把简短的、短语长度的引文埋入释义性的、解读性的行文中。

This chapter addresses the methods for and style of writing an award-winning thesis, one that will stand out as much for its flowing prose as for its persuasive exposition. You will be eager to begin, but understand that the task—particularly for a dissertation—will soon become arduous, even torturous, as you stare at a blank screen or fuss around the apartment, filled with doubts about your ability to complete one chapter let alone the entire project. Most dissertation writers start with what they consider to be the core chapter, and then use this as the basis for a conference paper and hopefully a journal article. They may then write one or two chapters that stress a particular methodology or field, such as film or gender. While this progression has practical merit, and may be inevitable, it often results in discrete chapters and a disjointed narrative. I explain later how to structure chapters, then integrate them into a seamless whole, but first I will begin at the sentence level, with an effective, modern method for presenting evidence that I call *textual immersion*, before discussing the concepts of structured précis and paragraphs as work units.

TEXTUAL IMMERSION

It will be instructive to mention two approaches to presenting and interpreting evidence within the academic disciplines of the humanities. Both have had their advocates yet both are outmoded, and they are far less effective than textual immersion. On the one hand, there are writers in the British tradition of the multi-sentence quotation, or worse, the block quotation (a lengthy extract, indented, without quotation marks). I recently reviewed a magisterial work of scholarship cast in this mold, representing two decades of prodigious archival study, yet so ubiquitous were the lengthy quoted passages and block quotes, which sometimes comprised all but three or four lines of the entire page, that there was little room left for interpretation. Instead of a work of analytical history, it read like an edited collection of primary sources. On the other hand, there are writers who follow the "thick description" approach pioneered by anthropologist Clifford Geertz. Detailed description is admirable, and Geertz could certainly bring a Balinese cockfight to life in gripping detail, yet he did so without using quotations, without presenting evidence that is, to support his assertions. Even though he stated—on quotation-less page 423 of *The Interpretation of Cultures*—that cockfighting lore was "written down in palm-leaf manuscripts," he did not quote from them. He claimed that no Balinese ever questioned an umpire's judgment nor charged a victor with unfairness, but he offered no textual evidence, such as excerpts from oral interviews. Textual immersion takes a sort of thick texting path between these two extremes, by embedding lots of short, phrase-length quotations into paraphrased, interpretive prose.

引言

　　我所推荐的写作方法的核心是短语长度的引文方式,理想状态是引用一个最好能够抓住你文中人物修辞特点的、掷地有声的短语,一个能使读者难以忘怀的短语,一个简明扼要的、能够最好表明你所要表达的主旨的短语。不要大段引用无聊的冗词,反之仅截取关键陈述和掷地有声的修辞——并在上下文中——用紧凑的语言改写余下的部分。文本置入的方法在你打算用一段或几段的空间深入描述或解读一个单一文本时是有效的,例如在解读一篇影响深远的演讲的时候。这样一来,文本的来源选择就显得十分重要。也许你手中有同一位人物有关同一主题的五篇演讲或说明同一观点的几封书信。不要这引用一点,那引用一点,仅选择一篇存在最丰富材料的演讲或者书信来进行集中引用。掌握此技巧需要大量练习和研读采用此种引用方式的高手们撰写的文章。请研读附录案例部分的有关例子,以了解在段落中怎样进行短语引用和其他部分的简洁改写,体会此种方式带来的累加的解读效果。

　　以短语长度进行引用、对其他部分进行简洁改写、累加解释为特点的文本置入方式具有以下三项优势。第一,文本置入方法更容易在不废话和打断叙述节奏的情况下介绍说话者本人。第二,它为行文中避免现在时态、第一人称或者单数复数不一致问题提供了方便。第三,它同时提升了引用的价值,为文本解读的最大化提供了空间。一些练习之后,你不但有能力令读者置身于你行文中人物的所在环境中,就像读者在现场聆听演讲或边读日记边联想一般;而且通过把引用内容的其他部分进行简洁改写的方式,你还有能力使你的论证更上一个台阶。文本置入的方式为史学提供了即时感和大段引用缺少的亲切感;事实上,很多读者都承认这样一个阅读习惯,每当他们读到引语段落的时候,会自行忽略,就好像小一号的字体所表述的内容即意味着无关紧要一般。

　　但是,与许多创新性的、强有力的技术相同,文本置入方法也有其潜在的、令人困扰的劣势,这是你需要警觉的。要警惕通过文中人物之口讲出自己的批判观点,或者超出上下文的文意或者进行有偏见的引用。一种解决方法是在行文中大量使用引文,使得没有批判者可以对你的资料产生不实的质疑。行文开始时就要呈现具有丰富引用的段落以确立方法的正当性并缓和质疑。谨记,在简洁诠释论述中呈现第一手资料引文这样一种有效的引用方式,如果运用到第二手资料时不能够做到有效和严格,就有被指控为抄袭的隐患。正如彼得·查尔斯·霍菲尔在 *Past Imperfect*(《过去的未完成》)中所指出的,美国的专业历史学在20世纪90年代后名誉扫地,起因是人们发现两位受欢迎的学问精深的历史学作家史蒂芬·安布罗斯和多丽

Quotations

At the heart of the system advocated here lies the phrase-length quotation, ideally a ringing phrase that best captures your actor's rhetorical style, a memorable phrase that will stick in your reader's mind, a pithy phrase that best illustrates the point you wish to make. Instead of quoting a long passage of dreary verbiage, chop out key statements and ringing rhetoric, and then paraphrase—closely, and in context—from the rest of the passage. Textual immersion is particularly effective when you devote a whole paragraph—or paragraphs—to an in-depth presentation and interpretation of a single text, such as an influential speech. Source selection is therefore important. Maybe you have five speeches by the same actor on the same subject, or several letters that make the same point. Instead of picking out quotes here and there, choose the one speech or letter that provides the richest material, and then draw intensively from it. Mastering the technique requires practice, as well as study of the kinds of quotations chosen by practitioners of the art. Study the samples in the Examples section to see how the quoted phrases and paraphrasing build up through the paragraph so that the interpretative effect is cumulative.

Textual immersion in phrase-length quotations, close paraphrasing, and cumulative interpretation offers three main advantages: First, it is easy to introduce the speaker without wasting words or disrupting the narrative flow. Second, it provides a convenient workaround for present tense, first person, or singular/plural inconsistencies. Third, it simultaneously elevates the value of the quote while maximizing space for your interpretation. After some practice, you will not only be able to immerse your reader in your actor's milieu, as if the reader were listening to the speech or thumbing through the diary, but by close paraphrasing around the quotations you will also be able to promote a step in your argument. Textual immersion lends historiography an immediacy, an intimacy that lengthy passages seem to lack; indeed, some readers admit that whenever they encounter a block quotation, they skip over it, as if its smaller typeface suggests its irrelevance.

Yet in common with many innovative, powerful techniques, textual immersion also has potentially troubling disadvantages for which you must be vigilant. Be on your guard against charges that you have put words into your actor's mouth, or selected quotations out of context or with a bias toward your thesis. One safeguard is to quote such a preponderant body of material that no critic could doubt that you had been untrue to your sources. Presenting an especially quotation-rich paragraph early in your paper will establish the method and allay fears. Be mindful, too, that a valid system for presenting primary-source quotations embedded in closely paraphrased prose can lay

丝·克恩斯·古德温之所以如此多产是因为他们有计划地窃取其他作者书中的整个段落，通过改变一些单词和把多页引用内容归于同一脚注来掩盖抄袭痕迹。自安布罗斯、古德温丑闻之后，诠释一词就变成一个忌讳的字眼，为其重新正名则需要花费很长时间，并且需要持一种负责的态度。无论你以何种原因使用第二手资料——无论是作为背景信息、理论支持，还是反面观点——皆要意识到，不仅包括资料事实，而且还包括文字风格，小到行文顺序和遣词造句，皆是该作者的知识成果或知识财产。如果你不去承认那些信息或者创造性内容的起源来自他人，尤其是如果你把那些内容作为自己的成果展示出来或者以其他的方式利用它为自己牟利，那么你的行为就属于剽窃。

谨记身为一位职业学者的道德责任感。仅按照你面前的原文资料一字不落地引证或引用——是身为学者所遵循的基本原则。换句话说，千万不能从第二手资料中照抄原始资料却使其看起来像你阅读过原始文本再进行引用一样。如果这样做，你违反了学者的道德伦理，并且如果第二手资料作者犯下引用错误的引言甚至故意更改了其本意——这两种现象，我碰到过不止一次，深感悲哀——你将会以讹传讹。所以，无论如何，引用第二手文献的时候，一定要在脚注中注明资料来源。例如：

105. Ralph T. O'Neil speaking on NBC Radio, 23 March 1931, cited in William Pencak, *For God and Country: The American Legion, 1919–1941* (Boston: Northeastern University Press, 1989), p. 79. （拉尔夫·T.奥尼尔在 NBC 广播中的讲话，1931年3月23日，选自威廉·潘查克，《为了上帝和国家：美国退伍军人协会，1919—1941年》。波士顿：东北大学出版社，1989年，p.79。）

或者，找到原始文本，但要谨记你的道德责任感，避免抄袭。就算我亲自前往 NBC 档案馆复印奥尼尔的原始手稿，我也一定需要在注释中提及潘查克的功劳，因为如果没有他的作品，我就无法找到原文。

尽管多句引用或引语段落的运用可以避免方法论和道德方面的隐患，但也要拒绝其诱惑尽量不使用。基本上，在文学批判领域，偶尔在古代史研究方面，正规的行文方式是以引用一段很长的原始文献篇章作为引语段落开端，然后以分析此一引语段作为正文内容。如果你的导师或学科训练坚持此一写作方法，你只能别无选择地遵循，但是我依然建议你在书写解读性段落的时候假装引语段落并不存在。这则建议也适用于你分析视觉图像，像建筑、雕像、绘画、照片、动画，而且还当然包括影音图像之时。用词丰富，栩栩如生地以文字描述图像——仅把实际图像当做额外的补充。这样一来，就算出版商因为空间或版权的原因不准你在文章中附加图像，你的文章依然完整。以下是总体原则，要看文本置入方法的具体应用实例请参看案例部分。

- **确认每位发言者**，换句话说，你需要介绍或者归类所有引文的出

you open to accusations of plagiarism when applied with insufficient rigor to secondary sources. As Peter Charles Hoffer details in *Past Imperfect*, the U.S. historical profession lost credibility in the 1990s following disclosures that Stephen Ambrose and Doris Kearns Goodwin, two popular yet scholarly authors, were so prolific because they had systematically lifted entire passages from other authors, covering their tracks by changing a few words and referencing multiple pages in a footnote. Paraphrasing became a dirty word after the Ambrose and Goodwin scandals, so its rehabilitation will take time as well as responsible treatment. When you are employing a secondary source for any reason—for background information, theoretical support, or counterpoint—be cognizant that not only the source's facts but also its literary style, right down to the level of word order and selection, are the intellectual creation or property of the author. If you fail to acknowledge the provenance of either the information or the creative content, particularly if you present that content as your own work or otherwise appropriate it to your benefit, then you are stealing.

Always remember your ethical responsibilities as a professional academic. It is essential that you only quote from—and cite—a source that you have physically in front of you. In other words, never copy primary material from a secondary source and then cite it as if you were looking at the original text. By doing so, you would commit an ethical violation, and you risk discovery in the event the secondary-source author copied the quotation incorrectly or, worse, changed its meaning, both of which, I am saddened to report, I have seen on more than one occasion. So, by all means, copy from the secondary source but be sure to reference that source in the footnote. [105. Ralph T. O'Neil speaking on NBC Radio, 23 March 1931, cited in William Pencak, *For God and Country: The American Legion, 1919–1941* (Boston: Northeastern University Press, 1989), p. 79.] Alternatively, locate the original text, only do remember your ethical responsibility not to plagiarize. Were I to visit the NBC archive to copy O'Neil's remarks from the original transcript, I must still credit Pencak's research in my footnote, because I would not have found the quotation otherwise.

Despite the potential for methodological and ethical pitfalls, resist the temptation to resort to multi-sentence or block quotations. Primarily in the discipline of literary criticism but occasionally in studies of ancient history, it is traditional to begin a section with a lengthy original passage, set off as a block quotation, that subsequent body paragraphs then analyze. If your advisor or discipline insists on this method then you have little choice, although I would urge you, nonetheless, to write the interpretive paragraphs as if the block quotation was not there. This advice holds when you are analyzing vi-

处。你的读者应该不查看脚注就能够了解谁在发言。在此方面，新闻业是一个典范，因为记者们深切了解，没有出处的引文是几乎没有价值的；若一则报道声称"根据五角大楼的一个匿名信息来源，加拿大部队将侵犯缅因州"，报纸的读者们难道会信以为真吗？在论文或章节中首次提到某个人物时，要提供其全名及其完整头衔，以后可以将其全名简化为姓氏。与此相同，行文中语境和日期的介绍也应该一目了然，使得读者不需追溯注释就能够清楚明白。例如：

Addressing West Point graduates on 1 June 2002, President George W. Bush asserted that, "Moral truth is the same in every culture."（2002年6月1日，总统乔治·W. 布什对西点军校的毕业生声称："道德真理在不同文化中具有普遍性。"）

- **引号的位置**是一个令许多作者困惑的问题，部分由于美式英语和英式英语的区别，也由于一些学者和大学出版社的草率编辑。不过该问题内容简单、逻辑凝练。即当结束一段引言时，应该把逗号或句号至于引号之内。请允许我重复一遍：在引文的结尾，所有的逗号和句号都应被置于引号之内，如"inside the quote marks."与中文语法不同，美国正式英语——或者说芝加哥模式——对于原始文本中逗号和句号的位置要求不留余地、十分死板。但是，在引文后加入其他符号的情况下，却存在一则例外，虽然在实际运用当中，很少有机会如此操作。只要分号、冒号或问号是你所添加的，就都要被置于结尾引号之外。例如：

Begemann said, "It is such a starry night"; Van Gogh wondered if she would ever come to bed. Van Gogh asked, "Why is it such a starry night?" What was behind van Gogh's question, "Why is it such a starry night?"[1]（贝格曼说："真是一个漫天繁星的夜晚"；梵高不知道她是否从不会来睡觉。他问："为什么夜晚漫天繁星呢？"梵高的问题的真实意图是什么？）

- **把引号留给引言**。在美国正式英语中，仅在真正引用文本时才使用引号，并辅以脚注。也就是说，不要在表示讽刺的语气时轻易使用引号，也不要在表示不确定的语气时随意地使用，或在表明暗示的语境时不负责任地使用。[2] 例如：

Despite seizing the Philippines, Americans have never been "imperialists."（"即使美国人侵略了菲律宾，他们也未成为过'帝国主义者'"。）

这个作者其实在暗示美国一直都是帝国主义者吗？故而，在行文中，不要用布什是一个"重生"的基督教徒这样的表述方式，而要或者运用事实论

---

[1]. 此示例中，第一个问号是引文就有的，第二个是你额外添加的。——译者注
[2]. 根据中文惯例，引号除了表示引用文本，也可用于表示强调等。因此本书中文部分的符号使用遵循中文惯例，英语部分严格使用英语的符号体系。——编者注

sual images—architecture, sculpture, paintings, photographs, cartoons—and of course films. Describe the image in words—bring it to life with the richness of your prose—and only include the actual image as a bonus. Then, should a publisher not let you use the image whether for reasons of space or copyright, your article still stands as written. General usage guidelines follow; for samples of textual immersion, see the Examples section.

- **Identify every speaker,** which is to say, you must introduce or attribute all your quotations. Your reader should always know who is speaking without having to search through the footnotes. Journalism is a model here because reporters understand that a quotation without attribution is next to worthless; what newspaper reader would take seriously a report that claimed, "According to an anonymous source at the Pentagon, the Canadian army is planning an invasion of Maine"? Provide the actor's full title and name at first mention in the paper or chapter, and then use just the family name thereafter. Similarly, contexts and dates should be obvious to your reader without recourse to footnotes. [Addressing West Point graduates on 1 June 2002, President George W. Bush asserted that, "Moral truth is the same in every culture."]

- **Quote mark position** is a source of confusion for many writers, due in part to variations between British and American English, as well as sloppy editing by some scholars and university presses. Yet the rules are elementary and the logic elegant. When closing a quotation, the comma or period goes inside the quotation mark. Please allow me to repeat myself: At the end of quotations, all commas and periods go "inside the quote marks." Unlike Chinese grammar, American—or Chicago-style—formal English makes no allowance for the position of commas and periods in the original text. But there is an exception for other punctuation marks that you add to a quotation, although in practice you should rarely, if ever, do so. If you add a semicolon, colon, or a question mark then it goes outside the closing marks. [Begemann said, "It is such a starry night"; van Gogh wondered if she would ever come to bed.] [Van Gogh asked, "Why is it such a starry night?"] [What was behind van Gogh's question, "Why is it such a starry night"?]

- **Quote marks for quotations.** Reserve quotation marks solely for actual quotations, backed up by a footnote. That is to say, do not use them cynically to denote irony, loosely to suggest uncertainty, or irresponsibly to make an insinuation. [Despite seizing the Philippines, Americans have never been "imperialists."] Is this author insinuating that Americans have always been imperialistic? So instead of writing, Bush was a "born-again" Christian, either state confidently—as a fact—that indeed Bush was a born-again

述的表达方式，即布什是一个重生的基督教徒，或者在该单词并非一个常用名词的情况下，表述为布什是一个所谓的重生的基督教徒。在正式英语中，用斜体字而非引号标示特殊用法的单词或词组性名词。例如：

Bush was a self-described *born-again* Christian, someone who had experienced a spiritual rebirth.（布什自认为是一个'重生的基督教徒'，是一个经历过灵魂重生的人。）

This paper defines *culture* as X.（在本篇论文中，'文化'一词被定义为 X。）

Cardinal Isidro Gomá used the word *red* five times in a single paragraph.（红衣主教伊西德罗·戈马在一段行文中，将'红'这个字用了五次。）

为遵守上述对于引号的运用规定，要为引用的短语注明一个配套的脚注。例如：

On the platform were isolationists like "Radio Priest" Charles E. Coughlin.（站在台上的是一群类似于"广播主教"查尔斯·E.科洛林那样的孤立主义者们。[6]）

6. For Coughlin as "'Radio Priest,'" see, for example, *Broadcasting* (15 November 1936), p.38.（6.科洛林被称为"广播主教"的例子，请参看《广播》（1936年11月15日），p. 38。）

- **双重引号**。用额外的引号将引言置于引言中。[1] 尽管乍见时会觉得奇怪，但这样的行文语法意义精确，并可明确显示出引言中包含的二手资料，也就是说，你引用的书籍或新闻报道中所包含的某部分本身亦是来源于其他来源的引言。例如：

In 1938, New York's *Herald Tribune* stressed Ellery Sedgwick's amazement at conditions "'in "White Spain,"'" where governance "'appeared perfect,'" prices were reasonable, food was plentiful, and Gen. Francisco Franco had "'an ambitious program of slum clearance.'"（1938年，纽约的（《先驱论坛报》）强调艾勒里·赛德维克对于在"白色西班牙"的生活条件感到难以置信，那里政府执政"貌似完美"，物价合理，食品充足，而且弗朗西斯科·佛朗哥将军心怀一个"宏伟的贫民区清除计划"。）

其中引号的使用是奇怪但必要的，其目的是引用"白色西班牙"一词，因为赛德维克首先引用过此一词语，而《先驱论坛报》记者则引用了赛德维克的说法。在这种情况下，要在行文中正确地置入引号则需要置入一套双引号表明引言，再置入一套单引号表明记者引用赛德维克的引言，最后置入一套双引号标志赛德维克引用的引言。注意引用中要遵循美式英语标点符号使

---

1. 文中写作中并无此类用法，故本书中文翻译采用中文的引号表达方法，英语部分请遵循英语规则。——编者注

Christian, or if the term is not yet in common usage then write that Bush was a so-called born-again Christian. To denote terms or words-as-words, use italics instead of quotation marks. [Bush was a self-described *born-again* Christian, someone who had experienced a spiritual rebirth.] [This paper defines *culture* as *X*.] [Cardinal Isidro Gomá used the word *red* five times in a single paragraph.] For phrases used at the time, maintain the rule by providing a supporting footnote. [On the platform were isolationists like "Radio Priest" Charles E. Coughlin.⁶] [6. For Coughlin as "'Radio Priest,'" see, for example, *Broadcasting* (15 November 1936), p. 38.]

- **Double quote marks.** Set quotations of quotations inside an extra set of marks. While this can sometimes look strange, it is grammatically precise and indicates when your source is second hand, as when you are quoting, say, a passage from a book or newspaper report that is itself a quotation. [In 1938, New York's *Herald Tribune* stressed Ellery Sedgwick's amazement at conditions "'in "White Spain,"'" where governance "'appeared perfect,'" prices were reasonable, food was plentiful, and Gen. Francisco Franco had "'an ambitious program of slum clearance.'"] Five marks are admittedly unusual but necessary, nevertheless, to close the quotation ending with *White Spain* because Sedgwick placed the term in quotation marks and the *Tribune*'s reporter was in turn quoting Sedgwick. So to embed the quotation correctly in prose requires an outside pair of marks to denote a quotation, an inside single mark to indicate that the reporter was quoting Sedgwick, and then a double mark for Sedgwick's term. Note the logic of the double–single–double quotation-mark system that is in use in American English (it reverses in British English, with single–double–single marks).

- **Brackets.** Render quotations with total fidelity, which means double-checking them for accuracy. Remember that even a misplaced comma can alter the meaning of a phrase. Whenever you need to make a change—to the tense of a verb, say, or to insert a point of explanation—do so inside a pair of square brackets, as in this example: Rebel commanders said that they had "call[ed] for Muammar [el-Qaddafi] to surrender immediately."

- **Ellipses.** Use a three-dot ellipse (. . .) to denote an omission within a sentence, and a four-dot ellipse to denote the omission of one or more complete sentences. [According to John Quincy Adams, commerce was "among the natural rights and duties of men. . . The moral obligation of commercial intercourse between nations is founded . . . upon the Christian precept to love your neighbor as yourself."] As this example suggests, ellipses create clutter and are best avoided, which is fine because textual immersion minimizes the need for them. [According to John Quincy Adams, commerce was

用方法，即双引号、再单引号、再双引号这样的顺序逻辑（而英式英语则与此相反，即单引号、再双引号、再单引号）。

• **方括号**。以完全忠诚的态度引用资料，就是说要检查两次其准确性。要记住，一个错放的逗号有可能改变一个短语的意思。在你需要更改内容的时候——例如改变一个动词的时态，或者插入一个解释性的观点——把此放在方括号里，正如该例子：Rebel commanders said that they had "call[ed] for Muammar [el-Qaddafi] to surrender immediately."（反政府军的将军说他们已经"要求[了]穆阿迈尔马[卡扎菲]投降"。）

• **省略号**。英语中，使用三点的省略号"..."表明一个句子中的省略，使用四点的省略号表明段落中一个以上句子的省略。例如：

According to John Quincy Adams, commerce was "among the natural rights and duties of men. . . . The moral obligation of commercial intercourse between nations is founded . . . upon the Christian precept to love your neighbor as yourself."（根据约翰·昆西·亚当斯所言，商业"存在于人的自然权力和责任之中……国家间商业交往的道德责任基于……基督教所遵循的爱邻如己的原则"。）

正如此例子所显示的，省略号会造成混乱，最好避免使用，而文本置入的引用方式正好减少了省略号的使用。这样一来，上文引用则可以改为：

According to John Quincy Adams, commerce was "among the natural rights and duties of men." Based on the "Christian precept to love your neighbor as yourself," he felt that nations had a "moral obligation" to participate in commercial trade.（根据约翰·昆西·亚当斯所言，商业"存在于人的自然权力和责任之中"。基于"基督教爱邻如己的原则"，他认为国家之间在参与商业活动时应心存"一种道德责任"。）

不要在句子的前方或后方使用省略号去开始或结束一句话的引用。当你的写作容量具有字数上限的时候，要注意：MS Word模式下，省略号被计算为三个单词。因为省略号中圆点与圆点之间皆存在一个空格，所以，为了避免自动换行，在每个圆点之间输入Word的不间断字符（按住Ctrl+Shift，再按下空格键）。

• **大写字体**。使用一堆烦琐的方括号，或者小写字体，虽然是被允许的，但更简单的做法是保持嵌入式引文中的首字母大写就好。不过，在以首字母为小写的引文为句子开头的情况下，要将其首字母改成大写。[1]

• **错误**。为了给读者标明在引用的原始文献中存在的语法和拼写错误，

---

1. 更改大小写字体的方式分为以下两种情况。第一种情况：把某一个段落援引到某一句话中，若原始引文中首字母为大写的话，不要把大写改成小写。例如："According to Lincoln's 'Four score and seven years' of family history..."第二种情况：把某一个段落援引到某一句话的开头，若原始引文中首字母为小写的话，要把小写改成大写。例如："'Everything you have, you owe to your name,' Homer quoted Anthony."——译者注

"among the natural rights and duties of men." Based on the "Christian precept to love your neighbor as yourself," he felt that nations had a "moral obligation" to participate in commercial trade.] Do not use leading and trailing ellipses (to begin or end a sentence-length quotation). Note that when you are writing to a word limit, MS-Word counts an ellipse as three words. Ellipsis points have a space between them, so to corral ellipses that partially wrap to the next line, insert Word's special non-breaking character between each period (hold down <Ctrl> and <Shift> then press <Spacebar>).

- **Capitalization.** Rather than using a pair of fussy square brackets, or lowercasing, which is permissible, simply retain the capitalization of embedded quotations, but do change to uppercase when beginning a sentence with a lowercased quotation.
- **Errors.** Alert your reader to grammatical and spelling errors in the original text by including a [*sic*] after the problem. ["When you wanted to pack the supreme court," New York Life Insurance executive Warren R. Evans of Shelby, Montana, later wrote to Roosevelt, "you turned me from a steady supporter of yours into a cynical and disallusioned [*sic*] antagonist."] Like ellipses, every [*sic*] is a distraction, so minimize their usage, which is easier anyway when quoting short phrases. Use a 2-em-dash for missing letters, and a 3-em-dash for missing words. [According to the chronicle, "King Harold swore that Wi—— was a ———."]

Citations

Whenever you include a quotation, present information that is not common knowledge, or refer to someone else's ideas, you must provide a citation that accurately describes your source. Citations maintain the academic principles of honesty and openness, enabling other scholars to both verify and employ your research. There are two basic systems: parenthetical referencing (Modern Language Association or MLA) and footnotes (Chicago). While the MLA author-date system may have advantages for the natural and applied sciences, source information in parentheses makes prose look ugly thereby spoiling the narrative's flow, is incomplete without a bibliography, and it precludes additional information, often resulting in a mixed parenthetical and footnoted hybrid. For these reasons, the MLA system is—in my opinion—unsuited

在错误后标注［*sic*］。例如：

"When you wanted to pack the supreme court," New York Life Insurance executive Warren R. Evans of Shelby, Montana, later wrote to Roosevelt, "you turned me from a steady supporter of yours into a cynical and disallusioned [*sic*] antagonist."[1]（"当你企图拉拢最高法院的时候"，来自蒙大拿州谢尔比郡的纽约人寿保险公司董事沃伦·R.埃文斯在过后写给罗斯福的信中说到："您把我从一个您的长久支持者变成了一个愤世嫉俗的、失望的对立者。"）

与省略号一样，每一个［*sic*］的使用都会分散读者的注意力，故应尽量减少其使用次数，而遵循引用简短的固定短语这一原则正好与其不谋而合。英语中，使用破折号标注缺失的字母，使用1.5倍破折号来标注缺失的单词。例如：

According to the chronicle, "King Harold swore that Wi—— was a ———."[2]（根据编年史记载，"国王哈罗德曾咒骂Wi——是一个———"。）

引文

在进行引用、提出非常识性知识的信息，或者提及其他人观点的情况下，必须提供一则能够确切描述信息来源的引文。引文秉持学术的诚实性和开放性原则，使得其他学者能够核实并利用你的研究成果。引文有两种基本系统格式：插入语引用系统格式（现代语言学会文体，MLA文体）和脚注引用系统格式（《芝加哥论文格式手册》文体）。尽管 MLA 文体在自然科学和应用科学的行文模式中具有优势，但以括号标注信息来源的形式并置于正文中使得行文容貌可怖，而且破坏了叙述的流畅性，同时没有书目就不完整，还阻止额外信息，最后导致文体系统格式变成了插入语引用和脚注引用的混合体。基于以上原因，虽然仍有一些学科领域坚持使用 MLA 文体，但在我看来，该系统格式不适用于人文学科的论文书写。以脚注引用为特征的芝加哥论文格式，以其最低程度的侵入性和最大程度的灵活性，现如今正成为主要领先国际的人文学科期刊行文的标准格式。

《芝加哥论文格式手册》存在具有微小差距的各个版本，在本指南中我罗列出的文体格式基于此理想模式，适用于所有的原创作品和大多数投稿文章所规定的格式，当然，在确定用稿之后，编辑有可能会要求再次修改格式以适应该期刊的要求。注意：你在已出版文本中看到的差别甚至错误，并不是提供给自己草率粗心工作的许可证。"哦，我只是照搬了 *Lower Tigris Geographical Society Review*（《下底格里斯河地理学会评论》）"这样的说法并不是为自己的疏忽和无知进行辩白的好借口。你确实该吸取顶级国

---

1. disallusioned 拼写错误，正确拼写应为 disillusioned。——译者注
2. 此处，Wi——，代表一个人的名字，但是全名缺失，故而用破折号标注缺失字母；was a 后边缺失一个单词，故而用1.5倍破折号标注缺失单词。——译者注

to the humanities, although some disciplines may still insist on its use. Chicago-style footnoting, the least intrusive and most flexible system, is now standard at leading international humanities journals.

Minor variations of Chicago style exist; I detail throughout this guide an ideal form that is suitable for all original work, as well as most article submissions, although, on acceptance, an editor may ask for reformatting to suit the journal's style. Note: variations, as well as errors that you may see in print, do not provide a license for sloppy work. "Oh, I simply copied my style from the *Lower Tigris Geographical Society Review*," is no excuse for ignorance or laziness on your part. For sure, pick up good habits from top international journals or university presses, but let *Chicago 16th* be your final arbiter of style. If a copy is not yet sitting on your desk then postpone buying that new winter coat and order one from an online bookstore. Remember, the golden rule of style is consistency. If you are going to abbreviate *chapter* to *chap.* in footnote 4 then you must say *chap.* in footnotes 21, 37, 66, and 110 as well, otherwise your reader will have no confidence in your eye for detail, and, to quote from an old mentor of mine, "It is the details that kill you."

Best practice is to reserve footnotes solely for the information necessary to provide the citation. In other words, you should avoid extended footnotes, the logic being that if the information is important then include it in the body paragraph, and if it is not important then do not clutter up your footnotes with it, making their sheer bulk ultimately unmanageable (and unpublishable). Kevin Kenny, a senior scholar at Boston College, would relate to students in his dissertation seminar how he had once submitted an article to a journal and was humbled when one of the reviewers commented acidly that the author had a poor command of the secondary sources, as evidenced by the plethora of extended footnotes. Sometimes, of course, an extended note is necessary or desirable. You may wish to remedy confusion over an actor's name, provide the original text of a problematic translation, or include references to additional works that a reader outside your field might usefully consult. And sometimes you will include information, particularly concerning methodology or theory, in the notes of an MA thesis or PhD dissertation that you later delete from a journal article or book manuscript. Strive, nevertheless, to minimize superfluous detail in notes. General usage guidelines follow.

- **Reference number.** Insert a footnote reference number—a superscripted Arabic numeral—at the end of the sentence containing the referent.

际期刊和大学出版社的好习惯,但却要把《芝加哥论文格式手册(第十六版)》作为疑难格式问题的最终裁决依据。如果该书现在还没有出现在你的书桌上的话,那么请延迟购买一件新款冬季外套的计划,去网上书店订购吧。记住,文本格式的重要原则是前后一致。如果你打算在脚注4中把chapter(章节)缩写成chap.,那么在随后的脚注21、37、66和110中也要比照办理,否则你的读者会怀疑你的细节处理,在此,引用我过去导师的一句话来说就是:"细节决定成败。"

最佳的方法是仅在那些必须提供引文信息的地方使用脚注。换句话说,避免过于长的脚注,其原则是如果该信息很重要,则把它置于正文段落当中,如果该信息不重要,不值得把它堆砌在脚注中,从而避免行文的净容量不可控制(从而导致不值得出版)。波士顿学院的资深学者凯文·肯尼往往在博士学位论文写作讨论班中为学生们讲这样一则经历:他曾把一篇论文投递给一份期刊却受挫,原因在于其中的一位评论者尖刻地宣称,笔者对第二手资料的掌控力很弱,从而导致散落于各处,还过度使用的过长脚注。当然,有时候过长的脚注也是必需的或者是可取的。你也许打算对一个人物名字所引起的混淆进行校正;为一段有争议的翻译提供其原始文本;或者为该领域外的读者在注释中推荐有用的书目。而且,尤其是有关方法论和理论方面的一些信息,在一篇硕士论文或者博士学位论文中是需要的,而在期刊文章或者成书的手稿中是需要被删掉的。不过,要争取尽可能少在注释中添加过多繁冗的细节。其总体标准如下。

- **注释编号**。在包含所引用对象的句子末尾为脚注添加注释编号——以阿拉伯数字上标的形式。注意,注释编号的位置要位于句末,在所有标点符号之外。例如:

During a speech to unveil a statue of Simón Bolívar in 1921, President Warren G. Harding averred that the New World "miracle" was part of a "divine plan," a "supreme scheme for developing civilization."(1921年,在为西蒙·玻利瓦尔的一尊雕像揭幕的演讲中,总统沃伦·G.哈丁宣称,新世界的"奇迹"是"神圣计划"的一部分,是一个"发展人类文明的上天安排"。[13])

"Censorship is necessarily a blunt instrument," writes film studies scholar Kevin Rockett, an "attempt at total repression" by state officials.(电影研究家凯文·罗基特写道:"审查制度必定会成为一种钝器,是由国家官员所奉行的全面压制的一种企图。"[24])

MS-Word具有自动生成注释的功能,虽然其中的默认参数功能有待改进。具体地说,在脚注中,要把注释编号的上标格式撤销,再在其后插入一个英语句号和两个空格;为了方便编辑格式,我对全部脚注皆进行复制、

Note that the reference number goes last, outside all marks. [During a speech to unveil a statue of Simón Bolívar in 1921, President Warren G. Harding averred that the New World "miracle" was part of a "divine plan," a "supreme scheme for developing civilization."[13]] ["Censorship is necessarily a blunt instrument," writes film studies scholar Kevin Rockett, an "attempt at total repression" by state officials.[24]] MS-Word has an automatic function for creating footnotes, although its default parameters bear improvement. In particular, in the footnote itself, remove the footnote number's superscripting and follow it with a period and then two spaces; for convenience of formatting, I invariably cut-and-paste footnotes. Reset footnote reference numbers (to 1) at the start of each new chapter.

- **Reference information.** Footnotes credit the author in given-name, family-name format, and set details of publication inside parentheses, as distinct from bibliographies, which alphabetize authors in family-name, given-name order, and provide publication information in discreet sentences. [13. Warren G. Harding, speech, Simón Bolívar Statue unveiling, *New York Times*, 20 April 1921, p. 2.] [24. Kevin Rockett, *Irish Film Censorship: A Cultural Journey from Silent Cinema to Internet Pornography* (Dublin: Four Courts Press, 2004), p. 13.] Asian authors whose family name comes first—Wang Xiaoyu—appear the same in footnotes and bibliographies, unless the author has adopted a Western-style name order.

- **Italicize published works.** This logical rule determines whether, and what part of a work's title appears in italics. In both footnotes and running text, set the title of any published work in italics, including books, journals, newspapers, plays, films, operas, and musical scores. [*War and Peace. Journal of Military History. New York Times. Hamlet. The Empire Strikes Back. Aida. Horn Concerto in No. 2.*] Conversely, the title of any unpublished work appears in roman type enclosed in quotation marks, including classified government reports, association minute books, memoirs, and PhD dissertations. ["War Plan Green." "Portland Elks Lodge Minutes, 2008." "My Nile Cruise, 1956." "Salsa in Santa Cruz: An Ethnography."]

Titles of articles in a journal, or chapters in an edited collection, similarly appear in roman enclosed in quote marks, because it is the journal or book that is the published work. ["Zhou Enlai and the Bandung Conference," *Journal of Cold War Studies*.] [Zuckermann's narrow study, "Pencil Buildings of Saigon," appeared in Shi Guanhua's magisterial *Architecture of Southeast Asia* in 2005.] It is clear from the typeface, therefore, whether a given title is that of a published work; a book with an ISBN number or a sixteen-page

粘贴的编辑方式。在每一章的开始重置注释编号的参数（从1开始）。

• **引文信息**。脚注中以先名后姓的排序方式标注作者，并把有关出版的细节性内容置于括号内，以区别于参考书目的罗列方式，因为参考书目是以先姓后名的字母顺序来进行作者排序，并在单独的句子中标注出版信息的。例如：

13. Warren G. Harding, speech, Simón Bolívar Statue unveiling, *New York Times*, 20 April 1921, p. 2.（13. 沃伦·G.哈丁，演讲，西蒙·玻利瓦尔雕像的揭幕仪式，《纽约时报》，1921年4月20日，p.2。）

24. Kevin Rockett, *Irish Film Censorship: A Cultural Journey from Silent Cinema to Internet Pornography* (Dublin: Four Courts Press, 2004), p. 13.（24. 凯文·罗基特，《爱尔兰电影审查制度：从无声电影到网络色情的文化之旅》。都柏林：四合出版社，2004年，p.13。）

亚洲作者的姓名通常以先姓后名的方式排序，例如"王小雨"，除非该作者采用其西式的姓名表达方式。

• **出版作品的斜体字标示**。以下逻辑规则告诉我们某作品名称是否该用斜体字进行标示，或者某作品名称中的哪部分需要用斜体字进行标示。在英语中，无论脚注还是正文，任何出版作品名称都要用斜体字进行标示，包括书籍、期刊、报纸、戏剧、电影、歌剧，还有乐谱。例如：*War and Peace*（《战争与和平》），*Journal of Military History*（《军事史杂志》），*New York Times*（《纽约时报》），*Hamlet*（《哈姆雷特》），*The Empire Strikes Back*（《帝国的反攻》），*Aida*（《阿依达》），*Horn Concerto in No. 2*（《第二圆号协奏曲》）。与此相反，任何未出版的作品名称都要以罗马正体字母在引号中对其进行标示，包括保密政府报告、协会记事簿、回忆录，以及博士学位论文。例如："War Plan Green."（《绿色战争计划》），"Portland Elks Lodge Minutes, 2008."（《波特兰麋鹿理事记事簿》），"My Nile Cruise, 1956."（《我在尼罗河上的漫游》），"Salsa in Santa Cruz: An Ethnography."（《圣克鲁斯的沙沙舞：一份民族志研究》）

期刊文章的标题或者编辑论文集中的章节，同样要以罗马正体字在引号中进行标示，因为期刊、书籍才是出版作品。例如："Zhou Enlai and the Bandung Conference," *Journal of Cold War Studies*.（周恩来和万隆会议，《冷战研究杂志》）；Zuckermann's narrow study, "Pencil Buildings of Saigon," appeared in Shi Guanhua's magisterial *Architecture of Southeast Asia* in 2005.（2005年，祖克曼的集中研究，"西贡的铅笔大楼"，见石冠华的作品《东南亚建筑》）。所以，从字体形式中可以很清楚地分辨所引用资料是否属于出版作品，也可以很容易地分辨出一本拥有ISBN书号的书籍或者一份容量为16页、发行

pamphlet printed in the thousands are easy to categorize as published, but less so would be thirty photocopies of a club's annual newsletter.

- **Short form.** Give the source in full for the first citation, and then in concise form (short form) for the second and subsequent citations. [27. Rockett, *Film Censorship*, pp. 119–20.]
- **Page numbers.** Give a single page in the form p. 22. To save space, many journal and book publishers omit the p., but you should include it in your manuscript to avoid confusion with other numbers, such as newspaper sections or government documents. Give two or more pages in the form pp. 6–8. Notice the use of an en-dash to denote a number range, in this case meaning *from* 6 *to* 8, and that there must be a single space after a p. or pp. For sentences containing two or more quoted phrases from different pages, list the page numbers in the footnote in the form pp. 256, 271. For those rare sentences containing two or more quoted phrases from different works, create a compound footnote with the references separated by semicolons.
- **Newspapers.** When citing newspaper sources, always include page numbers (column position is unnecessary). Be on your guard for multiple daily editions and page numbering across multiple sections. For consistency, italicize place of publication even if the city or town name is not part of the masthead. [29. *New York Herald Tribune*, 22 March 1938, morning edition, section IV, p. 22.]
- **Bibliography.** For projects requiring a bibliography—senior research papers, MA theses, PhD dissertations—every time you cite a new work be sure to add it to the bibliography, for this will save heartache at your project's completion. Most departments insist that the bibliography must contain—but only contain—any work cited in the footnotes, which is to say, do not pad the bibliography with works you have read but not cited. See the Examples section for bibliographic categories and sample entries.
- **Endnotes.** Unless a journal or press insists, always use footnotes rather than endnotes; footnotes not only make references accessible to your reader but when they are staring at you on the page they also discourage bad habits, like formatting them sloppily or turning them into essays.

Plug in the Actors

Even world-renowned scholars, most commonly in the fields of political science and international relations, make statements like, "After Germany invaded in May 1940, France confronted a dilemma," Germany invading,

量为千份的印刷手册属于出版作品。但一份只复印了30份的俱乐部的年鉴通讯录却不那么容易确定它是否为正式出版作品。

- **简化格式**。要在首次引用时以全称的方式介绍引文来源，然后在第二次和其后的引用时，对其以简化格式的方式进行介绍。例如：

27. Rockett, *Film Censorship*, pp. 119-20.（27. 罗基特，《电影审查制度》，pp. 119—20。）

- **页码**。以p.22的形式表示单页页码。为了节省空间，许多期刊和书籍的出版商在编页方式上省略掉p.，但你却要在初稿中保留p.以防止与其他引文数码发生混淆，例如报纸版面或者政府文献。用pp. 6–8 的方式表示两页或两页以上的页码。注意使用对开破折号标注页码范围，在上例中表示第6到第8页，而且在 p. 或 pp.的后边要留出一个空格的空间。对于含有从同一来源不同页数转引的短语的语句来说，要在脚注中以 pp. 256, 271 的形式进行标示。对于那些少见的从不同作品中引用短语的语句来说，要设置一个复合脚注，以分号的形式区分不同的引文来源。

- **报纸**。在引证报纸资源的时候，总是要标注报纸页码（专栏位置并非必要）。注意不同的日报版本和横跨于多个区块的引文来源的页码标注方式。为保持前后一致，即使某一份杂志的出版地并非其刊头名称的一部分，也要以斜体字的方式对其出版地进行标注。例如：

29. *New York Herald Tribune*, 22 March 1938, morning edition, section IV, p. 22.（29.《纽约先驱论坛报》，1938年3月22日，早报，第四部分，p. 22。）

- **参考书目**。对于需要列出参考书目的研究项目来说——高级研究性论文、硕士论文、博士学位论文——每次在脚注中添加新的引文来源时都要把它们添加到参考书目的目录中去，如此可以在项目完成时避免许多困扰。大部分的院系要求参考书目要包含——并且只能包含——在脚注中引用过的作品名称，也就是说，不要在参考书目中罗列那些你读过却没有引证过的文献名称。请参考案例中有关书目和范例方面的内容。

- **尾注**。除非一份期刊或者出版社对其提出要求，否则请使用脚注而非尾注；脚注不但可以使你的读者对引文来源一目了然，而且它们在每页的出现也在时刻提醒你避免某些恶习，例如草率地编辑脚注格式，或者错误地把脚注衍生成小论文。

插入人物

甚至连全球知名的学者，大部分在政治学和国际关系学领域的学者，也会作出这样的表述："在1940年遭到德国入侵后，法国就面临着困境。""德国的入侵"、"法国的面临"，这样的表述仅能像清道夫扫大街一样以粗略的线条勾勒出历史。一旦开始用没有思维，更无法展示表情、能力的

France confronting, paint history in strokes the size of a street sweeper. As soon as you start the process of replacing geographic entities, which have no capacity for thought let alone facial expressions, with organizations, you will have to admit that those organizations in turn consisted of actors who did not always think or express themselves in lockstep. Perhaps not most of the three million soldiers of the *Wehrmacht*'s Army Groups A, B, and C were intent on exacting vengeance for the Clemenceau government's punitive terms at Versailles in 1919. Plugging in the actors necessitates a lot more research, and will no doubt lengthen and complicate the project, yet it results in a different story, one that satisfies for its richness and nuance.

Actor-centric exposition raises the issue of viewpoints. Ideally, each body paragraph should contain only one viewpoint, that is, the thoughts, words, or deeds of a single actor. In a paragraph about Hitler dawdling over Operation Citadel, a pivotal battle at Kursk in July 1943, if you have just said, "He listened carefully to Manstein, yet he also factored Keitel's optimism into his calculations about a suitable launch date," then do not also go on to say, "Keitel, who habitually underestimated Soviet strength, felt that Hitler had obfuscated long enough." Your argument will gain weight and intelligibility if you break out what Keitel was thinking into a second paragraph. Authors of multiple-viewpoint mystery novels follow this method, ensuring that each chapter never has more than a single knower. Similarly, make certain that your reader can distinguish between the statements and thoughts of your actors and your own interpretation and analysis. Indeed, the pitfall of textual immersion lies in its power to convince, so you need to be particularly careful to distance your voice from those of your actors. One approach is to confine your opinion to the closing sentences of each paragraph, but for maximum separation, break out your interpretation into a second paragraph.

Banish the Passive Voice

Effective textual immersion in your actors' lives depends on the active voice. Again, even though some famous scholars, particularly European ones, bask in the anonymity of the passive voice, you have no excuse to follow suit. Old fashioned and woolly, the passive voice not only lengthens sentences but also masks actors and shifts responsibility. Especially with the increasing focus on bottom-up social history, it is critically important to identify your actors. "The Kongolese were converted to Christianity." Fine, but

地理现象代替具体的组织，你就要承认，那些组织也是由个体人物组成起来的，因此不一定具有统一的思考或表达方式。也许三百万"德国国防军"集团军 A、B 和 C 当中的大部分并非皆打算对克里蒙梭政府在凡尔赛会议中制定的针对德国的惩罚性条款实施报复。插入历史人物需要进行更多的研究，而且无疑会拓宽并加深研究计划的时间和复杂性，但是它也会形成不一样的故事，使其内容变得既充实又精细而令人满意。

  以人物为中心的叙述方式揭示了视角的问题。理想情况下，每一个正文段落仅能包含一个视角，也就是说，仅包含一个独立人物的思想、言辞或行为。例如，在有关希特勒筹划堡垒行动，即1943年7月交战于库尔斯克的关键性战役的描述中，如果你已经写道，"为确定一个合适的进攻日期，他仔细听取了曼斯特因的意见，但也把凯特尔的乐观精神纳入考量范围之内"，那么就别接着写道，"习惯性低估苏联力量的凯特尔，认为希特勒踌躇得够久了"。如果把凯特尔的想法另辟一段进行描述，就会加强该论证的分量和清晰程度。以多重视角为特色的悬疑小说的作者们遵循着这样一种方法，即确保每一章仅有一个单独的知情人。与此类似，你也要确保你的读者能够分辨出哪些论述属于文章中人物的主张和思想，哪些论述属于你自身的解读和分析。事实上，文本置入的缺陷就在于它的说服力，所以尤其要注意区分你自己的语气和文章中人物的语气。一种解决方法就是仅限于在每段结尾处写明自己的观点，但是，为了尽可能做到区分，可以把你对文本的解读内容另辟一段进行书写。

驱逐被动语态

  使用文本置入方式描述文中人物的生平要依赖于主动语态的使用。再次重申，尽管许多知名学者，尤其是一些欧洲学者们，欣赏被动语态的匿名性，但是你却没有理由去遵循这种习惯。被动语态过时又语意含糊，它的使用不但会增加句子长度，而且会在行文中掩盖人物主轴、转嫁历史责任。尤其在底层社会史学（bottom-up social history）受到越来越多关注的情况下，确认文中的人物变得至关重要。例如，"刚果人被迫改信基督教"。好吧，谁使得他们改变了宗教信仰呢？"葡萄牙传教士们使得刚果人改信基督教"，这样的表述才算完整的、主动语态的解读方式，但是这种表述行文时依然把刚果人改信基督教的责任归咎于外来机构。刚果人究竟是一群沉默的、意志消沉的行为主体，还是一群活跃的、热情的参与者？他们会为自己新找到的心灵归宿而欢欣鼓舞吗？"为基督教传递的解放思想和鲜明的一神教观念吸引，刚果人改变信仰聚集在葡萄牙传教会的周围"，这样的表述才能把聚光灯直接聚焦到刚果人身上。"在托莱多，神父们被谋杀了。"是的，此事已成事实，但谁做的呢？而改用主动语态，文中人物会

who converted them? "Portuguese missionaries converted the Kongolese to Christianity," is an adequate, active-voice explanation, but one that nonetheless places the onus on outside agency. Were the Kongolese mute and despondent subjects, or were they active, enthusiastic participants, dancing and singing for their newfound spirituality? "Attracted by Christianity's liberating message and clear-cut monotheism, the Kongolese flocked to the Portuguese missions seeking conversion," shines the spotlight squarely on the Kongolese. "Priests were murdered in Toledo." Yes, they were, but who did the deed? Revised to active voice, the actors become explicit: "Anarcho-syndicalists murdered priests in Toledo." "Of the four million dollars received by Lengthy Life, only a million was paid out to claimants." Revision to active voice identifies the payer and saves three words: "Lengthy Life received four million dollars yet only paid out a million to claimants." Uncertainty or ignorance is no excuse for passive voice constructions, because MS-Word will automatically alert you with its green wavy line, providing you check the "Passive sentences" box in the Grammar and Style settings section of Options. Banish the passive—be active. Always think: who is doing what to whom.

STRUCTURED PRÉCIS

Joining words into sentences, melding sentences into paragraphs, and arranging paragraphs into a narrative necessarily creates ever larger—often jumbled and verbose—blocks of text. Two features of the system I advocate will help you to order the chaos and trim the clutter: solid, explicit structure, teamed with tight, précised prose. *Structured précis*, as I call the resulting method, may appear overly formulaic to some readers and too dense to others, yet critics will have no difficulty navigating your narrative, just as the power of your thesis will not fail to impress them, packed as it is into such an accessible space.

Paragraphs as Work Units

Body paragraphs have a lot of work to do. They should begin with a topic sentence, present and interpret evidence in order to make a point that contributes to the larger argument, and end with a summation or conclusion before transitioning smoothly into the next body paragraph. Consequently, the most effective of them will be on the long side, around 250–300 words, sometimes even longer than 350 words. Note that unless you are a journalist or a novelist, two sentences do not constitute a paragraph. To take a body paragraph's elements in turn, the topic sentence introduces the paragraph and suggests or describes its function in the context of your thesis; a paragraph without a topic sentence will lack purpose and lack direction. Regard

变得直截了当："在托莱多，无政府主义工团成员谋杀了神父。""在人寿保险所收取的四百万美金当中，只有一百万被支付给索赔人。"在此，主动语态的改用明确了支付者的身份，并节省了三个单词的使用："人寿保险收取了四百万美金但是仅支付给索赔人一百万美金。"不确定或者不了解并不能成为使用被动语态结构的借口，因为假如你在MS-Word软件中位于选择菜单中语法和格式设置选项卡下勾取"Passive sentences"（被动态句子）文本框的话，MS-Word会自动以绿色波浪线的形式提醒你被动语态的使用。写作中一定要驱逐被动语态——改用主动语态。总要以这样的方式思考行文结构：谁对谁做了什么呢？

结构的精练

组词成句，合句成段，编辑段落组成叙述必然会使得文本内容不断增加，往往也会造成混乱和啰唆的文字表达。我所提倡的方法具有两大特色——夯实、明确的结构，以及紧凑、精致的辞令，可以帮助你行文秩序井然，并且去芜存菁。"结构性的精练"，即我所谓的终极方法，也许对于某些读者来说显得过于刻板，而对于另外一些来说又显得信息过于集中，但是这样会使得评论家在泛读你的叙述时驾轻就熟，并被你的论点的说服力所打动，因为它已在行文有限的可操作空间中被清晰地呈现出来。

以段落为工作单位

正文段落需要执行许多功能。它们应该以主题句开始，以论证的呈现和解读为主体，以便证明分论点，使之成为总论点的一部分，以概括或结论来结束以便顺利过渡到下一个段落。因此，最有效的正文段落，一段大概包括250—300个单词，有时或许会超过350个单词。值得一提的是，写论文不是写新闻稿、写小说，所以一段里边不能只有两句话。至于正文段落的基本部分，主题句相当于迷你版论点陈述，它提纲挈领，既概括了本段内容，又表明了分论点与论点之间的联系，没有主题句的段落会失去目的和方向。最好把论据集中在段落的前半部分，随着段落的推进再深入展开论证性的解读。尽量避免使用引语来结束段落；在我偶尔这样做的情况下，引语既能恰如其分地解释上文论据，又深刻地被下文解释。段落末尾的最后一两句话应该成为本段的结论句，结句可以通过使用概括主题的一两个关键词或短语来首尾呼应。本段的结句与下段的首句可以通过意译或直译地重复本段的某个短语或概念来承上启下。各段应该相互关联，浑然一体。只有这样，才能使一篇论文建立在一系列相关论点的基础上。如果你可以用不超过八个单词来概括本段的理由和作用，就证明这个段落可以很好地执行它的功能。但是假如你难以概括段落的作用或者标题，那你应

topic sentences as miniature thesis statements. Best practice is to concentrate the evidence early in the paragraph and then build up the interpretation toward the end. Strive to avoid ending a paragraph in a quotation; on the rare occasion when I do so, the following paragraph is substantively interpretive and the closing quotation reiterates or emphasizes the evidence presented beforehand. Use the last sentence, sometimes two, to summarize the paragraph's point, and, ideally, wrap back to the topic sentence by including one of its key words or phrases. In the closing sentence or the first part of the next paragraph's opening sentence, engineer a transition, typically by repeating a phrase or concept from the two parts, whether idiomatically or as a literal repetition of a word. Each paragraph should connect with and flow seamlessly into its neighbor, building the thesis from a succession of related points. To test whether you have made the paragraphs in a given section hard-working members of your project, try giving each one a temporary subhead of no more than eight words that describes its function. If reading through the subheads explains the section's purpose and argument then you have been successful. But if you struggle to summarize a paragraph's function, or the subheads, taken together across the paper, do not make sense in light of your thesis, then it is time to rethink the structure and rework the paragraphs.

Road Maps

Jumbled argumentation and stream-of-consciousness prose have no place in academic writing. If you are one of those creative types then remember that structure is still your friend. Even James Joyce's apparently formless *Ulysses* conformed to a plan. Err on the side of more structure, not less, because it is easy to replace "First . . . Second . . . Third" constructions with something less boilerplate, but making sense of chaos after the fact will rarely prove satisfactory. Editors of certain journals may ask you to remove subheads, but they will simply reject your submission out of hand if it is unstructured. From the outset, therefore, write with explicit confidence, not implicit vagueness.

Solid structure begins with this overarching schema: introduction, three to five main points, conclusion. By *main point*, I mean the primary components of your thesis (argument), the points that someone listening to a twenty-minute conference paper about your research would remember the next day. This structural schema operates primarily at the body-paragraph level, though the value of its logic applies just as well at the micro level of sentences and the macro level of multi-chapter dissertations. An ideal research paper of 6,500 words, or a somewhat longer dissertation chapter of 9,000–11,000 words, opens with three or four introductory paragraphs, contains four to six subheads beneath each of which follow the body paragraphs that present and interpret the evidence necessary to make each main point, and closes with a

该再考虑一遍结构，并且重新编辑段落。

脉络图

混乱的论证和意识流式的散文对学术写作毫无益处。假如你拥有很强的创新能力，也别忘记结构的重要性。即使詹姆斯·乔伊斯所著的 *Ulysses*（《尤利西斯》）行文看似毫无章法，其实也来源于谋篇布局。对于结构的重视宁可矫枉过正，也不可忽视，因为以一些并不是那么形式主义的词语代替"首先……其次……再次……"的结构不难，但是事后整合早已混乱不堪的行文结构所得到的结果往往并不是那么令人满意。某些特定期刊的编辑们可能会在决定用稿后要求你编辑行文时去掉副标题，但是如果行文结构混乱，他们更会马上退稿。因此从开始之时，写作目的就应该清晰明确，而非含混模糊。

夯实的行文结构要以中心策略的谋划作为其开端，具体包括：引言、三到五个主要观点、结语。"主要观点"是指你论文（论证）的基本成分，是那些某人聆听过一堂长达20分钟有关你研究的会议论文之后，第二天依然记忆犹新的观点。该结构策略首先要体现在正文段落的层面上，不过它的逻辑价值同样适用于其微观层面（即句子构成层面）和宏观层面（即多章构成的博士学位论文的层面）。一篇理想的包含6500个左右单词的研究论文，或某个稍长一些的包含9000—11000个单词的毕业论文章节，要以三或四段引导性段落作为开始，包含四到六段拥有副标题，且其下皆附有正文段落以呈现并解读必要的论据来证明每个主要观点，并以一系列结论段落作为结尾。一旦在引言中陈述了你的论点，就不要错过任何一个一点一滴、一段一段深化论点的机会；尽力为每一个总论点划分出它自身的分论点陈述，为每一段安排一个主题句，使其成为总论点的一个子部分。遵循同样的策略，每个具有副标题的部分都要以具有引言性质的一段开头以建立该部分的总观点；可能包含三到五个正文段落以陈述各自的分论点；并以能够形成过渡结论的段落结束。在每一个总结性段落的后一分，无论是论文/章节还是主要观点的写作层面，都要把行文内容归结到引言部分的关键短语上，从而完成其自身的修辞循环。

缺乏文章脉络图的引言是不完整的。脉络图的位置最好位于引言末段的后面，清晰明了，分别按顺序罗列出全文的主要观点（副标题），并附有一到两个词语的解释。文章脉络图会为读者提供一系列的提示语，以便使他们了解每个段落的起承转合，并且不会误失细节。简化版的脉络图观念也同样适用于段落层面的写作过程。写作过程中要注意结构设计的重要性，务必使得结构设计做到确认和明晰。从没有经验的作者到写作高手都会说出这样的话："包括……，还有许多原因导致 X 事件的发生"或者"对于 Y 事件的解读会产生许

couple of concluding paragraphs. Having laid out your thesis in the introduction, miss no opportunity to reinforce it point by point and paragraph by paragraph; work at giving each main point its own mini thesis statement, and each paragraph a topic sentence that is itself a subset of the thesis. Following the same schema, each sub-headed section should also open with a paragraph of an introductory nature that sets up the section's main point; it may well contain three to five body paragraphs that make respective sub-points; and its closing paragraph will offer an interim conclusion. Toward the end of each concluding paragraph, whether at the paper/chapter or main-point level, tie back to one of the introduction's key phrases, thereby completing the rhetorical circle.

No introduction is complete without a road map, preferably an explicit one, situated toward the end of the last introductory paragraph, which lists the main points (subheads) in their respective order, often with a word or two of explanation. Road maps provide a set of directions so that the reader knows what to expect at each junction and thereby does not become lost. Simplified versions of the road map concept also work at the paragraph level. Note here the importance of confident, explicit constructions. Inexperienced writers and even some old hands say things like, "There were many reasons why X happened, including . . ." or "There are several explanations for Y." Yes, of course there were. There may indeed have been twenty possible reasons for X and fifty explanations for Y. But you are the expert—you have studied the documents and formed an opinion. It is your job to choose a manageable number (three to five) of the most important reasons or explanations and present those to your reader. "X happened for three main reasons: First, . . . Second, . . . Third, . . ."

Practice the Fine Art of Précis

Lost art may be more apt, as few high schools today include methods for shortening written passages in their language curricula. A classic précis exercise requires taking a passage of a given length and rendering it in half as many words, without sacrificing content or meaning. Précis does not merely save words. It concentrates argument. Cutting out the clutter makes it easier for a reader to grasp your point. Writing long—as most writers do—is fine for a first draft, providing you then take time to précis, which may mean double the first draft's completion time. Effective précis comes only with practice, in part because every writer has a unique style, so certain techniques will pay greater dividends than others.

Précis embodies four main techniques: First, move to a longer, more complex sentence structure, concatenating adjacent sentences that say more

多观点"。是的，当然有。诚然，事实上确实会有20个原因导致 X 事件发生，并且对于 Y 事件的解读会有50种不同的观点。但是你在写作过程中，应该把自己视为该领域的专家——也就是说，你研究过所有的文献并形成了自己对于该问题的看法。你的责任就是在众多观点中选择你认同的那些（可能3种到5种）最重要的原因或观点并呈现给你的读者。"X 事件的发生是由以下3个主要原因导致的：首先，……其次，……再次……"

练习精练的技艺

把精练文字的艺术中的"艺术"这个词称为"失传的艺术"或许更为恰当些，因为现在几乎没有学校在他们的语文课程中进行缩写段落的训练。一个典型的精练文字训练要求把一个给定长度的段落缩写为其长度的一半，却不失其主要内容或观点。精练文字并非仅仅可以节省词语，还会使得论点更加集中。去芜存菁会使得读者更容易抓住你要表达的主旨。正如大多数作者那样，文章的初稿内容庞杂亦没关系，只是需要花时间进行精练，对此可能要花去写初稿时两倍的时间。有效的精练技艺只有通过训练才可以达成，因为大概是每个作者的写作风格各不相同，所以即使同样的训练每个人的付出和获得的收益也并不相同。

文字精练包含以下四个主要技巧。第一，将相邻并且大概具有相同意思的句子合并成长难句。就像以代词，尤其是以"这"开头的句子，很可能被合并成复杂句。还可以在长难句中置入分号或者成对的破折号，不过要量力而为。第二，尝试改变语序。以分词或者动名词短语开头的句子通常会节省单词用量，但是，像分号和破折号的使用一样，不要过度使用此技巧。第三，删除90%的副词和形容词。反正，像"非常"这种经常被滥用的单词也没有任何实质意义，不如把其作用留给要求特别效果的情况。第四，避免陈述众所周知的内容。不要写"美利坚合众国"，直接写"美国"就好了；而且还可以更精练，如果"美国"的概念在行文中不言而喻，就可以把它删掉。抓住每个去掉冗词的机会。例如，可以写"在那段时间"，"在那个阶段"，但千万不要写"在那个时间阶段"，不然会显得过度重复。尽量用单词替代短语，比如用"*before*"（从前）代替"*prior to*"（在此之前），用"*now*"（当今）代替"*at the present time*"（在现阶段）。"*As a result of*"（本着……缘故）之类短语往往存在其他选择，例如"*because of*"（因为）或"*consequent to*"（因而），"*in the process of*"（在……过程中）也算是不必要的冗词，对此完全有更加简化的说法。

润色的行文

假设目前含有论点陈述和文章脉络图的引言部分已写作完成；标题部

or less the same thing; sentences that begin with pronouns, especially *This*, are likely candidates. Aids to multi-clause sentences are semicolons and em-dashes in pairs, although limit these constructions. Second, experiment with changing the order of phrases. Beginning some sentences with a participial or gerund phrase typically saves a few words, but again, this is a tactic best not overused. Third, cut out 90 percent of adverbs and adjectives—hackneyed words like *very* are useless anyway—save their power for special effect. Fourth, avoid stating what is obvious to your reader. Instead of writing "the United States," write "America"; better still, if *America* is implicit, remove the reference altogether. Take every opportunity to cut superfluous words. Say either "during the time" or "during the period" but never "during the time period," which would be redundant. Look for two or more words you can replace with one, such as *prior to* with *before*, *at the present time* with *now*. There are usually alternatives for phrases like *as a result of*, such as *because of* or *consequent to*, and "in the process of" is unnecessary verbiage that you can simply jettison.

POLISHED PROSE

You now have an introduction with its thesis statement and road map; you have sub-headed sections, each of which makes a main point that advances your thesis through textual immersion in lots of skillfully interpreted, evidentiary quotations embedded in your prose; and you have a conclusion that reinforces the thesis while tying back to the introduction. But do not think for a moment that it is therefore time to relax. Just as in the production of a jade vase or silver chalice, you must now begin the exacting yet essential work of polishing, without which your exposition would be no more a work of art than any piece of grey stone or tarnished metal.

Scholarly Style

Your strategy should always be to gain recognition through quality—original research, polished prose, powerful argumentation—not glitz or gimmickry. Remember: nothing undermines quality and negates the hundreds of hours you devoted to your project faster than inconsistency, errors, and general sloppiness. Peppering your paper with spicy colloquialisms or printing it in a fancy font will distract your reader, detracting from your scholarship, not adding to it. Understand that there are internationally accepted standards, as outlined in *Chicago 16th* and reinforced in this guide. Despite what you may hear or see to the contrary in certain classrooms or publications, learn and implement those standards. Yet even within the ivory tower's established conventions, there is nonetheless plenty of scope for individuality

分已写作完成，呈现在你论文中的每一个主要观点都通过文本置入的方式在行文中获得了充分的嵌入引言论据和富于技巧的解读；加强论点的结语部分已写作完成，并且它与导论首尾呼应。此时看似大功告成，不过，却不是放松的好时机。正如置身于玉质花瓶或银质餐具的生产过程中一样，确切但是基本的润色文章的过程要开始了，丧失此一过程的话，你的行文只能是一块璞玉或玄铁，而不能称之为一件艺术品。

学术写作风格

你应当以通过论文质量获得业内认可——通过原创性的研究、润色的行文、强有力的论点为策略——而非通过浮夸和小聪明。记住：没有什么比一致性的缺乏、错误丛生或总的混乱更能迅速破坏你的论文质量并抹杀你几百小时的研究成果。在论文中加入野史中的绯闻白话，或印刷以花哨的字体只能令你的读者分心，不但不能提高反而损毁了自身的学术底蕴。要知道国际认可的行文标准已经存在，正如第十六版《芝加哥论文格式手册》中所列出的那样，也同样是本指南所强调的。就算你在其他课堂或出版界了解到与此相反的标准，也应该学会并应用国际认可的行文标准。但是，即使在传统的象牙塔内，亦留有张扬个性和创造性的足够空间。但是要在此生成一种意蕴丰富、行文悠远、自成一家的学问风格，是需要耗费作者大量时间和心血的。通过认真的磨炼，你自己的独特风格会在你发觉之前就隐隐呈现。保留自己过去写的旧文章，一年后再去读它们，你就会发现自己的进步。在此我恳请你注意：现代通俗语言是富于变化的，例如汉语、西班牙语，尤其是英语。所以，在你教育生涯和今后的职业生涯中，请始终保持对当代用语趋势和语法的密切关注，因为写作是一种尤其重要的沟通方式，而写作风格最好与时俱进。

学者们撰写的专业论文，对于那些习惯了阅读曾经的记者撰写的历史类畅销书的历史迷们来说，通常略显浮夸、匠气浓重，甚至是读不太懂。学者们或许部分出于某种程度的嫉妒，会批判畅销书作者缺乏学术严谨性，但是，严肃的历史学著作并非不可以变得适宜阅读。其实，行文风格从业内认同的学术性风格转向闲谈式的、老生常谈的新闻笔调是很容易的，就像通过查字典来翻译术语，通过术语来显示博学一样容易。行文风格需要在学究和通俗之间努力取得中间值，关键词就是"努力"。对此，要做到把写作看成一项艺术创作，就像绘画一样精益求精，画家永远觉得自己的画是下一幅的好，不要错误地认为杰出的作者来源于天赋，其他人望尘莫及。杰出的作品不可避免地乃是长时间努力的结晶，努力才能够润色出熠熠生辉的杰作。请学习本指南的语法及格式的基本知识部分，还要学习斯特伦克和怀特的依然

and creativity, but it does take considerable time and effort to develop a rich, flowing scholarly style. By really working at your style, it will develop before you know it. Save old papers, re-read them a year later, and you will be amazed at your improvement. A plea: popular modern languages, such as Chinese, Spanish, and particularly English, are dynamic, so, as you progress through the education system and down the path of your chosen career, keep abreast of current trends and usage; writing is far too vital a form of communication for your style to become passé.

When scholars write for their peers, their prose can seem turgid, pedantic, and even downright unreadable to history buffs who eagerly buy the latest best-sellers often penned by erstwhile journalists. Scholars, perhaps in part from envy, scorn popular writers for their lack of academic rigor, yet there is no reason why serious historiography cannot also be enjoyable to read. Still, it is easy to cross the line from acceptable scholarly style to chatty, clichéd journalese, just as it is tempting to demonstrate erudition by including jargon that requires a dictionary to translate. Work at finding a middle ground, with *work* being the operative word. Above all, treat your writing as an art form, like a painting that could always have been better, and will be when the artist begins the next canvas. Do not make the mistake of thinking that brilliant writers have a natural talent, one you could therefore never hope to emulate. Brilliant writing is invariably a product of hours of work, hard work devoted to polishing prose until it sparkles. Please study this guide's Grammar and Style Essentials, as well as Strunk and White's still excellent *The Elements of Style*, and note these additional points:

- **Gambits.** Just like the first bars of a Rolling Stones song, a sentence's opening gambit sets the stage for the drama to come. Work to make your gambits as interesting and different as possible, especially for the all-important first sentence—usually the topic sentence—of a paragraph. If you are beginning every third or fourth sentence with *The* then you are probably writing banal, unimaginative English. Notice how something as apparently simple as changing how you start a sentence has repercussions that fundamentally alter your style. Five years ago, I decided that I would never begin a sentence with *The*, a promise I have not yet broken, even in emails. Perhaps this writing trait is a silly eccentricity or conceit, and yet implementing it forced me to spend time thinking about word order and selection, phrasing, and sentence construction in general. As a result, my style certainly evolved, though whether it improved I leave to my reader to decide. But dislike my style as you may, please accept my challenge, which is to work constantly and consciously on your own style to make it more effective, interesting, and readable.

杰出的 The Elements of Style（《英文写作指南》），并注意以下几个要点。

• **开场白**。就像一首滚石摇滚乐队的歌曲开场一样，一句话的开场为即将开始的剧情奠定了基调。努力使你行文的开场变得有趣并有所创新——尤其是对于段首的第一句话——即通常所谓的主题句。如果你行文的第三或第四句话就以定冠词"*The*"（那个）开头，那么你的行文很可能流于庸俗，变成缺乏想象力的英文写作。请注意，行文开场如何起笔这一看似简单的行为却具有改变行文主体风格的效果。五年前，我做出一个决定，即写作时绝对不用定冠词 *The* 作为句子的开头，这个决定我一直遵循，甚至是在邮件的写作当中。或许这个写作癖好白痴、古怪又显得自以为是，但是执行它却迫使我不得不花时间斟酌词语的顺序和选择、短语的措辞和句子的总体结构等问题。结果是，行文风格肯定进步了，不过是否变好要留给我的读者来决定。但是，即使你可能不喜欢我的风格，也请接受我提出的挑战，持续并有意识地审视自己的写作风格，使其越来越表述清晰、语意丰富，并具有可读性。

• **人称代词**。尽量少用人称代词，必要时，也要用不定代词"*one*"而非特定人称代词"*you*"或"*we*"。仅在引言段落和解释性、论证性结构的语句中使用第一人称代词"I"。坚守自己的学术距离：在写作中请使用"美国入侵了伊拉克"，而非"我们入侵了伊拉克"。

• **取证**。不要以如下的方式向读者强加你的论点，例如，"我们可以看出威尔逊是一位自大的种族主义者"。要有自信心地写成"威尔逊是一位自大的种族主义者"，或者"如论据所言，威尔逊是一位自大的种族主义者"。同样，不要把你的观点隐藏在如下方式的陈述中，例如，"有人认为威尔逊本应该承认苏联"。如果此陈述确实是你希望得出的论点，那直接提出，因为有人可能认为得出过与此相反的论点。"我主张，威尔逊本应该承认苏联。"要努力使自己的行文风格在过度谨慎和过分自信中求得平衡。当你开始写作自己首篇主要的研究计划时，不完整的论据或仅仅是单纯的犹豫都会使你通过用"可能"、"也许"等字眼来分散风险。一旦你搜集的论据得到整合，你的自信心增长之后，再反过来浏览整个章节查找这些模棱两可的用词的时候，你也许会意识到这些用词只会迷惑你的读者并降低你观点的价值，除此之外，并无他用。但是，在间接论据或论据不那么充分的情况下，也要避免进行肯定的陈述。

• **强调**。在行文中不要再使用形容词最高级、惊叹号和类似"*fantastic*"（了不起的）、"*amazing*"（令人惊讶的）、"*great*"（杰出的）这类词语了，尤其是不要再使用已经被滥用无数并且不具有实际意思的单词"*very*"（非常）了。无论在行文中还是在引言中，请尽量避免添加强调（斜体字

- **Personal pronouns.** Be sparing with personal pronouns; when necessary, use *one* but not *you* or *we*. Limit the first person *I* to occasional use in introductory paragraphs and interpretational or argumentative constructs. Keep your academic distance: write, "Americans invaded Iraq," not "we invaded Iraq."
- **Forensics.** Do not impose your argument on your reader with statements like, "We can see that Wilson was an arrogant racist." Instead, say, with confidence, "Wilson was an arrogant racist," or perhaps, "Wilson, as the evidence indicates, was an arrogant racist." Similarly, do not hide your opinion behind statements like, "One might argue that Wilson should have recognized the Soviet Union." If that is indeed the argument you wish to make then say so, because one might just as easily argue the opposite. "Wilson, I argue, should have recognized the Soviet Union." Work to balance your style of argumentation between excessive caution and overconfidence. When you begin writing your first major research project, incomplete evidence or just simple hesitancy will prompt you to hedge your bets with *perhaps* and *maybe*. Once your evidence comes together, your confidence grows, and you scan through completed chapters for iterations of such fence-sitting words, you may realize that they were only serving to confuse your reader and devalue your point. Yet avoid making definitive claims when the supporting evidence is circumstantial or flimsy.
- **Emphasis.** Banish superlatives, exclamation marks, words like *fantastic, amazing, great*, and especially that much overused and wasteful word, *very*. Strain not to add emphasis (italics), whether to your own prose or to quotations. Instead, stress your points through the power of vocabulary. "It was cold on the summit of Mount Washington," sounds just as foreboding as, "It was very cold on the summit of Mount Washington." For those occasions when you can afford an extra word to make a point: "It was bitterly cold..."
- **Past tense.** Write entirely in the past tense, except to distinguish the work of a contemporary author on which you are drawing.
- **Contractions.** In formal academic writing, do not use contractions like *can't* and *won't*. Some scholars occasionally drop a contraction or two into a book-length work, but for effect rather than from nonchalance.
- **Vocabulary.** English has a rich vocabulary so there is no excuse for using vague or ugly words like *got*. [Smith wrote the letter when he got home. ✗] [Smith wrote the letter when he returned home. ✓] *Got* is often redundant anyway. [John got married to Susan. ✗] [John married Susan (and saved two precious words). ✓] Avoid all but the choicest colloquialisms, and then use them for effect or emphasis. Reword sentences that end

化)。反之，使用语汇的力量加强论点。"华盛顿山的山顶很冷"和"华盛顿山的山顶非常冷"听起来基本一样。这种情况可以在句中加上一个额外的单词以使其变得切题："天气冷得刺骨……"

- **过去时态**。除了提到你所研究的当代作家的作品时，通篇行文都要使用过去时态。
- **缩略语**。在正式的学术性写作中，请勿使用诸如"*can't*"（不能）和"*won't*"（不会）这样的缩略语。有的学者在写像书一样篇幅的作品的时候偶尔会在行文中放置一两个缩略语，不过他们这样做，通常是有意为之，而非对学术规范的无动于衷。
- **词汇**。英语词汇极其丰富，所以在行文中没有理由会使用诸如"*got*"（到）这样既模糊又难看的词语。例如，"史密斯到家后写了封信（*got home*）。✗" "史密斯回家后写了封信（*returned home*）。✓"而且，*got*经常是多余的，如"约翰和玛丽结婚了（*got married*）。✗" "约翰娶了玛丽（直接用*married*，还节省了两个单词的宝贵空间)。✓"除非深思熟虑，在行文中刻意使用口语词汇进行语意强调，一般来讲请避免在行文中使用它们。对于以介词结尾的句子或包含诸如"*had had*"（已经有）这样糟糕结构的句子，请重新遣词造句。
- ***That***。*That*不仅仅是一个连词，还是一个关键的先行词，其重要性随着句子长度和复杂性的增长而增长，所以请尽量一句话只使用一个*that*。对于具有两个*that*的句子，退一步并决定哪个分句更重要些（即你最希望强调的分句），并改写另一个*that*分句，或许使其以动名词的方式重现出来。例如，"史密斯写了一封包含了布朗所需求的所有证据的信（that contained all the proof that Brown sought）。✗" "史密斯写了一封包含布朗所需求的所有证据的信（containing all the proof that Brown sought）。✓"因为*that*的使用可以增强行文的精确性和可读性，至少在进入到严肃的精练行文阶段之前，对其宁可多用，也别少用。刚才的示例，*that*的使用是可选的，或许是没必要的，但是这仅是因为句子结构简单的缘故。
- **排比**。无论在句子结构层面还是在陈述三个主要观点方面，排比是一种吸引人的修辞美学，但是跟所有修辞技巧一样，需要避免过度使用，比如用到二组排比或者偶尔的四组排比。例如："靠着其掘石砌石员工的不息的智慧、有原则的价值观念以及训练有素的工作习惯，纪念碑所蕴涵的思想——通过象征和神话的力量所构筑的民族身份认同感——开始改变。"
- **抑扬顿挫**。有的单词和词组搭配起来会产生一种令人愉悦的韵律和节奏感，而另外一些单词在咬字吐音的时候，却听起来别扭拗口。试着大声朗读章节，以此来体验音韵的感觉，再尝试以不同音节长度的同义词进

in prepositions or include ghastly constructs like *had had*.

- ***That*** is no mere conjunction. It is a key pointing word the importance of which increases with sentence length and complexity, so strive to have never more than a single *that* in any given sentence. On writing a sentence with two *that*s, sit back and decide which of the clauses carries the most weight (the one you are most concerned to point to) and then recast the other *that* clause, perhaps to a gerund. [Smith wrote a letter that contained all the proof that Brown sought.] [Smith wrote a letter containing all the proof that Brown sought.] Because it adds precision and therefore enhances readability, err on the side of using more *that*s than less, at least before you enter serious précis mode. In the last example, *that* is optional, and perhaps unnecessary, but only because the sentence is so simple. [Smith wrote a letter containing all the proof Brown sought.]
- **Triplets** have an appealing esthetic, whether at the sentence level or in the case of three main points, but as with all stylistic devices, avoid overuse by employing doublets and occasional foursomes. [Because of the restless intellects, principled values, and disciplined work habits of those who quarried its stone and stacked its blocks, the ideology that the Monument embodied—and hence the kind of national identity it had the power to create through symbolism and myth—began to change.]
- **Cadence.** Certain words and phrases can develop a pleasing rhythm or cadence, just as other words sound downright ugly as they roll off the tongue. Try reading passages aloud to see how they sound, and experiment with interchanging words with similar meanings but different syllabic length. Alliteration is an equally important component of esthetically pleasing prose.
- **Tempo.** Parameters—over which you have considerable control—such as word choice, punctuation, and sentence length dictate the tempo of your writing, and hence the emphasis you decide to give to particular interpretive or argumentative passages. Sometimes you will wish to move your readers along, smoothly at a brisk pace, through evidentiary material. At other times, perhaps when you make a key observation or conclusion, it may be best to slow your readers down, bring them to a halt, or even force them to re-read a passage. *Although* reads slower than *though*, *still* reads quicker than *nevertheless*, and *but* reads quicker than *yet* despite being the same length. Many readers habitually stop at the word *paradox*, reading the passage a few times to ensure they have correctly solved the riddle. Adding optional commas slows the pace and creates a measured tempo. [She sprinted toward the president and from less than fifty feet opened fire.] [She walked deliberately

行替换，重新体验。在美学意义上，押韵是构成令人愉悦的散文体裁中同样重要的组成部分。

- **节奏**。能够置于你掌控中的参数，例如遣词、标点和句子长度决定了你的写作节奏，并因此决定了你打算进行特定解读或论证段落的强调力度。有时，你期望读者们通过你行文中的论据资料能够以一种轻快的节奏进行流畅的阅读。而另外一些时候，可能在你行文中作出关键性评论或结论的时候，也许最好能降低读者们的阅读速度，使他们的阅读暂缓，甚至迫使他们重读那一个关键章节。在阅读过程中，读者在读到"*although*"（尽管）时比读到"*though*"（然而）时速度更慢些，读到"*still*"（可是）时比读到"*nevertheless*"（虽然如此）时速度更快些，而且即使同样长度的句子，在读到"*but*"（但是）时也比读到"*yet*"（可是）时速度更快些。一些读者习惯性地在读到"*paradox*"（悖论）这个词时暂停，并重新再读几遍原文以确定他们已经解决了这个谜团。加入原本可有可无的逗号可以降低阅读速度并为行文建立一种标准的节奏。例如，"她全力奔向总统并在距其五十英尺时开火"；"她蓄意走向总统，并且，在距其五十英尺时，开火"。同样，行文中加入"一方面……另一方面"或"不但……而且"这样的关联词语虽然耗费了额外的单词空间却增加了内容的强调力度。例如，"不过多伊尔是一位有影响力的天主教徒和一位忠诚派的支持者"[1]；"不过多伊尔不但是一位有影响力的天主教徒，而且是一位忠诚派的支持者"。

- **隐喻**。优秀的作者们会花时间在行文中制造隐喻和明喻使得了无生机的段落变得令人难忘。你很可能会在乔治·奥威尔富有煽动性的文章"Politics and the English Language"（政治和英语语言学）中获得相关的灵感。

- **时间顺序**。针对过去进行的写作不可避免地需要针对一个特定时间点，讨论该事件发生前后的史实。注意到呈现一系列事件的必要性才能够使你的读者意识到时间顺序，从而在总体上把握该事件的总体意义。鉴于此，行文中"*had*"（已经）的使用是十分必要的，即使语法上它是可有可无的；我则倾向于在其使用上秉持宁多勿少的原则，即使这样一来，行文可能会变得烦琐无聊。例如："到了下午三点，豪已经准备好了他的进攻。狙击手在他左方从谷仓上开火迫使他已下令查尔斯河里的军舰投掷燃烧弹，此时烟雾从燃烧的城镇弥漫到了战场。他的后备军早已下船登岸，他所能指望的大约有3500人。将军罗伯特·皮戈特将对防守阵地进行正面攻击，与此同时，他将带领精锐部队沿着篱笆墙行进。"以上示例以"*now*"（此时，即下午三点）为界进行事件顺序排列，而以下的示例虽

---

1. 忠诚派（Loyalist）指的是美国独立战争时忠诚于英方的政治力量。——译者注

toward the president, and, from less than fifty feet, opened fire.] Similarly, adding "on the one hand . . . on the other hand" or "not only . . . but also" phrasing costs extra words but increases emphasis. [Yet Doyle was an influential Catholic and a Loyalist sympathizer.] [Yet not only was Doyle an influential Catholic but he was also a Loyalist sympathizer.]

- **Metaphors.** Good writers take the time to invent metaphors and similes to make memorable otherwise lifeless passages. You may find George Orwell's provocative essay, "Politics and the English Language," to be a source of inspiration.

- **Chronological sense.** Writing about the past invariably involves discussing events that occurred before or after other events, relative to a particular moment. Be cognizant of the need to present the train of events so that your reader can sense the chronology, thereby appreciating the significance of the events as a whole. *Had* is essential for this purpose, though its use is often optional; I lean toward overusing *had*, at the risk of producing boring prose. [By 3 PM, Howe had prepared his attack. Sniper fire from barns to his left had forced him to order the frigates in the Charles River to lob incendiaries, and now smoke was wafting over the battlefield from the burning town. His reserve had disembarked, and he could count on around 3,500 men. Gen. Robert Pigot would mount the frontal assault on the redoubt, while he would lead the grenadiers against the rail fence.] This example orders events either side of *now* (at 3 PM); the following example tells the same story in eleven less words yet conveys little sense of chronology. [At 3 PM, Howe mounted his attack. Sniper fire from barns to his left forced him to order the frigates in the Charles River to lob incendiaries. Smoke wafted over the battlefield from the burning town. His reserve disembarked, giving him around 3,500 men. Gen. Robert Pigot mounted a frontal assault on the redoubt, while he led the grenadiers against the rail fence.]

- **Creative writing.** Some paragraphs, typically those of an interpretive or concluding nature, will benefit from a more creative treatment. I do not wish to offend social sensibilities, so I will confine this observation to personal experience, that while I write better analytical paragraphs after a breakfast mug of strong black coffee, my creative writing blossoms over an evening glass of well-aged red wine.

- **Consistency.** Remember the golden rule of style: be consistent throughout. If you are using em-dashes in pairs——to demarcate sub-clauses——then avoid having a sentence with a single em-dash at the end; use a

然与上例内容相同，仅在英文行文中省略了11个单词，却无法很好地传递给读者时间之感。"在下午三点，豪发起了他的攻击。狙击手在他左方从谷仓上开火迫使他下令查尔斯河里的军舰投掷燃烧弹。烟从燃烧的城镇飘到战场上。他的后备军下船登岸，他所能指望的大约有3500人。将军罗伯特·皮戈特对防守阵地进行了正面攻击，与此同时，他带领着精锐部队沿着篱笆墙行进。"

- **创新性写作**。为写好某些段落，特别是那些承担解读性和结论性质的段落，要以一种创造性的心态去特别对待。我不打算冒犯社会通识，所以只是以自身的个人经历作为此评论的依据，即早餐的一杯高浓度的黑咖啡可以使我更好地进行分析性段落的写作；而晚餐的一杯陈年红酒则令我的创造性写作锦上添花。

- **一致性**。请记住行文风格的黄金法则，即自始至终保持行文的一致性。如果你使用破折号标注从句，那么要避免在整篇文章中只有一个位于句子结尾的对开破折号的句子，可以使用分号替代它。要在开篇时向读者介绍自己的行文风格。如果你惯于用分号对特别句式进行断句，那么不要等到行文进行到第四段才突然把三个分号紧邻着置于其中。要努力获得并维持读者对你的信任。

- **试验**。文法学者所遵循的规则本质上与其他规则没什么不同，偶尔还是可以在违反规则中前进的。而且英语，作为一种广泛使用的世界性语言，亦在无尽地发生着变化。故而如果你有充分的理由和格外的自信，当然可以试验去打破常规，但要确定此种对于常规的打破要建立在刻意为之而非无知者无畏的基础之上。

建构论证

段落的精练和行文的润色与论证的建构密不可分。要删繁去冗，精简剩余，突出主旨。你很可能会发现，随着研究和解读的进行，在独特方法论的指导下，你的研究主题被自己缩小到原主题下的一个子部分的同时，论点却逐步扩大，变成有力度的总体论证——理想的情况下，有一定独特性更好。对于我的博士学位论文来说，开始的暂定论点最终成为了支持新论点的三个子论证之一。随着各章的逐步完成，保持问题的清晰度和连贯性也随着研究计划的复杂性的增加而变得益发困难。此时，你已不再是一个业余的研究者，而成为了一个专业的项目经理，并且，在这样的身份下，应当充分利用现有的所有工具和协助手段。

MS-Word中的文档结构图功能是一个很有用的工具，故而我将其图标设在工具栏上。将每个副标题设为第二层，并将每一章设为第一层（在MS-Word的设置部分），然后点击该图标就可以立刻看清并了解你的文档结

semicolon instead. Introduce the reader to your style early on. If you like to break up the occasional sentence with a semicolon then avoid waiting until the fourth paragraph before throwing in three of them back-to-back. Work to gain and hold your reader's confidence.

- **Experiment.** Grammarians' rules are ultimately no different from others that occasionally one may break to advantage, and English, as a popular global language, is anyway perpetually in flux. So when you have a good reason, or are feeling particularly confident, by all means try an experiment, but be sure to break with convention by design rather than from ignorance.

Building the Argument

Précising paragraphs and polishing prose go hand in glove with building your argument. Cut the clutter, streamline the remainder, and sharpen the points. You may well notice that as your research and interpretation progresses, and in light of your particular methodological approach, your topic has narrowed to a subset of the original topic while your thesis has broadened into a powerful—and hopefully unique—overarching argument. In the case of my own doctoral dissertation, what began as a working thesis became one of three subsidiary arguments that supported a new thesis. Yet with every completed chapter, problems of clarity and continuity multiply amid the project's increasing complexity. No longer an amateur researcher, you have become a professional project manager, and, as such, you should employ all the tools and assistance available.

One useful tool is MS-Word's Document Map feature, an icon for which I keep handy on my toolbar. Set up each subhead at Level 2 and each chapter at Level 1 (as in the MS-Word Settings section), then click the icon to instantly see and navigate through your project's structure. At the same time, take a mental step back from your project to think deeply but with detachment about the function that each chapter, section, and even paragraph performs. How does each component advance your thesis? Still, the close involvement that comes with being a researcher/writer can make it difficult, if not impossible, to evaluate your own work. It is therefore essential to enlist the assistance of as many readers as possible, in addition to the members of your dissertation committee. You will find few people more willing to help than your peers, so join a departmental writing group, or, better still, form your own group with half-a-dozen fellow students. Meet each month, with two presenters circulating a chapter a few days in advance. Best practice is for every member to line edit (proofread) each presentation, which establishes a quid pro quo that all members will come to value despite the extra work entailed. Even if you meet in a restaurant over a couple of beers, maintain a collegial atmosphere; consider the black-box approach, with each member offer-

构。同时，从你的研究计划中退出一步进行思考，以便更深入、客观地把握每一章、每一部分，甚至每一段的功能。各部分是如何层层深入形成论点的呢？不过，处于研究者或作者的立场上，基于与作品的紧密关系，不容易，甚至不可能客观评价自己的作品。因此，必须邀请尽可能多的读者和答辩委员会的成员提供帮助。你将发现几乎没有什么人比你的同学们更愿意为你提供这样的帮助，所以参加一个系内写作小组，或者，最好组建一个由六七名同学组成的属于自己的写作小组。每个月见一次面，并请两位发言人提前几天提交一章发言以供他人传阅。最佳实践方式是每位成员都要逐条编辑（修改）每份发言，以便建立一种回报机制使得彼此互相欣赏，尽管如此一来大家皆需承担许多额外的工作。就算你们约在一家餐馆中见面，几杯啤酒之后，仍需要保持一种学院式的氛围；考虑采用"黑箱作业"（black-box approach）的方式，即发言者在所有成员发表评论时皆需冷静倾听等待，直到全部结束再进行回应。来自同道的压力不但可以提高自身的工作质量而且还可以提高效率。与学术会议评论者和那些甚至更加忙碌的博士学位论文导师相比，组员不久即会对你的整个研究的结构形成了解。

　　写作初学者一般会以一份新的 MS-Word 文档开始新一章的写作，有人持续这种一个文档一章的习惯直至整个研究项目结束。虽然处在不同文档中的章节更容易进行传阅，并且根据鸡蛋不能放在同一个篮子中的原理，电子档案也亦然，但是此种方法的弊端远远超越其益处。为了便于把各章融合成一个天衣无缝的整体，从而保证你研究计划的连贯性和取证能力，要尽快把所有单独章节的文档合并到一个文档中。把所有内容置于同一屋檐下，你就可以充分利用诸如文档结构图这样的 Word 工具，扫描重复的单词和短语，形成流畅的章节过渡。每一章都应该建立在前文的基础上，并介绍和发展出一个全新的主要观点，也许置于一个主要人物抑或事件的语境之下。保持相邻章节主要观点的连贯性和相关性，将其放在一个清晰的框架中以便有逻辑地一步步深化你的论点，如此一来，你就可以避免在行文中自曝其短，承认结构性失误，写出"正如我在第三章所提到的那样"这样的语句来。一旦你已经完成了其中几章的写作，并且思考过各章之间的关联，要试着在各章结语的最后一句中添加一个迷你过渡路线图，以便为你的读者翻开下一页作好铺垫。

- **语气**。在你行文论证成形的前提下，要确认行文语气以及行文中私人立场的使用程度。如果我写道："弗朗哥政府的游说集团成员在心理上将西班牙影射为美国，并默默地将蔓延着的、外国马克思主义引发的不道德的政治混乱与传统美国核心价值带来的文明秩序进行比照。"那么本句的

ing a critique and the presenter waiting dispassionately until the end before responding. Peer pressure to present will not only improve the quality of your work but also enhance productivity. In contrast to conference commentators or even busy dissertation advisors, group members soon develop an appreciation, chapter by chapter, of how your entire project hangs together.

Novice writers typically begin a new chapter with a new MS-Word document, and some continue until the project's completion on a document per chapter basis. While it is easier to circulate chapters if they are in discrete documents, and one does not have all one's digital eggs in the same electronic basket, the pros of this method lag far behind the cons. To facilitate the melding of chapters into a seamless whole, thereby ensuring your project's continuity and forensic power, migrate individual chapters to a single-document format as soon as possible. With everything under a single roof, you will be able to make full use of tools such as Document Map, scan for duplicate words and phrases, and develop smooth chapter transitions. Each chapter should build on the work of its predecessor while introducing and developing a new main point, perhaps in the context of an actor or an event. Maintaining continuity with and relevance to the main points in adjacent chapters, within an explicit framework that advances your argument step by logical step, will obviate admissions of structural failure like, "as I showed in chapter three." Once you have a few chapters in place, and thought about the connections among them, try adding mini road maps to the last sentence of each chapter's conclusion, thereby preparing your reader for what follows on the next page.

- **Tone.** Now that your argument is gelling, be cognizant of your tone, of the extent to which your personal opinion intrudes. If I write, "Franco lobbyists mentally mapped Spain onto the United States to contrast the amoral anarchy of encroaching foreign Marxism with the civilizing order of traditional American core values," then I am stating, perhaps without realizing it, a personal belief that in 1938 Marxism was amoral while American core values represented civilization. To keep my academic distance and maintain objectivity, I should write, "Franco lobbyists mentally mapped Spain onto the United States to contrast what they saw as the amoral anarchy of encroaching foreign Marxism with the civilizing order of traditional American core values." Even the most innocuous of word choices can carry huge meaning. Take the difference between *capture* and *recapture*. If I write: "On 10 March 2011, Col. Muammar el-Qaddafi's forces recaptured Ras Lanuf," then I make a value-added judgment, suggesting that Qaddafi was the legitimate ruler of Libya and that he had taken back or recovered what rightfully be-

行文，也许在我无意识的情况下，已经隐含了一个私人的主张，即在1938年，马克思主义是不道德的，而美国核心价值则代表了文明。欲确保学术独立以及维持其客观性，我要把行文改成："弗朗哥政府的游说集团成员在心理上将西班牙影射为美国，并默默地将他们当时所认为的蔓延着的、外国马克思主义引发的不道德的政治混乱与传统美国核心价值带来的文明秩序进行比照。"最无足轻重的用词都可能隐藏重大的含义。比较下"占领"和"收复"所存在的含义差别。如果我写道："2011年3月10日，穆阿迈尔·卡扎菲上校的军队收复了拉斯拉努夫。"在此行文中，隐含着我作出的一个附加价值判断，即卡扎菲是合法的利比亚统治者，而他仅是收回或者收复他正当拥有的东西。但是如果我写道："2011年3月10日，穆阿迈尔·卡扎菲上校的军队占领了反政府武装控制的拉斯拉努夫。"在此行文中，我则作出了一个价值中性判断，使我的观点不至于有所偏颇。同时也要注意，这几句话中的其他词语也会隐含着深意或者价值判断。不写"卡扎菲政府"，我可以写"卡扎菲陆军"，甚至"利比亚陆军"，二者在历史意义上也都是准确的。"军队"一词将卡扎菲领导的士兵与反对军赋予了相同等级的权威——或者道德的对与错——而"卡扎菲陆军"则暗示着此军队较之于反对军的乌合之众，更加正规和专业。"利比亚陆军"一词的使用则走得更远，通过在行文中除去卡扎菲的名字，暗示着那些士兵们，事实上是代表利比亚真正政府的合法军队，而反对军则一无是处，不过是一群毫无道德权威感的、借反叛崛起的、糟糕的群体。所以，不要不假思索地遣词造句。要衡量每一个主要单词的本意并思考其在上下文中的引申义。通过按下Shift+F7键的方式，充分利用MS-Word的同义词库功能。

打印—编辑—复查的循环

长久以来，每位作者皆会倾向于使用某些特定单词、短语和行文结构，它们合在一起形成了富于个人特色的行文风格，此种风格虽然既重要又有价值，但是优秀的作者也要预防行文中陈腐的重复和过度的使用。重复当然可以很有效，诚如在马丁·路德·金具有纪念价值的"我有一个梦想"演讲中所体现出来的那样，但是此种艺术实践是刻意为之，而非偶拾而得。重新浏览下80页有关一致性的部分，我在行文中确实有意在相邻两句中用了两个"如果你……那么要避免"这样的从句吗？确实，它们最初并非故意而为之，而是作为重点问题，我决定将其视为一种写作特色，这就是为什么第二次重复后面也存有一个有关读者的格言性短句。但是，我要承认，自己在行文中过分地依赖"如果……那么"从句（为了使其形

longed to his side. But if I say, "On 10 March 2011, Col. Muammar el-Qaddafi's forces captured rebel-held Ras Lanuf," then I make a value-neutral statement, keeping my opinion out of the equation. Notice, too, how other words in these sentences are potentially loaded with meaning or judgmental values. Instead of "Qaddafi's forces," I could say "Qaddafi's army," or even "the Libyan Army," both of which are historically accurate. Whereas *forces* puts Qaddafi's soldiers on the same level of authority—or moral right/wrong—as the rebel soldiers, *Qaddafi's army* suggests that this force was more formal or professional than the ragtag forces of the rebels. *Libyan Army* goes even further by taking Qaddafi out of contention, suggesting that those soldiers were, in fact, the legitimate force representing the true government of Libya, while the rebel forces were nothing but a lousy bunch of rebellious upstarts with no moral claim to power. So do not just toss words into your paragraphs unthinkingly. For every major word, evaluate its meaning and consider its context. Make full use of MS-Word's thesaurus by pressing <Shift><F7>.

Print–Edit–Review Cycle

Over time, every writer comes to favor certain words, phrasing, and literary constructions, which harmonize into a characteristic style. Developing a signature style is as important as it is valuable, and yet good writers will guard against banal repetition or over usage. Repetition, of course, can be effective, to wit Martin Luther King's memorable "I Have a Dream" speech, but practice the art intentionally, not accidentally. Look back at the Consistency bullet on page 79. Did I really intend to write two "If you . . . then avoid" sentences hand running? Well, actually not when I first wrote them, but having spotted the issue, I decided to make it a feature, which is why I followed the second iteration with a short maxim-like sentence about one's reader so as to mirror the prior construct. I admit, nonetheless, to an over reliance on *if . . . then* sentences (made the more obvious by my inclusion of *then* after every *if*, in order to stick with standard constructions), which borders on an addiction.

Spotting structural and stylistic issues, such as transitions and duplicate phrasing, is problematic when scrolling a video screen. Experiment with MS-Word's Draft view as well as the more popular Print Layout, and consider investing in a twenty-two-inch-plus display set vertically (in portrait mode) so that you can scan up and down multiple pages without scrolling; LCD displays have come down in price, and many now have built-in pivots to allow for easy rotation. To maximize my vertical display while composing as well as editing, I use Draft view and minimize my toolbars. To check for correct spacing between words, particularly in footnotes where there are so many ab-

成一个标准结构,我在每个"如果"从句的后面都加上"那么",使其在行文中表现得更加明显),以至达到上瘾的程度。

在翻页的电脑屏幕上检视行文的结构和风格问题会比较麻烦,例如是否存在过渡和重复短语的问题。尝试使用 MS-Word 中的草稿视图模式和更加常用的打印视图模式,并考虑买一个22英寸以上的显示器,竖向安置(设置为肖像模式)以便你不必翻页也可以上下浏览多页内容;LCD 屏幕的价格已下降了,而且当前许多这样的显示器会带有嵌入式支轴以方便旋转。在写作和编辑时要最大化地利用其竖向显示屏,为此我使用草稿视图模式,并将工具栏最小化。为了确认单词间的正确距离,尤其是在带有大量缩略词语的脚注中,需要调整 Word 软件中的显示/隐藏功能,为此我将其图标置于工具栏中,但是也可以使用热键 Ctrl+Shift+*完成此项操作。当你编辑脚注时,将其放大到140%倍以便使得标点符号比正常的12号字体显示得大些。不过,即使是用最大的电脑显示器的文档进行编辑亦存在严重的局限性,故而创造出高质量作品的核心方法是我所谓的"打印—编辑—复查"循环。此阶段至少要在论文初稿完成之后就开始进行,暂时忽略学术规范要求的双倍行距(28磅),用单倍行距进行打印以便使每页容纳更多行数以增强可读性,可以进行双面打印以节省纸张。在草稿的左上角装订,为自己配备一支自动铅笔,并抓紧所有机会——地铁上、走路时、用餐时间——逐条编辑打印文本。尤其要核查那些你用过一次以上的非常规单词以及过度使用的常规单词和短语。确认在第一次提到人物姓名时使用全称,以后皆使用姓氏。也要核查脚注中的错误,因为要使其变得完善可能需要几轮的复查。当完成纸面核查之后,再移至屏幕进行编辑修改,要充分利用 MS-Word 中的同义词库功能以便删除重复的词语、增加行文的变化。尽可能多地重复此一过程,直到产生出一篇结构精练、行文润色、正确无误的出版品的那一天。

完成项目

我恐怕,根据像本书这样的指南的描述,会使得一切听起来太容易了。没有几个人真正写过博士学位论文,甚至只有更少的人看到它们付梓印刷,因此难以体会其中的过程是如何的漫长而艰辛。有时你会对自己论文的论点是否合理产生质疑;有时你觉得整个过程应该重新来过或者要全盘放弃,但是这种自我质疑是具有建设性的,因为过度自信使人自满。但甚至在一切顺利,你即将完成研究整个计划的时候,也要时不时地抽出几个钟头用于自我反省。

breviations, toggle MS-Word's Show/Hide feature, for which I keep an icon on my toolbar, but there is also a hotkey: <Ctrl> <Shift> <*>. When editing footnotes, zoom in to 140 percent so that punctuation appears larger than regular 12-pt type. Still, even the biggest digital display will always impose severe limitations, so at the core of any method for producing quality written work lies what I call the print–edit–review cycle. At this stage, which should begin at the completion of your first draft, if not before, temporarily override academia's double (28-pt) line spacing in order to boost the lines-per-page thereby enhancing readability, and print double-sided to save paper. Staple the stack at the top left corner, arm yourself with a mechanical pencil, and take every opportunity—subway, walking, mealtimes—to line-edit the printed pages. Check, particularly, for unusual words that you have used more than once, as well as common words and phrasing that you are overusing. Ensure that you give names in full at first mention and then just family name thereafter. Check the footnotes for errors too, because it will take several passes before they are perfect. When you are through, review your edits on-screen, making full use of MS-Word's thesaurus to obviate duplicate words and add variety to your prose. Repeat the cycle as often as it takes to produce structured précis, polished prose, and an error-free publishable copy.

COMPLETING THE PROJECT

Guides like this one, I fear, make everything sound too easy. Few people write dissertations and even fewer see them in print, which indicates how difficult the process actually is. There will be times when you question whether your argument makes any sense, times even when you feel like starting over or quitting altogether. Yet such self doubt can be constructive, for overconfidence breeds complacency and hubris. But even when everything is going well and you are close to completing the project, every so often, put a few hours aside for introspection.

Introspection

Anxious thoughts scamper around the brain like a gerbil on a treadmill. Try marshaling them in a one- or two-page memo or *think-piece*. Looking back through my files, I see there were seven occasions when I felt a need to commit my worries to paper, then email the resulting think-piece to my advisor and readers for feedback. I usually caught them at a busy time, and sometimes their advice was brief, but the exercise always helped me over a difficult patch, or allowed me to understand, if not always solve, a complex problem. By chapter five, I was grappling with how to apply postmodernist theory and explain how it affected my actors' worldview. As the stack of specialized works on my desk grew, the faster the gerbil scurried. At a loss, I

反思

焦虑的思绪犹如奔跑在踏板上的仓鼠一般疾驰于脑海中。尝试着把它们归纳成一至两页的备忘录或者"思考片段"。通过那些文档回顾写作过程，我发现其中有七次我觉得有必要把自己的忧虑呈现于纸张，然后把最后的思考片段寄给我的导师和读者寻求反馈。虽然他们通常很忙，并且有时回复的意见十分简练，但是这样的过程总是帮助我度过瓶颈期，或者让我了解到问题的复杂性所在，即使不会总能彻底解决问题。我还记得当论文写到第五章时，我陷入如何利用后现代理论以及解释该理论如何影响了论文中人物们的世界观这样的一个困境中。随着相关专著在我的书桌上越积越多，我脑海中的仓鼠越跑越快。太纠结了，于是我把思绪整理成思考片段并邮寄给波士顿学院的著名思想史学家保罗·布赖内斯。在他颇具个人特色的回复中，告诉我"去他娘的理论"，也就是说他建议我不要过多关注怎样把后现代结构技术应用于论文当中，因为我在写给他的思考片段中显示出的深厚的理论功底完全有可能自然而然完成自己的论争。将之前纷繁复杂的思维整理成有序的思考片段，然后请教求助，帮助我了解了理论的作用，并帮助我的论文写作避免陷于烦琐术语之中的弯路。

最后几个步骤

当你完成了所有章节的写作（或者研究报告的正文段落），并运行过"打印—编辑—复查"的循环之后，就可以进入结语部分的写作了。一份优秀的结语不但需要总结论据、加强论点，还需要强调你的论点是如何深入并改变了主流的学术观点的。理想层面上，它将为未来更加深入的研究指明方向。然后，要重新回顾引言部分，就像你自从研究计划开始的那天起也许反复进行的那样。我的博士学位论文的引言部分需要全部重写，但是我不确定这算是对自己学术过程的肯定还是意味着我论文的部分失败。在进行包括对结语和重新审视过的引言进行的"打印—编辑—复查"的循环过程中，请运用以下技巧。

- **同上**。把针对同样来源的连续脚注改成同上（ibid.），另外，在有必要时，把具有相同作者的连续脚注改成作者同上（id.）。
- **复合脚注**。如果你打算使用复合脚注，就是在每个段落结束后撰写一个包括该段落所有来源的脚注，此阶段是一个把单个脚注合并成复合脚注的绝佳机会。
- **重置**。核查你重置的所有姓名简称、组织简称和简化脚注，确认其在每章第一次出现时是全称状态。确保甚至连 United Nations（联合国）被简称

worked up a thoughtful think-piece and emailed it to Paul Breines, Boston College's legendary intellectual historian. "F--- theory," was his characteristic reply, by which he meant that I should not obsess over how to incorporate postmodernist deconstruction techniques into my dissertation because the solid theoretical grounding I had just demonstrated to him in the think-piece would naturally inform my interpretation. Marshaling what previously had been random thoughts into order in the think-piece, and then soliciting advice, helped me to understand the theory and saved my dissertation from a plague of tedious jargon.

Concluding Steps

Once you have completed all the chapters (or body paragraphs in the case of a research paper) and run them through the print–edit–review cycle several times, you will be ready to write the conclusion. A good conclusion not only sums up the evidence and reinforces the thesis but also stresses how the thesis informs and modifies prevailing scholarship. Ideally, it will point the way to further research and directions that the field might take in the future. Then, revisit the introduction, as you may already have done several times since the project's inception. My dissertation's introduction required a complete rewrite, although whether that indicates a vindication of the scholarly process or a failure of vision on my part I am unsure. During the ongoing print–edit–review cycle, which can now include the conclusion and revised introduction, implement the following:

- **Ibid.** Change consecutive footnote references to the same work to ibid., and, where applicable, to a consecutive author to id.
- **Compound footnotes.** If you intend to use compound footnotes, with a single note at the end of each paragraph containing the citations for all of that paragraph's sources, then this is an ideal time to migrate the individual notes to the compound format.
- **Resets.** Verify that you have reset all shortened names, abbreviated organizations, and concise (short form) footnote references to their full-length state at their first mention in every chapter. It is good policy not to make exceptions, even for organizations as commonplace as the United Nations (UN) or Federal Bureau of Investigation (FBI), if only to indicate to your reader that you are as consistent as you are conscientious. Strike a balance between banal repetition and saving words on the one hand and losing your reader on the other hand. Having first mentioned "President Franklin D. Roosevelt" on page two of a forty-page chapter, you are unlikely to lose your reader by using the "Roosevelt" short form on pages ten, twenty-two, and thirty-five. But for an obscure actor that you reference on page five and then not again until page thirty, provide most of the name if not all of it. Sgt.

为 UN、Federal Bureau of Investigation（美国联邦调查局）被简称为 FBI 这样的常见名称也不例外，即使这样做仅是确保你的读者看到你写作的一致性和认真的态度。要在无聊的重复、节省词语和承担表达不清而使得读者混淆之间求得一个平衡。假设你已完成了容量为40页的一章，在其第2页第一次提到了"富兰克林·D. 罗斯福总统"的全名，则不太可能因为在其后的第10、22和35页使用"罗斯福"这个简称就令读者感到混乱。但是，对于仅在行文中第5页和接下来第30页提到的一个读者不熟悉的人物名字来说，就算不写全名，也要提供其名字的大部分，甚至全部姓名。例如，"中士爱德华·L.帕克·Jr."在第二次提到时可以缩写为"中士爱德华·帕克"。

- **参考文献**。假设你已把行文中提到的每一本新书都填入参考文献当中，那么现在所需要做的就只是将其纳入"打印—编辑—复查"的循环了，但是要注意已经在引文中删除却依然存在于参考文献中的书目。参考文献的标准做法是只包含那些在正文部分引用过的文书目录。

- **扉页**。在合适的时候，编辑一个包含目录、致谢、版权和标题页的表格。

- **院系格式**。使你的手稿符合院系要求的某些特殊标准。

- **打印**。对整篇手稿进行最后一遍"打印—编辑—复查"的循环，并最终确定下来。在最终稿打印之前，注意某些院系可能要求至少一份的无酸纸打印文本，不过现在不少牌子的激光打印纸既便宜又符合无酸打印的标准。在打印完要向学位委员会和学术委员会提交的文本之后，复查每一页以确保激光打印机正确地打印了所有页面；毕竟在你付出了那么多努力和所需的勤奋之后，如果发现留在大学档案馆的文本有6页空白，甚至更糟糕地缺了10页，将会感到多么沮丧。

要以从容不迫、有条不紊的态度对待收尾部分的所有工作。放慢节奏，保持细心和谨慎。避免制造以前不存在、以后再没有机会被察觉的失误。无意间用手指或者一捆纸碰触键盘而导致输入了不妥当的字母简直太容易了。无论何时你怀疑自己犯了这样的错误，点击撤销键入按钮（Ctrl+Z键）并检查光标所在的位置。我为我如此的吹毛求疵道歉，但是对于你的研究计划是否成功来说，每一个小细节的把握与整体论文的大论点一样重要。记住，正确的细节也许不会被评判你论文的忙碌的教授们记住，但是没什么比愚蠢的失误和无意的错误更能使他们记住，分散他们的注意力，影响他们理解论文的信息。在你欢庆自己的答辩成功——实至名归，同时开始准备使自己的成就更上一层，着手于出版第一篇文章或专著时——一种莫名的失落感会随之而来，这也许是此过程中理所当然的一部分。

Edwin L. Parker Jr. could be Sgt. Edwin Parker at second mention.

- **Bibliography.** Providing you added to your bibliography each time you referenced a new title, all that is necessary here is to include it in the print–edit–review cycle, but pay attention for any titles that should not be in the bibliography because you dispensed with the reference. Standard practice is to include only those works in the bibliography for which there are citations in the text.
- **Front matter.** Where applicable, compile a table of contents, and write the acknowledgements, copyright, and title pages.
- **Departmental format.** Bring your manuscript into conformity with any special departmental formatting guidelines.
- **Printing.** Run the print–edit–review cycle one final time on the entire manuscript, and set it in stone. Before printing the finished work, note that some departments require at least one copy on acid-free paper, although many brands of inexpensive laser-printer paper now meet acid-free specifications. After printing the copies for your committee and degree submission, go through each sheet to verify that the laser printer did its job correctly; after all that work and due diligence you will be disappointed if your bound copy in the university archives has six blank pages or, worse still, ten missing pages.

Throughout these concluding steps, operate in a deliberate, methodical manner. Slow down; exercise care and caution. Avoid introducing errors that were not there before and which you will not spot subsequently. It is all too easy to inadvertently tap the keyboard or brush it with a sheaf of papers, thereby entering rogue characters. Whenever you suspect you may have done so, click Undo Typing (<Ctrl> <Z>) and check where your cursor is sitting. I apologize for belaboring what may seem to be picky issues, and yet the details are every bit as crucial to your project's success as the big picture of your overarching thesis. Remember, attention to detail may not consciously impress busy professors who are evaluating a thesis or dissertation, but nothing will stick in their minds more, distracting them from the candidate's message, than silly mistakes and unforced errors. Soon after celebrating your successful—and well earned—defense, a feeling of anticlimax will settle in, which is perhaps as it should be, as you gear up for the consummate achievement of publishing your first article or monograph.

出版或发表
PUBLISHING AN ARTICLE OR MONOGRAPH

如果你已撰写出一篇由创新研究支持的原创文章，并已将其编辑成有说服力的高品质的稿件，那就没有理由不在硕士论文或博士学位论文答辩之前试着发表——而且也有可能发表成功一篇经专家评审的期刊文章。博士生们应该努力在答辩之前发表至少一篇文章，不过要是发表了二到三章内容，可能会使得大学出版社的编辑犹豫是否值得再为此出版一本专著。把目光锁定在你所在领域的顶尖国际性期刊上面，并致力于此。即使投稿遭拒的过程将会耗时很久，但你在此过程中将会得到有益的反馈，并形成对自己手稿价值的客观评价。

审稿时的同行评审

顶尖的国际性期刊——就是你唯一应该追求发表论文的场所，因为在其他更低级的期刊发表自己的论文只会贬低它的价值——秉持着严格的学者评审程序。在认定你提交的论文值得深思之后，编辑会以匿名的方式将你的论文发送给二至三位在该领域领先的专家学者，他们会写出详细的匿名评审书，内容包括或经过微小改动就得以发表的推荐，或经过彻底改动、重新投稿才可发表的推荐，或者干脆不可能发表的意见。

投稿

到准备好发表文章的时候，你要对所在领域的知名期刊已经有所了解，不过还是要浏览图书馆的书架以熟悉相关领域的期刊，或许还能发现你所在领域内的另一份有价值的期刊。文章最好能够发表在所在领域的顶尖期刊上，不过也要考虑到该期刊的压稿时间、你的文章与该期刊的吻合度和私人关系。从期刊编辑处或从其他学术圈的小道消息处打听该期刊是否存在压稿的问题，一些期刊可能会存在为期两年的压稿时间而另外一些可能在下一期就可以发表你的文章。如果你的文章采用了特殊的方法论或描述了一个地域性关心的问题，那么可以考虑在一个符合你文章特点的更低级期刊发表。同样，在缩减后仅存的几个顶尖目标刊物中进行选择的时候，要偏向于最近已发表过你导师的作品或者评论过你最近参加会议发表论文的编辑所在的期刊。

一旦确定了所要投稿的首选目标期刊，就要查阅该期刊最近的几期内容以便获得有关发表风格和格式的相关信息，并核实投稿要求（目前一些期刊仅将投稿要求发布在它们的网站上）。严守字数限制——要求6500个字的文章就不要投出7300个字的稿件——并注意出版字数与投稿字数可能存在的区别；若决定了该论文可以发表，评论人可能会要求作者添加更多

Providing you have an original thesis supported by innovative research and convincingly presented in a quality manuscript, there is no reason why you should not try to publish—and succeed in so doing—a peer-reviewed journal article before you defend your MA thesis or PhD dissertation. Doctoral candidates should aim to publish at least one article before their defense, although publishing more than two or three chapters may make a university press editor less inclined to consider a monograph. Set your sights on the top-ranked international journal in your field, and work your way down. Even though the submission–rejection process is time consuming, you will receive useful feedback along the way, and gain a sense of your manuscript's merit.

PEER REVIEW PROCESS

Top-ranked international journals—the only journals in which you should aim to publish your scholarship, because anything less only serves to devalue it—adhere to a rigorous peer review process. Having decided that your submission is worthy of further consideration, an editor will send your paper anonymously to two or three leading academics in your field, who will write detailed reports, also anonymously, including a recommendation to either publish the piece with limited changes, publish after a substantial rewrite and re-submission, or not publish at all.

Submission

By the time you are ready to publish an article, you will already be familiar with the leading journals in your field, although it is still worthwhile to browse your library's shelves to make the acquaintance of journals in peripheral fields and perhaps discover a new publication in your own field. It is always best to publish in your field's top journal, but also factor in backlog, suitability, and connections. Inquire from the journal's editor or on the scholarly grapevine whether there is a backlog; some journals have a wait time of two years but others can publish in the next edition. If your paper uses a particular methodology or speaks to a regional interest then you might consider a lower-ranked journal that matches your specialty. Similarly, when narrowing down a number of top contenders, favor the journal that recently published your dissertation advisor or which has an editorial board member who provided commentary for your last conference presentation.

Once you have selected the target for your first submission, look through the last few editions for hints on style and formatting, and check the submission requirements (some journals now carry this information only on their websites). Adhere to word limits—6,500 does not mean 7,300—and note that publication length can differ from submission length; having accepted

内容或者深化某一观点。将博士学位论文的一章改写成期刊文章的时候，可能要删除那些与文章论点不直接相关的句子、段落，甚至整个部分，该论点可能就是博士学位论文论点的分论点或者变化论点。将论文的一章精简成一篇具有期刊长度的论文是一项很有益的训练，将使你注意到多余的论据和长久以来形成的迷恋自己的资料来源的陋习。注意使你的文章的介绍段落适合目标期刊的读者。写一篇概括文章主题的约150字的独段摘要，包含使用资料介绍、解释论点和它在史学中的地位。你的投稿方式应尽可能地专业。在封面后的摘要页上，写明如下陈述："我保证本稿件不曾发表，现今亦不曾考虑在其他刊物进行发表。如果发表本稿件，我同意签署出版合同。"不但要把文章标题置于封面页，另外在正文第一页亦注明标题——但不注作者姓名。

准备出版一部专著会需要更多的考量，作者威廉·杰尔马诺的综合性著作 *Getting It Published*（《准备出版》）中有很全面的介绍。最基本的是，你应该承认，几乎没有不经过大量的重新整理就可以出版的博士学位论文。博士学位论文不可避免的是博士生们的激情再加上评审委员关注点的混合产物。它们一般皆包含着论著性质的理论、方法论和文献综述性质的内容，也就是那些更广泛的学术群体并不感兴趣也并不需要知道的内容。若没有经过修改和删节而直接将你的手稿提交给大学出版社的编辑，就会得到诸如"我恐怕此研究范围过于狭窄，不在本出版社的出版范围之内"这样的评论。首先，要尝试确认与你作品最匹配的受众群——学者、学生、政府机构、历史学爱好者，然后据此调整内容。向同事征求意见，在学术会议上发表其中的部分，而且将你的手稿就那样先放置几个月来思考其中的问题都是对修改来说很好的策略。我的情况是，出版论文比写完论文花了将近一倍的时间，其中我合并了两章，删除了整个一章，重新写了引言和结语，并对语气、语态、内容进行了大量修改。当你满意于所作的修改使得这个项目尽可能成形的时候，再按照期刊或者出版社的投稿要求提交并等待。

评审报告

学术界，正如我的导师经常说的那样，就是在焦虑不安的行动和令人烦恼的漫长等待中交替行进着的。耐心但要时刻准备快速对每一次事件的转折进行反应，如果幸运的话，期待着编辑开始关注到你的手稿并将其送交评阅，其过程一般历时四到十二周。不要梦想着那二到三个评阅人会

an article, reviewers may ask the author to add content or develop a particular point. When converting a dissertation chapter to a journal article, be prepared to axe sentences, paragraphs, or even entire sections that are peripheral to the article's thesis, which will probably be a subset of or a variation on the dissertation's thesis. Précising the chapter to article length will be a useful exercise, focusing your attention on excessive evidence, and the perennial problem of falling in love with one's sources. Tailor your article's introductory paragraphs to the target journal's readership. Write a 150-word single-paragraph abstract that summarizes your topic, mentions your sources, and explains your thesis and its historiographical importance. Make your submission as professional as possible; on the Abstract page following the cover sheet, include this statement: "I confirm that this manuscript has not been published elsewhere and is not currently under consideration for publication in any other journal. If the manuscript is accepted, I agree to sign a contract for the transfer of copyright to the publisher." In addition to including it on the cover sheet, give the paper's title—but not your name—on the first page.

Additional considerations apply when preparing a monograph for submission, which William Germano covers in his comprehensive *Getting It Published*. Most fundamentally, you should recognize that few dissertations make it into print without a major rewrite. Dissertations inevitably become the product of the doctoral candidate's passion, with an admixture of the committee members' pet interests. They tend to contain theoretical, methodological, and historiographical sections bordering on treaties, moreover, for which a broader scholarly public would have little interest and less need. Left unrevised and unexpurgated, your manuscript will solicit comments from university press editors like, "I am afraid this study is too narrow for our press's catalogue." Try to decide, at the outset, to whom your work will best appeal—scholars, students, government agencies, history buffs—and tailor it accordingly. Soliciting opinions from colleagues, presenting sections of your work at conferences, and generally sitting on the manuscript for a few months can all be productive strategies. In my own case, the path to publication took twice as long as producing the dissertation itself, requiring the melding together of two chapters, the cutting of one chapter entirely, and the writing of a new introduction and conclusion, in addition to a raft of revisions to tone, voice, and content. When you are satisfied you have done all you can to knock the project into shape, submit it in conformity with the journal or press's submission requirements and wait.

Reviewers' Reports

Academia, as my advisor often remarked, alternates between spells of feverish activity and agonizingly long waits. Be patient but prepared to re-

添油加醋地夸奖你的杰出学术成果,因为当他们的评阅书到手的时候,你唯一能做的只有尽量克制自己不要放弃学术生涯或者卧轨自杀。深吸一口气,解读编辑发来的评阅。诸如"评阅人对你的文章感兴趣但是认为其在出版之前尚需修改",这样的评论实质上是值得庆贺而非引发自杀冲动的褒奖,因为这是编辑在告诉你如果你能够作出必要的修改,他所在的期刊就会发表你的文章。当看到评论人诸如"行文过于陈词滥调"、"缺乏足够的论据支撑论点",或者"论点的重要性尚需更加清晰明了"这样的评论,你会气愤,并觉得羞愧,因为还存在三本你没有读到的专著,七个拼写错误的单词,以及十四个你错误阐述的事实。但是要理解,不管那些评论人多么挑剔你的论述、否定你的论点,正是你所在领域的顶尖专家,他们在为你将要出版的作品质量的提升方面,提出建设性的——而非毁灭性的——意见。

都说,没有什么比收到编辑拒绝出版的邮件、评论人否定的评阅书更令人沮丧了。但是就我自身的经历来说,这并不意味着你应该放弃学术去找一份快餐店的工作。当我将自己的第一本书提交给一家顶级美国大学出版社之时,编辑起初很兴奋,但是两个评论人却从私人立场(错误地)理解了我的政治立场,指责我是一个反犹太主义宣传家,是个罗列参考文献,将文章中主要人物的谎言解读成真实,以明显的双重标准进行论证,放弃了身为专业史学研究者所持的责任感的知识失败者。当意识到这些恶毒的——不专业的——人格诋毁的评论是出于评论人自身的政治偏见之后,我将自己的开题报告提交给了二十多个大学出版社,收到了六位热心编辑索要手稿的邀请,并从第一位编辑手中得到了一份出版合同。

修改和准备出版

理解了评阅书的相关内容后,写邮件给编辑解释你很乐意修改评阅人所提出的问题。在发送邮件之前给自己至少一天的缓冲时间,以便使你的血压稳定下来,还有在发送之前重读邮件内容,千万不要做出任何过河拆桥的行为,因为学术圈其实很小。评阅人的意见大致可以分为三个主要方面。首先,语法、事实和解读层面的失误,这些都是你应该并能够轻易纠正的内容。少数情况下,错误在评阅人而非你自己,此时要找到至少两个以上的可靠资料来佐证你的立场,并小心和礼貌地向编辑进行解释。其次,论据和论证中存在的问题——从论据论证薄弱到论据论证缺乏——很可

spond quickly with each turn of events, which hopefully will begin with a notification that the editor has sent your manuscript out for review, a process typically taking four to twelve weeks. Put aside your dreams that the two or three reviewers will wax lyrically about your brilliant scholarship, because when their reports arrive it will be all you can do not to abandon your scholarly career or stand in front of an express train. Take a deep breath and decode the editor's email. A comment like, "the reviewers are interested in publishing your article but feel that it needs work before they are able to accept it for publication," is actually cause for celebration not suicide, because the editor is saying that providing you make the necessary changes, his journal will publish your article. You will feel angry at the reviewers who say, "the writing is excessively clichéd," "there is insufficient evidence to support the argument," or "the argument's importance needs clarification," and embarrassed that there were three new monographs you failed to read, seven words you misspelled, and fourteen facts you stated incorrectly. But understand that the reviewers, however much they may pick holes in your exposition or disagree with your argument, are top scholars in your field, and they are making constructive—not destructive—comments designed to improve the quality of the published piece.

That said, there is nothing more demoralizing than an email from an editor declining publication, and reviewers' reports that are destructive. Yet as my own experience indicates, this does not mean you should give up and seek employment in a fast food restaurant. When I submitted my first book manuscript to a leading American university press, the editor was initially enthusiastic, but the two reviewers took personal offense to what they (incorrectly) believed my politics to be, accusing me of being an anti-Semitic Nazi propagandist and an intellectual failure who padded bibliographies, presented actors' lies as truths, argued to a gross double standard, and abdicated professional responsibility as a historian. Once I had accepted that the vicious—and unprofessional—character assassination was a product of the reviewers' own political biases, I sent my proposal to two dozen university presses, receiving six requests for the manuscript from eager editors, the first of which resulted in a book contract.

Revision and Pre-Press

Having digested the reviews, write an email to the editor explaining how you will be happy to rectify the problems raised by the reviewers. Sit on the email for at least a day to allow your blood pressure to stabilize, and read it again before sending; do not burn any bridges as the academic universe is surprisingly small. Reviewers' comments fall into three broad categories: First, grammatical, factual, and interpretational errors, all of which you should and

能，还包括背景和文献综述方面的问题。重申，你应该，也无疑会解决这些问题。虽然它也考验着你的耐性，但是不要在没能全面解决所有批评意见的情况下就再次提交手稿，因为编辑比你还缺乏耐性，并可能以最终的拒绝来回复你。反之，向一个独立读者寻求帮助，一个以前从来没有接触过这项研究的人，他可能是你曾经听过课的一位教授，或者是你曾在学术会议上遇到的一位学者。我提交的第一篇文章，是向一个欧洲期刊投稿的有关美国历史的文章，但缺少非美国读者的阅读语境，为此，我向一位英国历史学研究者征求意见，他很快确认并帮我解决了此问题。最后，你、编辑、评阅人三方默认可以选择性修改的意见，即那些暗示着基于你已有的论据，若评论人自己写，那么他会撰写出什么样的文章，诸如此类的意见。在你认为妥帖的情况下，尽可能地根据这些评论进行修改，但是不要为了取悦评论人而出卖了自己的学术独立性。确认哪些意见是你必须处理的关键性问题，哪些意见是可选择性完善的，当然，这些决断十分微妙，但要记住编辑担任仲裁的角色；在你业已完善和没有完善的意见之间提供一个相对平衡的意见——并说明理由——还有向编辑讨教。

在你再次提交经过修改的手稿不久之后，编辑会确认（或者不会）它符合了评阅人的要求，并向你解释出版程序和时间安排。一个文字编辑将会通过电子邮件发送给你文章的样稿，其形式正如印刷模式一样，通常为 PDF 文档。只要你所提交的手稿达到本指南所要求的标准，文字编辑将不会对其作出很大改动，但是不但要仔细重新通读编辑稿件，还要再次核实整篇手稿，因为在编辑和修改格式的过程中，错误有可能不知不觉再次出现。

专业道德

无论你是一个三年级的本科生还是一个院系的领导者，把自己看做专业人士，还有把自己所选的学科看做自己的职业对自己最有利。在历史学的学科体系下，最严格并最具影响力的政府性社会团体之一是 American Historical Association（美国历史学协会，简称 AHA），其公开网站提供了免费的 *Statement on Standards of Professional Conduct*（《专业行为标准声明》），是每一位具有英文阅读能力的历史学研究者都应该学习的，尤其要注意其中的"抄袭"和"名誉及信任"部分。

will easily rectify. In the rare event that the reviewer is in error, corroborate your position with at least two other reliable sources and explain it with care and politeness to the editor. Second, problems—ranging from weaknesses to omissions—with your evidence and argumentation, and perhaps, too, with background and historiography. Again, you should, and will no doubt, fix all these problems. Although it will try your patience, do not resubmit without fully addressing the criticisms, because the editor has less patience than you do, and may respond with a final rejection. Instead, seek help from an independent reader, someone who has never seen the project before, perhaps a faculty member with whom you took a class, or a scholar you met at a conference. My first article submission, a piece on U.S. history to a European journal, lacked context for a non-American reader, which a scholar of British history whom I asked for advice quickly identified and helped me to address. Third, comments that you, the editor, and the reviewer tacitly understand to be optional, the kind of comments suggestive of an article the reviewer would like to have written based on your evidence. Incorporate as many of these optional changes as you see fit, but do not sell out your scholarship simply to please the reviewer. Deciding which issues are critical problems you must fix and which are optional enhancements is, of course, tricky, but remember that the editor's role is arbitration; provide a balanced commentary on the enhancements you have and have not made—and why—and ask the editor for guidance.

Shortly after you re-submit the revised manuscript, the editor will confirm (or otherwise) that it met the reviewers' concerns, and explain publication procedures and schedules. A copy editor will then email to you page proofs of the article, as it will appear on the printed page, typically as a PDF. Providing your submission was to the quality advocated in this guide, the copy editor will have made few changes, but be sure to not only review the edits carefully but also check the entire manuscript one more time, because errors can creep in during the editing and formatting process.

PROFESSIONAL ETHICS

Whether you are a third-year undergraduate or a departmental head, it is in your best interests to consider yourself a professional, and your chosen discipline as a profession. In the case of history, one of the strictest and most influential governing bodies is the American Historical Association (AHA), whose open-access website provides without charge the AHA's *Statement on Standards of Professional Conduct*, which all historians capable of reading English should study. In particular, note the sections on "Plagiarism" and "Reputation and Trust."

水分和抄袭

仅仅因为你所在国家的大学制度打造了一个要么出版、要么淘汰的氛围，或者你的同事皆如此，这些并不能作为你的借口，以至利用期刊文章、编辑作品集的章节、纲目分录等，或者基于你几年前就进行的研究，将其改头换面成你的最新成果以丰富自己的个人履历。更严重的是，正如时常在东亚发生的情况那样，要避免抄袭其他学者观点的诱惑。不要陷入主流体制中，在此机制中贱卖自己的学术成果，而要成为你所在机构中追求最高学术标准和抄袭零容忍度的倡导者。每当说服一个同事追随你的脚步，你就增加了所在机构成为该领域领导者的机会，而且你所在机构的名誉会影响别人对你自身的作品和名誉的认可程度。

Padding and Plagiarism

Simply because your country's university system has created a publish-or-perish climate, or because your colleagues do so, is no excuse for padding your curriculum vitae with journal articles, chapters in edited collections, entries in compendia, and so forth that rehash arguments you previously made, based on research you conducted years earlier. Worse still, as happens too often in East Asia, avoid the temptation of copying the ideas of other scholars. Rather than succumb to the prevailing system, selling your scholarship short in the processes, become an advocate at your institution for the highest professional standards and a zero-tolerance policy toward plagiarism. Each time you convince a colleague to follow suit, you increase the chances of your institution becoming a leader in your field, recognized the world over for an excellence that will soon devolve onto your own work and reputation.

语法及格式的基本知识
GRAMMAR AND STYLE ESSENTIALS

十种最常见的写作方面的问题

1. 被动语态掩盖了行为主体。
2. 多重时态：从过去时跳转到现在时。
3. *that* 和 *which* 用法的混淆。
4. 代词的不搭配。例如，"国会开了会而且他们通过了法案 ✘"，"……它通过了法案 ✓"。
5. "不过"的误用/过度使用，反之，可以尝试使用"*but*"（但是）、"*yet*"（可是）、"*although*"（尽管）、"*still*"（依然）。
6. 列举时在"和"之前逗号的省略。[1] 例如，"红、白和蓝 ✘"，"红、白，和蓝 ✓"。
7. 大写方式。例如，"西班牙的*president*（总统）对*President*布什说 ✓"。
8. 缩略语和口语的使用场合。例如，"*can't go wrong*（没法搞错）✘"。
9. 世纪、100以下数字的书写不使用阿拉伯数字，而用英文拼写。例如，"20世纪已经过了20天 ✘"。
10. 脚注编号位置的错误，应放在引号的外边。例如，"布什把此称之为'邪恶轴心'。[4] ✓"

句首的开场白

回去翻阅每一段落的初稿，颠倒特定词语的顺序，而不要每两句话皆以"那个"或者"在1776年"开头。例如，将"那些威尔士龙骑兵，与往常一样，在鲁莽的狂热状态下冲了进去"修改为"与往常一样，那些威尔士龙骑兵在鲁莽的狂热状态下冲了进去"。英语富有多彩的语句起始策略，不过在此要注意，类似于"*nevertheless*"（虽然如此）这样的单词往往更适合用于句中而非句首。下面有在一些场合下适用的单词，还包括逗号：

可是 |反正, |还有, |虽然如此, |虽然如此, |简单地说, |
总之, |另外, | 与此相反, | 确实, | 且, | 而且, | 然而|
尽管| 依然, | 一直到这时, | 兹, | 于是| 因此| 那么 |日益 |
此外, |与此同时, | 与此同时, | 当时, | 而 | 事实上, |
在……范围内 | 无论 | 虽然 | 只要 | 很重要的是, | 最终, |
值得一提的是 | 尽管 |

"和"、"但是却"、"但是"都可以用在正式的写作中，不过要偶尔为之，只在特殊场合和强调时使用。把诸如"还有"、"而且"和"确实"放在句中与以它们为句首相比，会显得没那么学究。另外，千万不要以下列的单词作为句首：

不过, | 举个例子, |

---

1. 此原则不适用于中文写作，中文写作中一般用顿号表示并列词语间的停顿，具体用法参见《中华人民共和国国家标准标点符号用法》（GB/T 15834–2011）。——编者注

Ten Most Common Stylistic Problems

1. passive voice masks action.
2. multiple tenses: flipping from past to present tense.
3. confusion over that/which usage.
4. pronoun disagreement. [Congress met in session and they passed the act ✘] [. . . it passed the act ✓]
5. *however* misuse/overuse (instead, try *but, yet, although, still*).
6. lists omit comma before *and*. [red, white and blue ✘] [red, white, and blue ✓]
7. capitalization. [Spain's president said to President Bush ✓]
8. contractions and colloquialisms. [can't go wrong ✘]
9. centuries, and numbers less than 100, spelled out. [the 20th century was 20 days old ✘]
10. misplaced footnote reference number; punctuation outside quote marks. [Bush called it an "Axis of Evil."[4] ✓]

Opening Gambits

Instead of starting every other sentence with *The* or *In 1776*, scan back through the rough draft of each paragraph and invert the word order of selected sentences. [The Welsh dragoons, true to form, charged in with reckless abandon.] Revised: [True to form, the Welsh dragoons charged in with reckless abandon.] English has a wealth of introductory gambits, although be careful here, for words such as *nevertheless* are often better employed within a sentence rather than at the beginning. Some possibilities, with commas where typically applicable:

Yet | Besides, | Moreover, | Nevertheless, | Nonetheless, | In short, | In sum, | In addition, | In/by contrast, | Indeed, | Further, | Furthermore, | Though | Although | Still, | Hitherto, | Hereby, | Therefore | Thus | So | Increasingly | Additionally, | Meanwhile, | At the same time, | At this time, | Instead | In fact, | Insofar as | Whatever | Despite | Given that | Importantly, | Ultimately, | It is noteworthy that | Notwithstanding |

And | And yet, | But | are allowed in formal writing, only use them sparingly, and then for effect or emphasis. You make opening gambits such as *Moreover, Furthermore,* and *Indeed* sound less pedantic when you embed them within a sentence, and you should never use the following to open a sentence:

however, | for example, | for instance, | also |

Instead, embed them in the sentence. [Patton had already decided, however, to . . . ✓] [On the morning of the sixteenth, for instance, Patton . . ." ✓]

打比方，|还有|

　　反之，要把它们放在句中。例如，"巴顿已经作出决定，不过，去做……✓"，"在16日早上，打比方，巴顿……✓"。虽然如此，要尽量减少类似于"*for instance*"（打比方）、"*such as*"（诸如），尤其是"*for example*"（例如）这一类词的使用，因为它们会浪费两三个单词的空间而且效果通常有待商榷。反正，你所提出的论据自然成为一则示例。甚至一些高明的作者都会误用到"*however*"（不过），其实他们想表达的是"*but*"（但是）、"*yet*"（可是）、"*although*"（尽管）或"*though*"（然而）之意。而且，"*however*"一词属于那种令读者的思绪停顿的词语，故而要把它留到特殊场合使用。像"*clearly*"（很明显）这类词不适用于引言段落，也最好节制其在正文段落中的使用；只要你所选择的论据和取证的技术足够支撑论点，或许到结语时叙事会不言自明。仅在行文中宣称很明显却不足以达到这种目的。

标准结构

　　英语本身具有表达明确而且简洁的短语规范，所以要遵循。
　　如果 X 那么 Y。（要注意，中间没有逗号）
　　不仅 X 而且 Y。（同上，中间没有逗号）
　　是 X 而非 Y。
　　一方面，X。另一方面，Y。
　　第一，……第二，……第三，……［或］最后，……

逗号

　　一方面，语法规则规定了逗号使用的很多场合，但另一方面，与写作方式的改进随之而来的是长难句的写作，使用逗号以增强可读性也是必要的。归根结底，依据《芝加哥论文格式手册》所言："逗号的有效使用依赖于良好的判断，以增强可读性为其旨归。"因此，我列出逗号使用的如下几则规范，不过我要承认自己在写作时存在过度使用和偶尔错用逗号的问题。

- 总是在一系列列举中的倒数第二位事项前使用逗号。例如，"美国国旗由红色、白色，和蓝色构成。✓" "你冷吗、饿吗，还是渴吗？✓"
- 在主语和动词之间用逗号分隔副词性短语。例如，"红衣主教戈马，收到电报之后，坐下回了一封长信。✓"
- 以少于四个单词的副词性短语作为句首，其后的间隔逗号并非是必需的。例如，"回家后红衣主教戈马起草了回信。✓"
- 历史学者却通常在介绍性日期之后添加一个逗号。例如，"1930年5月，戈马撰写了一封主教信函。✓"
- 除非位于句首的分词短语后接续的是一个动词，否则要在其后添加一个逗号。例如，"以身先士卒来说，亚历山大树立了一个高贵的榜样。✓" "身先士卒的是亚历山大自己。✓"

Still, work at reducing instances of *for instance*, *such as*, and especially *for example* because they cost you two words and are frequently moot. After all, if you are including evidence then it is automatically an example. Even advanced writers sometimes use *however* when they really mean *but*, *yet*, *although*, or *though*. And *however* is one of those words that stops your reader cold, so reserve it for special occasions. Words like *clearly* do not belong in introductions, and do limit their use in body paragraphs; providing that your evidence selection and forensic skills adequately support your thesis, then things may well be clear by the time you reach your conclusion. Saying that something is clear does not make it so.

Standard Constructions

English has tried and tested phrasal patterns that simply sound right, so stick with them.

If *X* then *Y*. (Note, there is no intervening comma.)
Not only *X* but also *Y*. (Similarly, no intervening comma.)
This *X* but not that *Y*.
On the one hand, *X*. On the other hand, *Y*.
First, . . . Second, . . . Third, . . . [or] Finally, . . .

Commas

On the one hand, grammatical rules govern many aspects of comma usage, while on the other hand, with advanced style comes longer sentences and the need for commas to enhance readability. Ultimately, as *Chicago* says, "Effective use of the comma involves good judgment, with ease of reading the end in view." So, below, I list some of the rules, but I admit to overusing—and occasionally misusing—the comma in my own writing.

- Always include a comma after the penultimate item in a series. [American flags are red, white, and blue. ✓] [Are you cold, hungry, or thirsty? ✓]
- Set off adverbial phrases that lie between the subject and the verb with commas. [Cardinal Gomá, on receiving the telegram, sat down and wrote a lengthy reply. ✓]
- A comma is not strictly necessary after short introductory adverbial phrases of less than four words. [After returning home Cardinal Gomá drafted his reply. ✓]
- Historians, though, commonly include one after an introductory date. [In May 1930, Gomá wrote a pastoral letter. ✓]
- Set off introductory participle phrases with a comma, unless followed by a verb. [Charging into battle, Alexander set a noble example. ✓] [Charging into battle was Alexander himself. ✓]
- Avoid commas where they might limit or restrict meaning. [Cardinal

- 避免逗号的使用局限或妨碍了对于整句的理解。例如,"红衣主教戈马的主教信函,*Grave Hours*(《严肃的时光》),是一篇修辞学的杰作"暗示着他仅写过一篇主教信函。而在"红衣主教戈马的主教信函《严肃的时光》是一篇修辞学的杰作"则暗示他写了很多。
- 以逗号分隔插入短语,而以破折号分隔独立的分句。例如,"梅尔的书,大部分,很难理解。✓""梅尔的书——像很多其他从法文译本一样——很难理解。✓"

破折号、空格

在复合词——如果是形容词而非名词——如 "high-fidelity sound system"(高保真音响系统)或者 "nineteenth-century wartime experiences"(19世纪的战争经验)等之间要加入一个正常破折号或连字符。注意形容词和名词之间的区别。例如,"Tom carried machine-gun bullets, Dick carried the machine gun."(汤姆携带了机枪子弹,迪克携带了机枪。✓)遵循《芝加哥论文格式手册》的指导,如果破折号的使用可能影响可读性,那宁可用连字符来构成合成词。

对开破折号。书写数字或日期时,像 "1914—1918年"、"第519—605页" 或者 "1942年7—8月" 使用对开破折号进行分隔(同时按Ctrl键和-键)。如果你打算使用"从",那么就不要使用对开破折号;换句话说,要写成"从7月到8月",却绝不能写成"从7月—8月"。战争或协议的双方也要用对开破折号而非连字符进行标示。例如,"俄—日战争;罗马—柏林轴心;亚当斯—欧尼斯协议。✓"

破折号。为分隔独立的分句——如本句一般——使用破折号(按Ctrl+Alt 的同时按下-键)。[1] 随着句子的长度和复杂性的增强,可以尝试使用成对的破折号。例如,这个论点陈述的案例就使用了破折号分隔一篇论文的五个主要观点: 本文将证明——通过对于托马斯·莫尔有关财产所有权、宗教宽容、煽动性行为、犯罪和惩罚和智者统治的见解讨论——*Utopia*(《乌托邦》)既是一篇警告革命迫在眉睫的檄文又是一篇有关社会控制的指南。

与《芝加哥论文格式手册》不同,我主张整句与整句之间以**双倍空格**进行分隔(但不包含冒号之后的情况);在 MS-Word 中设置其检测功能,并在草稿中的每一个句号之后插入双倍空格。句子之后添加一个额外的空格令人感到顺眼,能增强可读性,并避免与以缩略语或单一字母结束或开头的邻句之间发生混淆。与此类似,不在个人姓名的多个单一字母之间添加空格。除非会发生混淆,否则省略缩略词之间的句号。例如,"D.F. 史密斯

---

1. 使用笔记本电脑的时候,你首先需要按住功能键以激活数字键盘;这样的操作虽会带来略微的不适应,但经过实践之后,会逐渐习惯成自然。MS-Word也会自动地产生这个符号,只要输入:字母,空格,破折号,空格,字母,空格,可是这个方法要花几次额外按键,还有你需要回去删掉两个非必要的空格。至于苹果电脑:按Apple+Minus=对开破折号;按Apple+Alt+Minus=破折号。注意,MS-Word允许你根据习惯设置自己的快捷键盘操作(快捷键)。

Gomá's pastoral letter, *Grave Hours,* was a rhetorical masterpiece.] Implies he wrote only one pastoral. [Cardinal Gomá's pastoral letter *Grave Hours* was a rhetorical masterpiece.] In fact, he wrote many.
- Use commas to set off parenthetical elements; use em-dashes for independent clauses. [Maier's book, for the most part, is hard to follow. ✓] [Maier's book—as with so many other French translations—is hard to follow. ✓]

Dashes, Spacing

For compound words—when they are adjectives but not nouns—as in "high-fidelity sound system," or "nineteenth-century wartime experiences," use a plain dash, or hyphen. Note the distinction between adjectives and nouns. [Tom carried machine-gun bullets, Dick carried the machine gun. ✓] Following *Chicago*'s guidance, when readability is an issue I err on the side of hyphenating compounds.

En-dash. For number and date ranges, like "1914–18," "pp. 519–605," or "July–August 1942," use an en-dash (hold down <Ctrl> while pressing <-> on the numeric keypad). If you want to say *from* then you do not use the en-dash as well; in other words, "from July to August," never, "from July–August." Wars and treaties between parties also use en-dashes not hyphens. [Russo–Japanese War; Rome–Berlin Axis; Adams–Onís Treaty. ✓]

Em-dash. To set off independent clauses—as here—use the em-dash (hold down <Ctrl> and <Alt> while pressing <->).[1] As your sentences become longer and more complex, practice using pairs of em-dashes. Sample thesis statement using em-dashes to set off a paper's five main points: [This paper will argue—through a discussion of Thomas More's views on property ownership, religious tolerance, seditious behavior, crime and punishment, and meritocracy—that *Utopia* was both a warning of impending revolution and a manual for social control.]

In contradistinction to *Chicago*, I advocate **double-spacing** between sentences (though not after colons); set MS-Word to check for this, and double-space after each period consistently throughout your manuscript. An extra space after a sentence is esthetically pleasing, improves readability, and avoids confusion when a sentence ends or begins with an abbreviation or initial. Similarly, for multi-initial personal names, I do not insert a space between the initials. Remove periods from abbreviated entities, unless it creates

---

1. With laptops, you first need to hold down the function key that activates your numeric keys; this is a tad awkward but, with practice, soon becomes automatic. (MS-Word will also generate this automatically if you type: character, space, dash, space, character, space, but this method takes several extra key strokes and you have to go back and delete out the two unwanted spaces.) On Apples: <Apple> <Minus> = en-dash; <Apple> <Alt> <Minus> = em-dash. Note that MS-Word lets you customize your own keyboard shortcuts (shortcut keys).

是U.S.（美国）向UN（联合国）派驻的大使。✓"

日期、数字

目前的大部分美籍历史学研究者使用《芝加哥论文格式手册》所推荐的日–月–年格式，以便省去中间插入的逗号。例如"红衣主教戈马在5 November 1936（1936年11月5日）前往托莱多。三天后，即8 November（11月8日），他回到潘普洛纳去。两天以后，即10日，他会见了自己的秘书。✓"这种现代的格式更适用于扫描并且可以节省逗号的使用。

MS-Word会自动把序号转换为上标，例如"《时代》的115th期✗"；为了避免这样的错误，要在数字和字母之间先按空格键，再按退格键"115th期✓"，或者，更好的做法是，撤销自动更改功能选项。只是偶尔的情况下，你才总是必须拼写99以下的数字，而不使用阿拉伯数字。

年代不是所有格形式的，所以要拼写成"the 1930s"（20世纪30年代）而非"the 1930's"（后者的标记方式曾流行于20世纪50年代至60年代）。当被标记为形容词时，需要添加连字符；而被标记为名词时，则不需要连字符，例如，"Nineteenth-century（19世纪）的战争与the twentieth century（20世纪）中发生的战争不同。✓"规则当然存在例外，诸如百分比、武器系统和军事部队称谓，例如，"第5装甲师的88毫米口径机枪射杀的死伤率为27%。✓"

标示页数范围时，不要缩略书写100以下的数字，例如"pp. 77–93"；标示100的倍数时要写清所有数位，例如"pp. 200–204"；在标示100的倍数加十位以内的非零数字时可以简写后一个数字成个位，例如"pp.301–7"。按要求，用两个数位来简写其他页数，例如"pp. 344–51, 596–602, 613–20"。注意，需要在页数标码 *p.* 或 *pp.* 和页数之间添加一个空格。

独立分词（动名词）从句

为使写作更加生动，可以尝试偶尔在句中添加分词性短语，但是这个短语必须修饰该句语法意义上的主语。例如，"身处在越来越多元的社会中，民族的多样性而非政治意识形态的多样性日益成为政策成功与否的仲裁。✗"本句中，作为主语的民族多样性，在语法意义上是无法身处在多元化的生活中的，只有人而非概念，能够生活在社会之中。

That/Which 的用法

That 要应用于限制性从句，而 *which* 则要应用于非限制性从句，非限制性从句需要以逗号与主句相分隔。换句话说，要是删除从句，主句则变得失去意义，此种情况下要使用 *that*，但是即使删除从句也不会破坏主句的表达，此种情况下要使用 *which*。例如，"Boston has a climate that chills you to the bone"（波士顿具有一种刺骨的气候）。"Boston, which is a windy city, is my

confusion. [D.F. Smith was U.S. ambassador to the UN. ✓]

Dates, Numbers

Most American historians now use the *Chicago* recommended day-month-year format, which does not require any intervening commas. [Cardinal Gomá went to Toledo on 5 November 1936. Three days later, on 8 November, he returned to Pamplona. Two days after that, on the tenth, he met with his secretary. ✓] This modern format scans better and saves commas.

MS-Word wants to superscript ordinals [the 115th edition of *Time* ✗]; stop it from doing this by leaving a space and then backspacing [the 115th edition ✓], or, better still, by turning off the option in Auto-Correct. Only rarely, though, will you find yourself in this situation, for you should always spell out numbers of ninety-nine or lower.

Decades are not possessive, so write "the 1930s" and never "the 1930's." (Popular in the 1950s and 1960s, this latter format has been anachronistic ever since.) Centuries, when adjectives, are hyphenated, and when nouns, are un-hyphenated. [Nineteenth-century warfare was different from war in the twentieth century. ✓] There are, of course, exceptions to rules, such as, percentages, weapon systems, and military units. [Casualties were 27 percent after the 88s of the 5th Panzer Division opened fire. ✓]

When giving page ranges, do not abbreviate numbers less than 100 [pp. 77–93]; use all digits for multiples of 100 [pp. 200–204], and the last digit for the first nine numbers in a century [pp. 301–7]; abbreviate other numbers using two digits, as required [pp. 344–51, 596–602, 613–20]. Notice the space after a *p.* or *pp.*

Orphaned Participle (Gerund) Clauses

To make your writing more interesting, practice opening the occasional sentence with a participle phrase. But the phrase must modify the sentence's grammatical subject. [Living in an increasingly pluralistic society, ethnic diversity rather than varied political ideology had become the arbiter of successful policy. ✗] Here, ethnic diversity, which is the subject, cannot live in a pluralistic society; people not concepts live in a society.

That/Which Usage

Use *that* for restrictive clauses and *which* for non-restrictive clauses, with the latter set off by a pair of commas. In other words, if the sentence would not make sense were the clause removed then use *that*, but if you could omit the clause without crippling the sentence then use *which*. [Boston has a climate that chills you to the bone.] [Boston, which is a windy city, is my

home"（波士顿，这个经常刮风的城市，是我的家）。将这两则例文删除从句之后，会变成"Boston has a climate"（波士顿具有一种气候），"Boston is my home"（波士顿是我的家），前一句毫无意义，后一句却句意完整。

不完整的英文表达

如果你容易写出不完整的句子，那首先，为使自己对于此猛于虎的恶习加深印象，尝试如下的方法：大声朗读自己的作品并感觉它；或者更好的方法是，请一位朋友背对你朗诵它。总是要特别注意指示代词、反身代词和代词的使用（这个、他们的、他/他、它、它的）；要对所指代的人或事物了如指掌。一旦段落中出现了一个以上的人物（语态），了解谁对谁做了或说了什么会变得尤其困难，诸如你在行文中涉及相同性别的三个人物的行为的情况。要在行文中指明人物的姓名以避免发生此种混淆，尽管这样一来，会存在重复或显示过分精确的风险。虽然同义词的使用（如罗斯福；总统；FDR；椭圆形办公室的主人）可以减少重复，却要避免使用过多传媒性语言；你的读者情愿接受行文中的重复也不愿意接受语意的模糊。两难之时宁可矫枉过正。

代词的不搭配

即使高明的作者也会因代词的搭配问题而感到烦恼。为了减少该问题的发生，一方面可以使用专有名词，尤其是，一定要在行文中嵌入真实的、活生生的历史人物，而非组织或国家。例如，"1898年，美利坚合众国入侵古巴，但是特罗尔修正案阻止了他们合并该岛。✘"把"他们"改成"它"会纠正不妥的语法，但如果把"美利坚合众国"改成"美国人"则不但符合语法要求，而且还可以节省两个珍贵的单词空间。更妙的是，还可以明确侵略者，你可以意指，诸如"美国军队、将军威廉姆·R.沙福特的部队、沙文主义者们"，或者甚至"西奥多·罗斯福的莽骑兵队"。

称呼的首字母小写

减少大写字母的使用成为行文的趋势。"大写字母的节约使用"即《芝加哥论文格式手册》中所谓的"向下"的行文方式。目前，一些宗教史学研究者会在行文中写 *the Catholic church*（天主教会），仅仅在头衔位于称呼的紧前面的情况下才会将头衔的首字母大写。例如，"阿根廷的 president（总统）与 President George W. Bush（乔治·W.布什总统）会面了。""美国内战期间，大部分 *southerners*（南方人）为 *the South*（南方）而斗争。"再次强调首尾一致的原则，如果你将"Blacks"（黑人）一词首字母大写，那么请贯彻始终。第一次提到某一人士时，需写清全名和所有的官方头衔，如：理查德·M.尼克松总统、陆军元帅伯纳德·罗·蒙哥马利、代表约翰·W.麦科马克（民主党-马州）、红衣主教弗朗西斯·斯佩尔

home.] In these two examples, [Boston has a climate.] hardly makes sense, but [Boston is my home.] is a complete sentence.

Fractured English

If you are prone to the problem of fractured sentences then first, to impress on yourself the nature of the beast, try this: read your work aloud and see how it sounds; better still, ask a friend to read it back to you. Always be careful with carry-overs, stand-ins, and pronouns (this, their, he/him, it, its); make clear to whom or to what you are referring. Once you have more than one actor (voice) in a paragraph, knowing who is doing/saying what to whom becomes especially problematic, as when you have three persons of the same gender. Avoid confusion by using actors' names, even at the risk of repetition or appearing excessively precise. While synonyms (Roosevelt; the president; FDR; the man in the Oval Office) may alleviate repetition, avoid excessive journalese; your reader will much prefer repetition to bewilderment. If in any doubt then write explicitly not implicitly.

Pronoun Disagreement

Even advanced writers struggle with pronoun agreement. One way to minimize the problem is to use proper nouns, and, especially, by plugging in real, live historical actors instead of groups and nations. [In 1898, the United States invaded Cuba, but the Teller Amendment prohibited them from annexing the island. ✗] Changing *them* to *it* would fix the bad grammar, as would changing *the United States* to *Americans*, which also saves two precious words. But by specifying the invaders, you could implicate, say, U.S. forces, Gen. William R. Shafter's troops, Jingoes, or even Theodore Roosevelt's Rough Riders.

Down-Style, Naming

Trends are toward less capitalization, a "parsimonious use of capitals" that *Chicago* calls "down" style; some historians of religion are now writing, "the Catholic church." Uppercase titles only when directly preceding a name. "The president of Argentina met President George W. Bush." "During the Civil War, most southerners fought for the South." Again, consistency is the rule. If you are going to uppercase Blacks then do so throughout. On first mentioning a personage, give full name and any official title: President Richard M. Nixon, Field Marshal Bernard Law Montgomery, Rep. John W. McCormack (D-MA), Cardinal Francis Spellman. But in subsequent paragraphs, just give family name: Nixon, Montgomery, McCormack, Spellman. Handle terms and organizations that you will use more than once like this: "Congress of Industrial Organizations (CIO) . . ." When used as a noun, spell

曼。但是在余下的段落中，只需给出其姓氏就好，如：尼克松、蒙哥马利、麦科马克、斯佩尔曼。以如下的方式处理你不止一次使用的专有名词和组织名称：CIO（产业工会联合会）……。若美国一词作为名词被使用，则需要拼写其全称the United States（美利坚合众国），但当作为形容词使用时则可缩写："尼克松将美国外交政策理解为……"。注意：即使"美利坚合众国"作为单数名词被使用，它的所有格形式也会打破原有的规则："根据the United States（美利坚合众国）的想法，越南是……"。但是，通过在句中插入人物，可以避免此种尴尬结构的产生："根据Policy makers（决策者）的想法，越南是……"。

大写字体和格式——美国视角下的示例

the Western Hemisphere　西半球　　the East Coast　东岸边
the South　南方　　southern Baptists　南方浸礼教徒
redcoats　英国士兵　　Britons　英国人
laissez-faire　自由放任政策　　realpolitik　现实政策
the colonial period　殖民时代　　the Progressive Era　新政时期
the Jazz Age　爵士时代　　the Roaring Twenties　兴旺的20年代
the Industrial Revolution　工业革命　　the New Deal　新政
World War II　第二次世界大战　　the Cold War　冷战
the Fourth of July　美国独立日　　Sept. 11 or 9/11　9月11日或者"9·11"
the Monroe Doctrine　门罗主义　　the doctrine　教条
USS *Maine*　美国军舰"缅因号"　　the U.S. Constitution　美国宪法
Chiang Kai-shek　蒋介石　　Mao Zedong　毛泽东
Guomindang　国民党　　Chinese Communist Party　中国共产党
art deco　装饰派艺术　　modernism　现代主义
postmodernism　后现代主义　　church and state　政教
the State Department　国务院　　the secretary of state　国务卿
the Senate　参议院　　the senators　参议员
the United States Army　美国陆军　　the army　陆军
the Communist Party　共产党　　the communists　共产主义者
the Right　右派　　the right wing　右翼
the West　西方　　Western world　西方世界

魔咒性的单词和短语

"看见"和"看到"等词只能跟人物搭配。别说"新的一天目睹了许多流血事件"或者"美国对中国的政策皱眉"，因为时光是盲目的，国家是不会皱眉的土地；嵌入人物会使行文生动起来。排除委婉的表达，不说"里根过世了"，而简明扼要写成"里根死掉了"。不要删掉介词，例如，"the student graduated college ✗"（学生毕业本科学院了），"the student

out "the United States" but abbreviate when used as an adjective: "Nixon understood U.S. foreign policy to mean . . ." Note: while "the United States" is a singular noun, its possessive breaks the rule: "in the United States' opinion, Vietnam was . . ." but you can avoid this awkward construction by plugging in people: "in policymakers' opinions, Vietnam was . . ."

Capitalization and Style—Examples from a U.S. Perspective

the Western Hemisphere	the East Coast
the South	southern Baptists
redcoats	Britons
laissez-faire	realpolitik
the colonial period	the Progressive Era
the Jazz Age	the Roaring Twenties
the Industrial Revolution	the New Deal
World War II	the Cold War
the Fourth of July	September 11 or 9/11
the Monroe Doctrine	the doctrine
USS *Maine*	the U.S. Constitution
Chiang Kai-shek	Mao Zedong
Guomindang	Chinese Communist Party
art deco	modernism
postmodernism	church and state
the State Department	the secretary of state
the Senate	the senators
the United States Army	the army
the Communist Party	the communists
the Right	the right wing
the West	Western world (as cultural term)

Anathemous Words and Phrases

Reserve words like *saw* and *viewed* for people; never say, "the new day witnessed much bloodshed," or "America frowned on China's policy," because days are blind and countries are eyebrow-less chunks of land; plug in actors and watch your prose come alive. Banish euphemisms; instead of "Reagan passed on," say simply "Reagan died." Do not drop prepositions [the student graduated college ✗] [the student graduated from college ✓]. Say either "during the time" or "during the period" but never "during the time period," which would be redundant.

banish:	use instead:	banish:	use instead:
amidst	amid	and more	[TV-speak]

graduated from college ✓"（学生毕业于本科学院了）。写成"在那段时间"或"在那个阶段"，但不要写成"在那个时间阶段"，不然会使得行文繁冗。

不要用：	而要用：	不要用：	而要用：
amidst 之间	amid	and more 什么的	（TV-speak）（电话广告语言风格）
amongst 之间	among	as of yet 至今	yet
dove 潜入	dived	at the present time 现在	now
etc., i.e., 等	[be explicit] [要明确]	at the time that 当……时	when
ex（boss）以前的领导	former (boss)	due to the fact that 由于	because
ongoing 持续着	continuing	firstly, secondly 首先，第二	first, second
pled 恳求	pleaded	got, gotten 获得	[ugly; reword] [行文粗陋，需要重新考虑]
prior to 在……之前	before	had had; that that 已经有；就那个	[rephrase] [重新写]
spark 引起	incite	one of the methods 一种方法	one method
spilt 溢出	spilled	plus（he was...）且（他是……）	and（he was）
towards 向	toward	somewhere 某一个地方	[often superfluous] [经常过剩的]
upon 在……上	on	utilize 使用	use

美式英文 vs. 英式英文

阅读许久以前或美国以外印刷的书籍时会很容易挑出其中的行文恶习。英式英语中，引言位于单引号之间，而引言之中的引言才会被置以双引号；标点符号位于引号之外；一系列示例中的倒数第二项与后项之间不会以逗号分隔；that 和 which 可以互换。英式英文的行文方式是：'Be sure to buy parsnips, turnips and Swedes', she shouted after him, 'and a bag of those "Spanish" onions'（'一定要买到牛蒡、萝卜和包菜'。她朝着他喊道：'还有一袋那种"西班牙"洋葱'。）

amongst	among	as of yet	yet
dove	dived	at the present time	now
etc., i.e.,	[be explicit]	at the time that	when
ex (boss)	former (boss)	due to the fact that	because
ongoing	continuing	firstly, secondly	first, second
pled	pleaded	got, gotten	[ugly; reword]
prior to	before	had had; that that	[rephrase]
spark	incite	one of the methods	one method
spilt	spilled	plus (he was . . .)	and (he was)
towards	toward	somewhere	[often superfluous]
upon	on	utilize	use

American vs. British English

It is easy to pick up bad habits when reading books printed some time ago or outside the United States. In British English, quotations go between single marks, while quotations-within-quotations are in double marks; punctuation goes outside the quote marks; the penultimate item in a series has no separating comma; *that* and *which* are interchangeable. British English looks like this: 'Be sure to buy parsnips, turnips and Swedes', she shouted after him, 'and a bag of those "Spanish" onions'.

TIPS FOR EAST ASIAN WRITERS

Adopt the grammar and style of American rather than British English, including the simpler and more logical American spelling, and pay particular attention to the following points:

- do not use the so-called royal, Victorian, or perhaps Mongol *we*. [McNeill's argument is insightful, although we should not consider his three variations as separate parts. ✗] Either use the first person singular or recast the sentence to remove the opinionated pronoun. [McNeill's argument is insightful, although I do not consider his three variations as separate parts. ✓] [McNeill's argument is insightful, although his three variations hardly constitute separate parts. ✓]

- italicize published works (but not the titles of journal articles).
- minimize uppercasing—practice down-style.
- *that* and *which* are not interchangeable as in British English.
- ensure that punctuation is inside quotation marks, and footnote reference numbers are outside the marks.
- triple check that you have transcribed quotations verbatim from the original source.
- be careful, particularly in footnotes, to use the standard Asian font (Songti

对东亚作者的写作建议

请采用美式英语而非英式英语的语法和表达方式，包括更简单、更富逻辑性的美式拼写方式，并特别注意以下几点。

- 请不要使用所谓的"国王之我们"[1]这样错误的写法。例如，"麦克尼尔的主张富有洞察力，尽管我们不应该将他三次观点转换看做各自独立的部分。✗"纠错有两种方法：要么采用第一人称单数，"麦克尼尔的主张富有洞察力，尽管我并不把他三次观点转换看做各自独立的部分。✓"要么去掉形容词性物主代词，重新造句，"麦克尼尔的主张富有洞察力，尽管他的三次观点转换很难被看做各自独立的部分。✓"
- 用斜体字标示出版作品名称（但不是期刊文章的题目）。
- 作品名称中尽量减少大写字母的使用量——使用down-style。[2]
- 美式英语不像英式英语具有可相互替换的 *that* 和 *which*，用法不一致。
- 请确保标点符号位于引号之内，而脚注参考号码位于引号之外。
- 请再三逐字核查索引资料是否与原始资料相符。
- 请注意，尤其在脚注中，只有中文字体能选择亚洲字体形式（仿宋体或新宋体）。

定冠词

不少东亚作者在英文写作中会误用定冠词 *the*。经验会产生一种直觉告诉你哪些名词前需要 *the*，但特定的规律会使你在学习过程中避免许多失误。定冠词 *the* 用于单数名词或者复数名词之前表示一个群体中的一个或一些特定成员。例如，"The boy（那个男孩子）跑过了the road（那条马路）。✓"不定冠词 *a* 和 *an* 用于单数名词之前表示一个群体中的任意成员，例如，"A boy（一个男孩）跑过了a road（一条马路）。✓"请不要在不定复数名词前使用任何冠词——无冠词。"Boys（男孩们）喜欢跑过 roads（马路）。✓"。同时请注意，专有名词前没有冠词。"David（大卫）跑过了 Fulham Road（富勒姆马路）。✓"当然，此种规律也有例外，如形容词作专有名词时就是一则例外，但最好熟记规律后再逐渐在个别案例中熟悉例外。"大卫把它称之为 Great Britain（大不列颠）而苏珊则将其称之为 the United Kingdom（联合王国）。✓"

---

1. 中世纪欧洲的国王或贵族习惯于称自己为"我们"。例如，We hereby sentence the prisoner to the gallows for tarnishing our courtly reputation.（因为玷污了我们国家的名誉，在此，我们判决此囚犯绞刑）。即在英语习惯中，用"我们"代表"我"的用词方式称之为"国王之我们"。——译者注
2. Down-style是仅大写作品名称中整个标题的首字母和专有名词的首字母，其余保留小写字母。详细说明请参照第114页。——译者注

宋体 or SimSun) only for Chinese characters.

Definite Article

Many East Asian writers misplace *the* when writing English. Experience develops a natural sense of which nouns require a *the*, but there are rules to make the learning process less of a hit-or-miss affair. Use the definite article *the* in front of singular or plural nouns referring to a specific member of a group. [The boy ran across the road. ✓] Use an indefinite article *a* or *an* in front of a singular noun referring to any member of a group. [A boy ran across a road. ✓] Do not use an article—the zero article—in front of an indefinite plural. [Boys like running across roads. ✓] Notice, too, that there is no article in front of proper nouns. [David ran across Fulham Road. ✓] Naturally, there are exceptions, as when adjectives behave like proper nouns, but best practice is to memorize the rule and just learn the exceptions as you encounter them. [David called it Great Britain but Susan called it the United Kingdom. ✓]

MS-Word 2010 设置

度量标准设置：毫米

1-正文　为建立正文段落的全新格式，要在 Word 菜单栏中点击：开始—样式—（点击右边的箭头）—新建样式（左下方）；{名称：1-正文}，{样式类型：段落}，{样式基准：无样式}，{后续段落样式：1-正文}。格式—字体—{字体：Times New Roman}，{字号：12磅}—确定；段落—缩进和间距—{对齐方式：左对齐}，{段前：0磅}，{段后：0磅}，{左侧：13毫米}，{右侧：13毫米}，{行距：固定值}，{设置值：28磅}，{特殊格式：首行缩进}，{磅值：10毫米}—确定。

2-副标题　开始—样式—新建样式（左下方）；{名称：2-副标题}，{样式类型：段落}，{样式基准：无样式}，{后续段落样式：1-正文}。格式—字体—{字体：Times New Roman}，{字体：加粗}，{字号：12磅}—确定；段落—缩进和间距—{大纲级别：1级}，{对齐方式：左对齐}，{段前：16磅}，{段后：0磅}，{左侧：13毫米}，{右侧：13毫米}，{行距：固定值}，{设置值：15磅}—换行和分页—{与下段同页：☑}—确定。

3-章节标题　开始—样式—新建样式（左下方）；{名称：3-章节标题}，{样式类型：段落}，{样式基准：无样式}，{后续段落样式：1-正文}。格式—字体—{字体：Times New Roman}，{字体：加粗}，{字号：13磅}，{效果：☑全部大写字母}—确定；段落—缩进和间距—{大纲级别：1级}，{对齐方式：左对齐}，{段前：0磅}，{段后：6磅}，{左侧：13毫米}，{右侧：13毫米}，{行距：固定值}，{设置值：20毫米}—换行和分页—{与下段同页：☑}—确定。

脚注文字　开始—样式（点击箭头）—引用—更改（突出，然后点击下小箭头）—格式—字体—{字体：Times New Roman}，{字号：10磅}。段落—缩进和间距—{对齐方式：左对齐}，{段前：2磅}，{段后：2磅}，{左侧：13毫米}，{右侧：13毫米}，{行距：固定值}，{设置值：16磅}—{特殊格式：首行缩进}，{磅值：10毫米}。

脚注、延续格局符及延续标记　视图（草稿）—脚注—[点击页面下方脚注区的左上列表框]—脚注分隔符—突出分隔符—格式—段落—缩进和间距—{左侧：13毫米}。（重复设置脚注延续分隔符和脚注延续标记）

MS-Word 2010 SETTINGS

Measurements setting: mm.

1-Body Text   To create a new style for your body paragraphs, on Word's menu bar, click: Home—Styles—(click arrow on right)—New Style (bottom left); {Name: 1-Body Text}, {Style Type: Paragraph}, {Style based on: No Style}, {Style for following paragraph: 1-Body Text}. Format—Font—{Font: Times New Roman}, {Size: 12 pt}—Okay; Paragraph—Indents and Spacing—{Alignment: Left}, {Before: 0 pt}, {After: 0 pt}, {Indentation Left: 13 mm}, {Indentation Right: 13 mm}, {Line Spacing: Exactly}, {At: 28 pt}, {Special: First Line}, {By: 10 mm}—Okay.

2-Subhead   Home—Styles—New Style (bottom left); {Name: 2-Subhead}, {Style Type: Paragraph}, {Style based on: No Style}, {Style for following paragraph: 1-Body Text}. Format—Font—{Font: Times New Roman}, {Font Style: Bold}, {Size: 12 pt}—Okay; Paragraph—Indents and Spacing—{Outline Level: Level 1}, {Alignment: Left}, {Before: 16 pt}, {After: 0 pt}, {Indentation Left: 13 mm}, {Indentation Right: 13 mm}, {Line Spacing: Exactly}, {At: 15 pt}—Line and Page Breaks—{Keep with next: ☑}—Okay.

3-Chapter Heading   Home—Styles—New Style (bottom left); {Name: 3-Chapter Heading}, {Style Type: Paragraph}, {Style based on: No Style}, {Style for following paragraph: 1-Body Text}. Format—Font—{Font: Times New Roman}, {Font Style: Bold}, {Size: 13 pt}, {Effects: ☑ All caps}—Okay; Paragraph—Indents and Spacing—{Outline Level: Level 1}, {Alignment: Left}, {Before: 0 pt}, {After: 6 pt}, {Indentation Left: 13 mm}, {Indentation Right: 13 mm}, {Line Spacing: Exactly}, {At: 20 pt}—Line and Page Breaks—{Keep with next: ☑}—Okay.

Footnote Text   Home—Styles (click arrow)—Footnote Text—Modify [highlight, then click Down-Arrow]—Format—Font—{Font: Times New Roman}, {Size: 10 pt}. Paragraph—Indents and Spacing—{Alignment: Left}, {Before: 2 pt}, {After: 2 pt}, {Indentation Left: 13 mm}, {Indentation Right: 13 mm}, {Line Spacing: Exactly}, {At: 16 pt}, {Special: First Line}, {By: 10 mm}.

Footnote Separator, Continuation Separator, Continuation Notice   View—Footnotes—[click the Listbox at the top left of the footnote area]—Footnote Separator—[highlight the separator]—Format—Paragraph—Indents and Spacing—{Left: 13 mm}. (Repeat for Continuation Separator, and Notice.)

页面布局 页面设置（右下边的箭头）—页边距—{上：25 毫米}，{下：20毫米}，{左：13毫米}，{右：13毫米}，{装订线：0 毫米}；版式—{页眉：15毫米}，{页脚：0毫米}。

页码 视图（页面视图）—把光标放在页眉上再双击—页码—页码顶端—输入数字3。

语法 Word 选项—校对—语法和格式—设置—{Comma Required: Always}，{Punctuation Required: Inside}，{SpacesRequired: 2}，{所有语法和样式复选框：☑}。

自动更正 Word选项—校对—自动更正选项—键入时自动套用格式—键入时自动替换—{☑直引号替换为弯引号}，但是，{☐序号（1st）替换为上标}。试用别的选项。

重要注意事项：不要使用 Word 的双倍行距设置，因为此间存在的一个诡异的软件编写失误将使你的该页脚注不可避免地转向下一页；反之，要设置 {行距：固定值}，{设置值：28磅}，正如"1-正文"所示。也要注意：如果你要插入图片，那你须为该段落设置 {行距：最小值}，否则文档中仅可显示一行图片的画面。

文档结构图：除了事先各自设置"3-章节标题"和"2-副标题"为1级标题和2级标题，正如上一页所表示的，你还可以定制某些文字、段落或者标题的级别，只要将视图模式转换成大纲视图，然后点击大纲栏即可。

管理你的 Normal.dot 模板：Word选项—加载项—管理—转到—模板—管理器；这样一来，文档会弹出一个分割窗口，右边有正常格式，左边有当前文档所存在的格式。如此一来，你就可以借助你文档的修改后的格式来更改任何其他文档的正常格式，当然，反之亦可。

Page Layout   Page Setup (arrow on right)—Margins—{Top: 25 mm}, {Bottom: 20 mm}, {Left: 13 mm}, {Right: 13 mm}, {Gutter: 0 mm}; Layout—{Header: 15 mm}, {Footer: 0 mm}.

Page Number   View (Print Layout)—place cursor at top of page and double-click—Page Number—Top of Page Number—Plain Number 3.

Grammar   Word Options—Proofing—Grammar & Style—Settings—{Comma Required: always}, {Punctuation Required: Inside}, {Spaces Required: 2}, {All Grammar and Style checkboxes: ☑}.

AutoCorrect   Word Options—Proofing—AutoCorrect Options—AutoFormat As You Type—Replace as You Type—{☑ Straight Quotes with Smart Quotes} but {☐ Ordinals (1st) with superscript]. Experiment with other options.

Important note: do not use Word's Double Space setting because a strange software bug will invariably carry your footnotes over to the following page; instead, set {Line Spacing: Exactly}, {At: 28 pt}, as shown in 1-Body Text. Also note: if you are inserting a picture then you must set {Line Spacing: At least} for that particular paragraph, otherwise only one line's worth of the picture will be visible.

Document Map: In addition to presetting 3-Chapter Heading and 2-Subhead at Levels 1 and 2 respectively, as shown on the prior page, you can customize the level for particular text, paragraphs, or headings by switching to Outline view and then clicking the Outlining tab.

Managing your Normal.dot template: Word Options—Add Ins—Manage—Templates—Organizer; this pops up a split pane, with Normal styles on the right and the styles that exist in your current document on the left. Now you can overwrite any Normal style with your document's modified style, and vice versa.

修辞结构

缩略首字母的单词 用一组字母来代表一个词语或词组,例如:"UN"(联合国)。

头韵 若干个词语的首字母或首音之间互相重复。

时代错误 编年史上的错误;不符合真实时间的历史事件或顺序有误的历史事件。

自相矛盾 貌似必要的推论或者结论之间相互矛盾(好似陷入一个悖论)。

格言 座右铭。

平庸 用来表示平庸的、泛滥的、琐碎的短语。

名言 其字面意思是"好话",可以理解为俏皮话。

诡辩术 沿着道德或伦理路线,通常通过偷换或延伸基本概念形成的一种微妙的、带有欺骗性质的论证方式。

第二十二条军规 主要由于过多的规矩和缺乏逻辑的情况而导致,形成不可避免的进退维谷的状态。

滥调 老套的、陈腐的表达方式。

对位法 对立或对抗观点之并列。

愤世嫉俗 批评或质疑他人表现出的美德或善良。

二分法 一分为二,对立的概念、观点或结构。

警句 简练的、尖刻的或富有启发性的话或短诗。

绰号 形容词意义的短语构成的,具有感情色彩的昵称。

委婉的说法 涉及令人不愉快的情形时,以中性、无害的词语代替敏感的、伤人的词汇。

同音同形异义词 发音相同但意思不同的两个单词;或者拼写相同但意思不同的两个单词。

夸张法 (或许故意为之的)过度夸张。

虚伪 极度地不真诚,掩饰真正意图的意思。

习语 无法从语法或者语言结构这些字面文意中了解其真正含义的一类短语。

不一致的 不合适或者不一致的意思。

反语 呈现出一种与意思的真实表示或隐义表示相反的说法或状况。

间接肯定法 一种用夸张或反讽的方式来掩饰真实意思的表示的方式,例如:这并非一件无关紧要的事情。

多种语言混合的诗文 由真实的或意想中的外来语混杂而成的表达方式。

RHETORICAL CONSTRUCTS

acronym use of a group of letters to represent a word or phrase in shortened form ("UN").

alliteration the repetition of an initial letter or first sound of several words ("wicked witch of the west").

anachronism an error of chronology; an event out of time or order.

antinomy the irreconcilability of seemingly necessary inferences or conclusions (as in a paradox).

aphorism a maxim.

banality a commonplace, overused, or trivialized phrase.

bon mot literally, *good word*; a witticism, a wisecrack.

casuistry subtly deceptive argumentation, along moral or ethical lines, often through the application or extension of basic principles.

catch-22 an inescapable dilemma, typically caused by excessive regulations or illogical conditions.

cliché a stereotyped, hackneyed expression.

counterpoint the juxtaposition of contrapuntal or oppositional themes.

cynicism contempt or criticism for virtues and generous sentiments of others.

dichotomy a division into two parts or moieties; oppositional concepts, ideas, constructs.

epigram a pithy, caustic, or thought-provoking saying or short poem.

epithet a phrase used adjectivally; an evocative nickname.

euphemism the substitution of an inoffensive term for one with unpleasant associations.

homonym two words that are pronounced or spelled the same but have different meanings.

hyperbole inordinate exaggeration, perhaps calculatedly so.

hypocrisy extreme insincerity; dissimulation.

idiom an expression not readily analyzable from its grammatical or linguistic construction.

incongruity an unsuitable or inharmonious statement.

irony a statement/situation that signifies the opposite of what it means or implies.

litotes an exaggerated or ironic understatement ("it was a matter of no little importance").

词语误用　说错或用错不适当的单词。
隐喻　把一种观点或事物用单词或短语表示为另一种观点或事物。
转喻　用比喻的方式或用其他概念或事物表达事物的本意，例如：用"功劳簿"指代荣誉，用"布鲁塞尔"指代欧盟总部。
新词汇　创造一个全新的单词；从外来语中引入的词汇。
象声词　模仿自然界的声音而形成的单词（如"嘶嘶"、"咔嚓咔嚓"）。
矛盾修辞法　由互相矛盾的词语组成的表达方式（如"他经历着人间炼狱"）。
悖论　貌似矛盾但实际上却真实存在的陈述或特质；难以解释却可以解释的谜团。
谬论　被认为是错误的知识或未知的领域。
源于父名的名字　一个人的名字取自于父辈的男性祖先，或来自于同一个行业的著名人物的名字。
冗言　多余词语的使用（不简单地说"盔甲，"而说"锁子盔甲"）。
挖苦　用轻蔑、辱骂的方式进行的刻薄讽刺。
符号学　对符号和标志，以及它们所代表的象征意味的研究。
明喻　用"好像"、"正如"这些比喻词进行两种观念或东西之间的比照。
绰号　昵称，被赋予一个充满想象力或幽默感的名字。
提喻　用部分代表整体或用整体代表部分的表达方式例如：用"马鞍"来指代"马匹"，用"壁炉"指代"房屋"。
同义词　大体意思相近的单词。
同义反复　多余的、重复的陈述方式，修辞学意义上的明显道理，例如"这部历史使得国际关系变得国际化"。
比喻　一个词语的形象用法；用一种东西指代另外一种东西。
自明之理　陈词滥调，或者明显的道理。

macaronic a medley of foreign words, either real or imaginary.
malapropism a verbal blunder or inappropriate word usage.
metaphor a word or phrase denoting one kind of idea/thing in place of another.
metonym a figurative expression or attribute standing in for another concept or thing, such as *laurels* for *honor* or *Brussels* for *the capital of the European Union*.
neologism coining a new word; borrowing a word from another language.
onomatopoeia imitation of natural sounds by words ("hiss," "crack").
oxymoron combination of contradictory words ("he endured a living death").
paradox a statement that appears contradictory yet is true in fact; a weighty, solvable riddle.
paralogism admittedly false knowledge; refers to the unknown.
patronymic deriving one's name from a male ancestor; one's name is the same as a famous person in a similar calling.
pleonasm the use of needless words ("chain mail" instead of simply "mail").
sarcasm the practice of keen irony; contemptuous or taunting language.
semiotics study of signs and symbols, and their relationship to ideas (adj. semiotic).
simile comparison by means of *like* or *as* between two kinds of ideas/things.
sobriquet a nickname; a fanciful or humorous name.
synecdoche a part standing in for a whole, or vice versa (as in, a saddle for a horse, or a hearth for a house).
synonyms words with common meanings.
tautologism needlessly repetitive statements; rhetorical self-truths ("this history internationalizes international relations").
trope the figurative use of a word; something standing in for something else.
truism a platitude, or self-evident truth.

有用——但经常弄错的词汇　（GRE 词汇）

abstruse　深奥的，难懂的
accidie　倦怠，精神上或身体上的迟钝，懒惰
anathema　禁令或诅咒；被诅咒的对象
anodyne　止痛的；抚慰的；解除痛苦的
anomie　认为社会的价值观不重要（或不存在）的态度
aphorism　格言
apodictic　可明确标明的
appetence　倾向，天性
apposite　适当的，合适的
asperity　严酷，艰苦
assiduous　勤勉的
aver　断言，证明是真的
bathos　由极好降为平常的突然过渡
credulous　轻信的，易受骗的
cupidity　贪财；对拥有物品的过分渴望
demotic　群众的（不是贵族的）；通俗的
diachronic　随着时间的持续而存在的
didactic　教学的；提供道德上的教训
disabuse　纠正错误的见解，讲清楚
dissemble　假装，掩饰
dissipation　放纵，无节制
efficacy　产生希望获得某种结果的能力
encomium　正式赞美的表达
enervation　失去活力
entrepôt　贸易港口，商栈；市场
epigraphy　研究墓志铭、碑文的识读等
equable　稳定的，均匀的
estimable　值得尊敬和佩服的
excoriation　以辛辣的词语来严厉指责的行为
exculpate　解除责怪或罪行
exegesis　文学作品的解释
exigent　紧急的，需要及时关注的
extirpate　根除，灭绝
gainsay　否认，反驳
gnomic　关于格言的
gnostic　具有知识和顿悟
hagiography　圣徒传；学习圣徒的生活的学科
holistic　赞同机能整体性的自然倾向

USEFUL—AND MISUSED—WORDS learn for GRE

abstruse	hard to understand
accidie	mental or spiritual torpor; sloth
anathema	a ban or curse; something detested
anodyne	soothing; relieves pain
anomie	society's values are irrelevant (absent)
aphorism	maxim
apodictic	clearly demonstrable
appetence	tendency; instinct
apposite	appropriate
asperity	harshness, severity
assiduous	hard working
aver	claim to be true
bathos	from lofty to banal discourse
credulous	easily deceived
cupidity	avarice; inordinate wish for possession
demotic	of the people (not aristocratic); popular
diachronic	persisting, existing through time
didactic	nature of teaching; morally instructive
disabuse	correct a fallacy, clarify
dissemble	pretend, simulate
dissipation	intemperance
efficacy	power to produce the desired effect
encomium	formal expression of praise
enervation	lack of energy
entrepôt	trading port, post; market
epigraphy	study of inscriptions, epitaphs
equable	steady, uniform
estimable	worthy of esteem and admiration
excoriation	act of condemning with harsh words
exculpate	to free from blame or guilt
exegesis	explanation of a literary work
exigent	urgent, requiring immediate attention
extirpate	root out, destroy
gainsay	contradict or oppose
gnomic	dealing in maxims
gnostic	possessing knowledge, insight
hagiography	reverential biography; study of saints' lives
holistic	natural trend toward organized synthesis
hermeneutics	interpretation of texts, esp. Biblical ones

hermeneutics 诠释学，文字作品，尤其是《圣经》的解释
impecunious 没钱的；永远贫穷的
inchoate 未完成的，没有完全发展或计划的
incommensurable 缺乏比较标准的，不能比较的
ineluctable 不可避免的
inimical 不友好的，敌视的；不利的，不易相处的
insouciance 漠不关心、不注意的态度
involution 纠缠；修辞的复杂性
irenic 安抚的
irredentist 主张和祖国统再次统一
laconic 简洁的
limn 描述；具体地概述；勾画
litotes 曲言法；夸张的少报
lugubrious 悲哀的；夸饰伤心的；令人沮丧的
macaronic 由不同语言词语组成的混合物
manqué 不完备的，不充足的
meme 文化基因；遗传下来的文化特征
mendacious 对说谎上瘾的；不诚实的
minatory 威胁性的，恫吓的
misanthrope 不喜欢并且不相信所有人的人
moot 未决议的，不重要的
neologism 新词，旧词新义
noisome 恶臭的，有害的
novum 暗指新制度或范式
ochlocracy 暴民制度；暴民统治
paean 赞美歌
paleography 古文书学
panegyric 颂词；正式的公开赞美（写的或者说出的）
particularism 完全忠于自己国家、政党的人
pedantic 卖弄学问的，学究的
peripatetic 徒步游历的
perspicacity 敏锐
philology 语文学，语言学
picayune 无价值的，不重要的，微不足道的
probity 正直，诚实
prodigality 浪费
prolixity 啰唆，冗长
propitiating 劝解的，抚慰的
proscribe 指责，禁令，禁止
protean 变化多端的，易变的

impecunious	having no money; perpetually poor
inchoate	not fully developed or formulated
incommensurable	lacking a standard of comparison
ineluctable	inescapable
inimical	unfriendly, hostile; adverse, difficult
insouciance	careless unconcern; indifference
involution	entanglement; rhetorical complexity
irenic	conciliatory
irredentist	advocating reunion with the mother country
laconic	concise, sparing with words
limn	to outline in detail; to delineate
litotes	exaggerated understatement
lugubrious	mournful; exaggeratedly sad, doleful
macaronic	medley of words from different languages
manqué	defective; inadequate
meme	inheritable cultural characteristic
mendacious	addicted to lying; deceitful
minatory	menacing, threatening
misanthrope	one who hates or distrusts all people
moot	subject to discussion; unimportant
neologism	new word, new meaning for old word
noisome	putrid, noxious
novum	implies a new order or paradigm
ochlocracy	mob rule; government by populace
paean	joyous expression of gratitude
paleography	science of deciphering ancient writing
panegyric	formal public eulogy (written or spoken)
particularism	fidelity to interests of one's state, party
pedantic	academic, bookish
peripatetic	always on the go
perspicacity	keenness of perception
philology	study of written records, linguistics
picayune	worthless, petty, trifling
probity	goodness, integrity
prodigality	wastefulness
prolixity	rambling, verbose quality
propitiating	conciliatory, mollifying
proscribe	denounce; prohibit; interdict
protean	readily assuming different forms, changing
putative	supposed, reported, reputed
quiescent	state of rest or inactivity

putative　假定的，据报告的，据说的
quiescent　平静、静止或不活跃的状态
quotidian　每日的，平凡的
recidivism　复发，再犯，累犯
recondite　艰深的，深刻的，深奥的
refractory　执拗的，固执地抗拒权威
restive　烦躁不安，不安；没耐心
salutary　有恢复健康作用的，有益健康的
sectary　持异议者，不符合传统规范者，派系主义者
sedulous　勤奋的，勤劳的
semiotics　符号学，研究符号以及符号意义的学科
sidereal　关于星或星座的
sphragistics　印章学
sublime　壮丽的，令人崇敬的
swidden　刀耕火种
sybaritic　奢侈享乐的，放纵的
synchronic　限于一个固定时间的研究
tendentious　有目的的
teleology　目的论
trenchant　锐利的，尖刻的
turpitude　恶劣，邪恶
tyro　初学者
unalloyed　不掺杂的，纯粹的
urbanity　文雅，有礼貌的，品位
veracious　诚实的，诚恳的
viscid　胶粘的
vitiate　污染，损害
vituperative　口头辱骂人的，侮辱的

容易引起歧义的词语及短语

beg the question（回避问题实质）　意味着本人认为自己的争论是有根据的，并非意味着提出问题或者促请别人提出问题。

biannual（每年两次的）、**semiannual**（每半年的）　应该直接写"*twice a year*"[*biennial*（每两年一次）、*biweekly*（每两周一次）、*semiweekly*（每周两次）等与此类似]。

bring（带来），**take**（带去）　朝观察者方向移动时用"*bring*"，远离观察者所在方位时用"*take*"。他把笔记本电脑带到档案馆去（*took*）并把档案带回来了（*brought back*）。

cull（挑选，剔除）　不但指从集合中挑出来，也指从集合中挑出去。

quotidian	occurring every day; commonplace
recidivism	backsliding into a former (bad) state
recondite	profound, deep, abstruse
refractory	stubbornly resisting control or authority
restive	restless; impatient
salutary	restorative, healthful
sectary	dissenter, nonconformist; a sectarian
sedulous	diligent, industrious
semiotics	study of symbols and their meaning
sidereal	relating to the stars or constellations
sphragistics	study of signet rings, engraved seals
sublime	grand or solemn to an awesome extent
swidden	slash-and-burn agriculture
sybaritic	proclivity to luxury; voluptuous
synchronic	a study at a fixed point, rather than over time
tendentious	having a purposed aim
teleology	philosophy of purposive causation
trenchant	caustic and incisive
turpitude	depravity, wickedness
tyro	novice, amateur
unalloyed	unqualified, pure
urbanity	sophistication, suaveness, and polish
veracious	truthful, earnest
viscid	sticky
vitiate	pollute, impair
vituperative	verbally abusive, insulting

Ambiguous Words and Phrases

beg the question   means to assume the validity of one's argument; it does not mean to pose or prompt a question.

biannual, semiannual   write: "twice a year" (biennial, "every two years"; biweekly, "every two weeks"; semiweekly, "twice a week").

bring, take   for actions directed toward the observer use *bring*, and away use *take*. He took his laptop to the archive and brought files back.

cull   can mean to choose from a group (to keep) as well as to select from a group (to discard).

emigrate, immigrate   viewpoint dependent. In a study about nineteenth-century Ireland: "conditions became so dire that Colleen O'Reilly decided to emigrate to America." But in a study on nineteenth-century America: "Colleen O'Reilly was one of nine hundred new immigrants

emigrate（移出）、**immigrate**（移入） 根据不同立场，使用不同词汇。例如，有关20世纪爱尔兰的一份研究报告中指出，"环境糟糕到使得科林·奥瑞利决定移居（*emigrate*）到美国。"但在有关20世纪美国的研究报告中，则指出，"科林·奥瑞利是在那一天于纽约港登陆的900名新进移民（*immigrants*）之一"。

moot（未决议的，无实际意义的） 在形容问题时（moot question）指的是可论证的问题；在形容议题时（moot issue）时却是指不值得讨论的话题。

sanction（允许，处罚，批准） 如果用做动词，意思是允许，如果用做名词，指的是处罚或批准。

table a motion（提出再审动议，搁置动议） 威斯敏斯特或布鲁塞尔：提出动议；美国国会山：搁置动议。[1]

---

1. 在英式英语和美式英语里，这个短语存在截然相反的两种含义。——译者注

who disembarked at the Port of New York that day."

moot a moot question is an arguable point, but a moot issue is an irrelevancy.

sanction as a verb, means permit, but as a noun, either penalty or approval.

table a motion Westminster or Brussels: put a motion on the table for discussion. Capitol Hill: remove the motion from the table and shelve it.

参考文献

Burke, Peter. *Eyewitnessing: The Uses of Images as Historical Evidence*. Ithaca, NY: Cornell University Press, 2007. Also in Chinese, Yang Yu, trans. Beijing: Peking University Press, 2008.

Chapman, James. *Cinemas of the World: Film and Society, from 1895 to the Present*. London: Reaktion, 2003.

The Chicago Manual of Style. 16th edition. Chicago: University of Chicago Press, 2010.

Germano, William. *Getting It Published: A Guide for Scholars and Anyone Else Serious about Serious Books*. Chicago: University of Chicago Press, 2008.

Hoffer, Peter Charles. *Past Imperfect: Facts, Fictions, Fraud—American History from Bancroft and Parkman to Ambrose, Bellesiles, Ellis, and Goodwin*. New York: Public Affairs, 2007.

Kingery, W. David, ed. *Learning from Things: Method and Theory of Material Culture Studies*. Washington, D.C.: Smithsonian Institution Press, 1996.

Marius, Richard. *A Short Guide to Writing About History*. 3rd edition. New York: Longman, 1999.

New Oxford Dictionary for Writers and Editors: The Essential A–Z Guide to the Written Word. Oxford: Oxford University Press, 2005.

Orwell, George. "Politics and the English Language." *Horizon*, 13:76 (April 1946), pp. 252–65. Commonly available on the web.

Oxford English Reference Dictionary. Judy Pearsall and Bill Trumble, eds. Oxford: Oxford University Press, 2003.

Riffe, Daniel, Stephen Lacy, and Frederick G. Fico. *Analyzing Media Messages: Using Quantitative Content Analysis in Research*. Mahwah, NJ: Lawrence Erlbaum Associates, 1998.

Ritchie, Donald A. *Doing Oral History: A Practical Guide*. New York: Oxford University Press, 2003.

Schlereth, Thomas J., ed. *Material Culture Studies in America*. Nashville, TN: American Association for State and Local History, 1982.

Siegal, Allan M., and William G. Connolly. *The New York Times Manual of Style and Usage*. New York: Three Rivers Press, 1999.

Strunk, William, Jr., and E.B. White. *The Elements of Style*. 4th edition. New York: Longman Publishers, 2000.

BIBLIOGRAPHY

Burke, Peter. *Eyewitnessing: The Uses of Images as Historical Evidence.* Ithaca, NY: Cornell University Press, 2007. Also in Chinese, Yang Yu, trans. Beijing: Peking University Press, 2008.

Chapman, James. *Cinemas of the World: Film and Society, from 1895 to the Present.* London: Reaktion, 2003.

The Chicago Manual of Style. 16th edition. Chicago: University of Chicago Press, 2010.

Germano, William. *Getting It Published: A Guide for Scholars and Anyone Else Serious about Serious Books.* Chicago: University of Chicago Press, 2008.

Hoffer, Peter Charles. *Past Imperfect: Facts, Fictions, Fraud—American History from Bancroft and Parkman to Ambrose, Bellesiles, Ellis, and Goodwin.* New York: Public Affairs, 2007.

Kingery, W. David, ed. *Learning from Things: Method and Theory of Material Culture Studies.* Washington, D.C.: Smithsonian Institution Press, 1996.

Marius, Richard. *A Short Guide to Writing About History.* 3rd edition. New York: Longman, 1999.

New Oxford Dictionary for Writers and Editors: The Essential A–Z Guide to the Written Word. Oxford: Oxford University Press, 2005.

Orwell, George. "Politics and the English Language." *Horizon*, 13:76 (April 1946), pp. 252–65. Commonly available on the web.

Oxford English Reference Dictionary. Judy Pearsall and Bill Trumble, eds. Oxford: Oxford University Press, 2003.

Riffe, Daniel, Stephen Lacy, and Frederick G. Fico. *Analyzing Media Messages: Using Quantitative Content Analysis in Research.* Mahwah, NJ: Lawrence Erlbaum Associates, 1998.

Ritchie, Donald A. *Doing Oral History: A Practical Guide.* New York: Oxford University Press, 2003.

Schlereth, Thomas J., ed. *Material Culture Studies in America.* Nashville, TN: American Association for State and Local History, 1982.

Siegal, Allan M., and William G. Connolly. *The New York Times Manual of Style and Usage.* New York: Three Rivers Press, 1999.

Strunk, William, Jr., and E.B. White. *The Elements of Style.* 4th edition. New York: Longman Publishers, 2000.

缩 写 词

军事名词缩写
Adm.　海军将领。
Capt.　上尉。
Cmdr.　准将，指挥官。
Lt.　中尉。
Col.　上校。
Maj. Gen.　少将。
Sgt.　中士。

有关脚注和书目等术语的缩写
b.　盒子（box，以下称为 b.）。
c.　纸壳箱（carton，以下称为 c.）。
ca.　大约，差不多；ca. 1934 表示日期是一个估计值。
chap. chaps.　一章，几章。
Cong.　美国国会。
ed. eds.　一名编辑，几名编辑。
esp.　尤其是，特别是。
et al.　（等人，以及其他人），有四名以上的作者，先提供第一作者的全名，然后写 et al。
f. ff.　一个文件夹，几个文件夹（folder，以下称为 f.）。
fn.　脚注。
ibid.　（同上）与前一脚注同源。只能用于出版来源。
id.　（同上，出自同一位作者）与前一脚注同作者。
min.　一分钟或几分钟；电影放映时间。
n. nn.　一个脚注，一些脚注。
n.d.　来源没有确定的日期。
no.　号码。
n.p.　没有出版地点，或没有出版社，意思是缺失相关信息。
passim　（各处）几页中的分散引用。
repr.　重印，指的是曾经出版作品的重新印刷。
sess.　开庭，会期。
trans.　译者。
U.S. GPO　美国政府印刷局。
vol. vols.　一卷，几卷。

正文中
sic　（原文如此）表明原文中复制的内容用过时或不正确的说法；以区别于 [*sic*]。

ABBREVIATIONS

Military Abbreviations
Adm. Admiral.
Capt. Captain.
Cmdr. Commodore, Commander.
Lt. Lieutenant.
Col. Colonel.
Maj. Gen. Major General.
Sgt. Sergeant.

Footnote and Bibliography Abbreviations and Terms
b. box [box, hereafter b.].
c. carton [carton, hereafter c.].
ca. (*circa*), about, approximately; ca. 1934 indicates that the date is an estimate.
chap. chaps. one chapter, several chapters.
Cong. Congress.
ed. eds. one editor, several editors.
esp. especially.
et al. (*et alia*, and others) for four or more authors, give the first author's name in full, followed by et al.
f. ff. one folder, several folders, [folder, hereafter, f.].
fn. footnote.
ibid. (*ibidem*, from the same source) same source as prior footnote; you can only use ibid. for published sources.
id. (*idem*, from the same) same author as prior footnote.
min. minute or minutes; for runtime of movies.
n. nn. footnote, footnotes.
n.d. no date.
no. number.
n.p. no place, or no publisher, meaning the information is absent.
passim (here and there) for scattered references over a range of pages.
repr. reprint, of a previously published work.
sess. session.
trans. translator.
U.S. GPO U.S. Government Printing Office.
vol. vols. one volume, several volumes.

In Text
sic (thus) to denote text copied verbatim from the original that is archaic or erroneous; to differentiate [*sic*] from the parent quotation, set it in italics inside square brackets, as here.

案　　例

论点陈述：期刊文章，迈克尔·E. 查普曼，2006年

  在描述了塞奇威克与他的朋友W.卡梅伦·福布斯在西班牙所进行的富于开创的巡视并讨论了 *Atlantic*（《大西洋》）自由论散文家们的选集之后，本篇文章记录塞奇威克对于国会认可弗朗哥的激进主义和他与凯利的工作合作关系。文章突显大论战中红色法西斯主义者的极端修辞方式，从而证实了该修辞方式使自由主义先进分子蜕变为保守分子的转向，并且奠定了1950年代麦卡锡主义的话语基础。其中认为，福布斯和塞奇威克对于弗朗哥本人不感兴趣，却支持他的事业是因为他们企图证明在史无前例的不安全时期，国际共产主义对于美利坚民族的身份认同造成了威胁。迈克尔·H.亨特曾观察到国家精英们——经常是那些具有最强烈民族身份认同感的精英们——会对外交事务危机作出回应，但他们根植于历史性的爱国主义可能会限制其回应的规模和适当性，有关形成民族身份认同的高潮时刻就兴起在此一渐进的、高对抗性的过程中。本文表明，这些行为的主角们在心里把西班牙影射为美国，从而把侵蚀着外国马克思主义的、不道德的、无政府主义的他者与传统的、美国核心价值观中的文明化秩序进行对照。像后来的冷战分子一样，支持弗朗哥的议会游说者们在面对其必要敌手的态度上显示出这样一则悖论，即只有当国际共产主义最终呈现出威胁的情况下，持续的斗争才会为民族安全提供最完美的辩护理由。[1]

  我以行文路线图开始这个五段引言中的最后段落，其中表明，本文将首先记录一些历史事件。对此，我做出了一个明确的论点陈述，然后通过明确另外一位历史学家的观点，勾勒出大历史观的框架。然后，我作出结尾阐述，表明，我所进行的案例研究与一段重要的历史时期有关——而且有可能其中心人物对此一历史时期的形成作出过贡献。我必须承认，自己实在是花了相当长的时间来写这一段，本段的语言结构并非一蹴而就而是经过深思熟虑的。此段落存在着一个计划过的进度——"描述"、"讨论"、"记录"、"认为"、"表明"——而且第一句中 *ah-dee-ess* 的头韵性/节奏性短语修辞是刻意而为之的。"After describing Sedgwick's . . . and discussing a selection . . . article documents Sedgwick's . . ."（在描述了塞奇威克的……在讨论了此一文选……本文记录了塞奇威克……）注意我如何在介绍福布斯和亨特的时候运用了全

---

1. Michael E. Chapman, "Pro-Franco Anti-Communism: Ellery Sedgwick and the *Atlantic Monthly*," *Journal of Contemporary History*, 41:4 (October 2006), pp. 641–62.

EXAMPLES

Thesis Statement: Journal Article, Michael Chapman, 2006

After describing Sedgwick's seminal tour of Nationalist Spain with his friend W. Cameron Forbes, and discussing a selection of the *Atlantic*'s libertarian essayists, this article documents Sedgwick's activism for State Department recognition of Franco and his working association with Kelly. It highlights the Great Debate's polarized red–fascist rhetoric, which backed liberal progressives into the conservatives' corner as well as laying the discursive groundwork for 1950s McCarthyism. It argues that Forbes and Sedgwick were not interested in Franco per se, but promoted his cause because they sought to demonstrate the danger that international communism posed to American national identity during a period of unprecedented insecurity. Michael H. Hunt has observed that climactic moments in the gradual and highly contested process of national-identity formation can arise when elites—often those with the strongest sense of national identity—respond to a foreign affairs crisis, yet their historically rooted patriotism may limit the scope and appropriateness of their responses. This article suggests that its actors mentally mapped Spain onto the United States, to contrast the immoral and anarchic Other of encroaching foreign Marxism with the civilizing order of traditional American core values. Like later Cold Warriors, Franco lobbyists confronted the paradox of the necessary enemy, for while international communism represented the ultimate danger, continually fighting it provided the perfect justification for national security.[1]

I begin this concluding paragraph of a five-paragraph introduction with a road map, suggesting in the process that the article will document something for the first time. I provide a clear thesis statement, which I then frame in a bigger-picture concern, as identified by another historian. And I close by suggesting that my case study has relevance to—and perhaps its actors contributed toward—an important historical period. This paragraph took longer to write than I care to admit, its constructions being deliberate rather then happenstance. There is a planned progression—*describing, discussing, documents, argues, suggests*—and the *ah-dee-ess* alliterative/rhythmic phrasing in the first sentence was intentional. [After describing Sedgwick's . . . and discussing a selection . . . article documents Sedgwick's . . .] Note how I give names in full for Forbes and Hunt, but not for Sedgwick, Franco, or Kelly, as I introduced them in prior paragraphs; my original manuscript had "Historian Michael H. Hunt," which in this version I edited out to save words, although "has observed" suggests that Hunt is a contemporary scholar.

---

1. Michael E. Chapman, "Pro-Franco Anti-Communism: Ellery Sedgwick and the *Atlantic Monthly*," *Journal of Contemporary History*, 41:4 (October 2006), pp. 641–62.

名，但对于塞奇威克、弗朗哥或者凯利，因为在先前的段落中已经介绍过，所以不再使用其全名。我的初稿中曾把亨特介绍为"历史学家迈克尔·H.亨特"，但在本版中，为了节省字数，我删除了历史学家一词，不过"曾观察到"所使用的现在完成时暗示出亨特是一位当今的历史学者。

文本置入：沃尔特·拉夫波，2008年

霍华德曾警告说，侵略伊斯兰君主制国家并称之为一场反恐"战争"是一项最糟糕的政策。他相信，恐怖分子不应该"被抬高到［国家层面上］的交战方地位上去：他们是罪犯"，而且不应该被给予"他们自身追求却不配拥有的地位和尊严"。他敦促布什要避免"情绪宣泄"的行为，换句话说，他不应该运用如此庞大的军事行动来作为报复"9·11"攻击的手段。这场反对伊斯兰国家的战争会使得那些目前甚至蔑视基地组织的伊斯兰民众与美国渐行渐远。而且攻打伊拉克的行为仿佛"一个醉汉在漆黑的巷子里丢了手表，却在路灯下寻找，仅因为那里比较亮堂"。基地组织，哈罗德写到，并非仅存在于伊拉克，而确实存在于许多其他国家中。布什应该与其他情报机构合作，逮捕并粉碎恐怖分子的网络，然后或者消灭他们或者把他们送上法庭。侵略伊斯兰国家会使得这些国家转变为哺育恐怖分子的温床，同时因在攻击中导致的无罪平民丧生会"侵蚀"美国的"道德威信"。此种侵略仿佛"试图用焊枪根除癌症细胞"。重点地区（土耳其、埃及、巴基斯坦）可能会在战争的火焰中被毁灭，而癌症的病因，奥斯马·本·拉登则可能逃脱并"不受损失"。[1]

本段来源于1967年出版的一本书的最后一章，证明现代文本格式渐渐趋向于采用文本置入的形式。拉夫波摘录关键词"战争"、"情绪宣泄"和一些难忘的短语如"一个丢失了手表的醉汉"、"用焊枪根除癌症细胞"，并把它们置入自己的段落中——"消灭恐怖分子或者把他们送上法庭"，而其原文则为"被追捕到然后被带到国际法庭上"——使得一篇较为晦涩的演讲浅显易懂。注意：为确保读者明白行文所采用的语气是属于霍华德的而非作者的，拉夫波在行文中曾四次把霍华德置于行为人的位置之上——"霍华德曾警告说；霍华德相信；霍华德敦促；霍华德写道"。大部分情况下，拉夫波忠实于他所运用的资料，不过他确实在行文中把自己的话借霍华德之口表述出来，"侵略伊斯兰国家会使得这些国家转变为哺育恐怖分子的温床"，因为霍华德最接近此含义的表述可见于下一自然段，"［电视中］西方军事行动的影像将加深彼此的仇恨并为恐怖分子之

---

1. Walter LaFeber, *America, Russia, and the Cold War, 1945–2006* (Boston, MA: McGraw-Hill, 2008), p. 418.

Textual Immersion: Walter LaFeber, 2008

Howard warned that the worst policy would be to invade sovereign Islamic nations, then call it a "war" against terrorism. Terrorists, he believed, should not be "dignified with the status of [country-based] belligerents: they were criminals" and should not be given "a status and dignity that they seek and that they do not deserve." He urged Bush to avoid a "catharsis"; that is, he should not try to avenge the 9/11 attacks with spectacular military actions. Such wars against Islamic nations would alienate even those Muslims who now despised al Qaeda. And to attack Iraq would resemble "the drunk who lost his watch in a dark alley but looked for it under a lamppost because there was more light there." Al Qaeda, Howard wrote, was not in Iraq, but did exist in many other countries. Bush should cooperate with other intelligence agencies, seize and break up the terrorist networks, then either kill the terrorists or bring them before the courts. To invade Islamic nations could turn those nations into breeding grounds for terrorists, while "eroding the moral authority" of the United States as it killed innocent civilians in the attack. Such an invasion would resemble "trying to eradicate cancer cells with a blowtorch." Vital areas (Turkey, Egypt, Pakistan) could be consumed in the flames, while the cancer's cause, Osama bin Laden, could escape and "cannot lose."[1]

This paragraph from the final chapter of a new edition of a book that first appeared in 1967, illustrates the modern trend toward textual immersion. LaFeber extracts key words [war, catharsis] and memorable phrases [the drunk who lost his watch] [eradicate cancer cells with a blowtorch] and embeds them in his own paraphrasing—"kill the terrorists or bring them before the courts" versus, "hunted down and brought before an international court" in the original—to make sense of what was a rather opaque speech. To ensure the reader understands that the voice is Howard's and not his own, notice how LaFeber posits Howard as doer on four occasions [Howard warned; he believed; he urged; Howard wrote]. For the most part, LaFeber is true to his source, although he does rather put words into Howard's mouth with his phrase, "To invade Islamic nations could turn those nations into breeding grounds for terrorists," for the closest Howard came to making such an assertion was in the next paragraph, with "[Images on television of] Western military action will strengthen the hatred and recruit for the ranks of the terrorists." A truer paraphrase would have been something like, "To invade Islamic nations would only strengthen local hatreds of Americans while increasing the supply of eager recruits to the terrorists' ranks."[2]

---

1. Walter LaFeber, *America, Russia, and the Cold War, 1945–2006* (Boston, MA: McGraw-Hill, 2008), p. 418.
2. Address by historian Sir Michael Howard to the Royal United Services Institute, October 2001, and article, "What's in a Name? How to Fight Terrorism," *Foreign Affairs*, 81 (January–February 2002), pp. 8–13; "hunted down," p. 9.

流招募到更多的新人"。一份更为吻合原意的改写可能更倾向于:"侵略伊斯兰国家只会增强当地人民对于美国人的仇恨之情,并为恐怖分子之流提供更多的热血的新兵。"[1]

文本置入:赛思·雅各布斯,2010年

帕森斯的傲慢与目光短浅对于美国的政策破坏力有可能会没有现实的大,只要他在万象的同僚行政人员有不一样的看法,但是大使馆、USOM[2]、USIS[3],以及其他主要的美国组织留下来的记录则表明,大使的大部分看法,皆曾与其他职权相近的官员分享过。他们皆认为老挝人是不受同情心之节制的愤怒、谦虚和嘲弄气质的混合体。文森特·西里斯,身为老挝国家警察局的最高美国顾问,在1958年写的"最终报告"认为:"老挝人本性上有些懒惰,很可能由于使人无精打采的气候,削弱了他们心理上和生理上的活力从而形成了一种'明天'哲学。"无论成因为何,他观察到,"大部分老挝人"是"可悲地体质虚弱的"、"非常懒惰的"、"缺乏野心的"。USOM 副会长戈登麦索格曾于1957年年末抱怨称,他面临的最大问题是"老挝人盛行的思考方法和意识形态"。对此,他说:"与技术性文明所要求的不完全一致。"麦索格告诉代理外勤务部长官的罗伯特·史密瑟:"老挝人[sic]倾向于顺其自然、追求适度,一个工业文明却要求其民众富于野心……[他们]把精确和精密看做是一种美德,预计未来的问题,有耐性静候有赖于当前投资而在未来形成的利益。"根据麦索格所言,这些要求明确地站到了东道主国人民的对立面上。USIS 领导人汉克·米勒在1958年所著的"老挝的国家计划案"中曾为老挝人的"政治幼稚"感到悲哀,认为他们"意识不到好公民和好政府要承担的责任"。他注意到,老挝国内不存在"有历练的、能够清晰表明立场的领导者",而且国人对于"自立的价值取向"缺乏信心。甚至在1958年前期被国际合作总署(ICA)派驻到老挝评估援助计划的专家组成员亦无法掩饰他们的轻蔑。尽管他们报告的大部分内容皆是准确的并令人意外的诚实——他们谴责美方资金的管理失当,"外勤计划的安排随意"以及"计划执行技能显示的低水准"——同时也描述了老挝人的"不成熟"、"目不识丁"、"无知"、"不谙21世纪的状况"和"不具有有强壮的体魄"。他们尤其对老挝佛教不屑一顾,声称,它"导致对生活自满,安于现状"。"老挝人对于经济发展确实毫无渴望",ICA 报告坚

---

1. Address by historian Sir Michael Howard to the Royal United Services Institute, October 2001, and article, "What's in a Name? How to Fight Terrorism," *Foreign Affairs*, 81 (January–February 2002), pp. 8–13; "hunted down," p. 9.
2. 美国援外使团。——译者注
3. 美国新闻处。——译者注

Textual Immersion: Seth Jacobs, 2010

Parsons's arrogance and narrow-mindedness might have been less damaging to U.S. policy had his fellow administrators in Vientiane seen matters differently, but the record left by the embassy, USOM, USIS, and other major American organizations indicates that the ambassador's views were, for the most part, shared by those officials whose authority approached his. They all regarded the Lao with a mix of irritation, condescension, and scorn untempered by empathy. Vincent Cillis, top U.S. adviser to the Lao National Police, noted in his 1958 "Terminal Report" that, "The Lao by nature is somewhat indolent, perhaps due to the enervating climate, which reduces mental and physical vigor and produces a 'manana' philosophy." Whatever the reason, he observed, "Most Laotians" were "woefully weak," "strongly indolent," and "unambitious." USOM Deputy Director Gordon Messegee complained in late 1957 that his biggest problem was "the prevailing method of thought, the ideology of the Lao people," which, he said, was "not completely in harmony with that required by a technical civilization." Messegee informed Robert Smither, acting chief of the field service division, that, "While the Laos [sic] tend to let matters take their own course and to seek moderation, an industrial civilization requires people who are ambitious, . . . [who] make a virtue out of precision and exactness, who anticipate the problems of the future, and who have the patience to wait for the benefits in the future derived from investments in the present." As far as Messegee was concerned, those requirements defined the antithesis of the host population. USIS leader Hank Miller's 1958 "Country Plan for Laos" bewailed Lao "Political naïveté" and "unawareness of the responsibilities of good citizenship and good government." There were no "tested, articulate leaders" in the country, he noted, and citizens put no stock in "the value of self-help." Even the team of experts sent to Laos by the International Cooperation Administration (ICA) in early 1958 to evaluate the aid program could not disguise their contempt. While much of their report was accurate and bracingly honest—they condemned the mismanagement of American funds, the "haphazard programming in the field," and the "low level of skill displayed in program execution"—they also described the Lao as "immature," "illiterate," "benighted," "unfamiliar with the twentieth century," and "not vigorous as to health." They were especially dismissive of Lao Buddhism, which, they claimed, "leads to the complacent acceptance of life as it is." "There is certainly no desire on the part of the Lao for economic development," the ICA report averred. "At the very most, they would like more whiskey and more new cars."[1]

---

1. Seth Jacobs, "The Universe Unraveling: United States Policy toward Laos, 1954–62," draft manuscript, January 2010. Jacobs is associate professor of history at Boston College.

称。"他们顶多希望得到更多的威士忌和更多新车。"[1]

本篇重量级的论据性段落将来自四种不同资料的22个独立引文,整合成转述性质的语篇和解读性质的行文。雅各布斯作为外交史家,处于所谓的文化转向的20世纪90年代的传统,关注的是决策者的修辞还有他们的政策,故而在行文中用对位法同时引用具有句子长度的几个段落和个体引用的单词。注意行文中雅各布斯是如何标识发言者身份,明确向读者传达他们的语气,还有通过评注词,例如"他观察到"、"他们谴责"、"他们声称"等评论来令读者明确说话者的身份。

文本置入:迈克尔·E.查普曼, 2009年

埃弗里特思绪下隐藏的是这样一种预设,正是"由于神的旨意,为人类谋利益的考量,美洲应该由文明族群来定居",为此,他进一步断定,美国"天才性的"国家制度——它独特的政府组织形式——是出于"神的最终意愿"。正如他所倾心的古希腊和古罗马时代,他们的共和国皆短命、摇摇欲坠、外敌环伺;古人无论在任何情况下,都没有能力充分利用其"人口众多、幅员辽阔的优势,拥有有保障、有条理、自由的享乐和言论权利的制度",就像当时的美国人有能力做到的一样。膨胀的人口享有无垠的土地这一观点对于埃弗里特的逻辑演算至关重要,但如果美洲的殖民者曾是欧洲人,神的最终意愿并不会完满。"美国性格中的一个最幸福的指徵"在于它人口的"独特性",因为它是在"英国文明的基础上"经年累月"嫁接了其他文明国家的语言、艺术和品味"。要是美国人是"任何一个欧洲国家的纯种后代",那么——即使在拥有完美的治理方式下——他们也会保留对"那个国家道德上和智能上的依赖性",而且他们的实验也会失败。美国人最"具吸引力和美好的独特性"之一,在于他们继承了英国定居者所具有的所有"盎格鲁-撒克逊人的显著品质",即欧洲国家中"融合了几乎所有珍贵的品质"。这就是共和主义在法国失败的原因,在那里君主制暴政的"昔日邪恶"大多以最"积习的形式"继续存在。所以即使美国为其提供了"示范的力量",法国的反应必然是粗暴的,伴随着如此"可怕的多余行径",几乎使自由之名本身都变得可憎。只剩下美国人独自作为"典范":他们定不忘却因为"全世界的目光"将会转向他们,如果他们失败,那么他们将会"摧

---

[1]. Seth Jacobs, "The Universe Unraveling: United States Policy toward Laos, 1954–62," draft manuscript, January 2010. Jacobs is associate professor of history at Boston College.

This weighty evidentiary paragraph contains twenty-two separate quotations from four different sources, integrated into paraphrased context and interpretive prose. Jacobs, a diplomatic historian in the tradition of the so-called cultural turn of the 1990s, is concerned with policymakers' rhetoric as well as their policies, hence his presentation of individual quoted words in counterpoint to a couple of sentence-length passages. Notice how Jacobs identifies all his speakers, and makes clear whose voice the reader hears, with comments such as, *he observed, they condemned, they claimed.*

Textual Immersion: Michael Chapman, 2009

Underlying Everett's thinking was the premise that it was the "will of Providence, and for the interest of humanity, that America should be settled by a civilized race of men," to which he added an assumption that the "genius" of America's institutions—its unique government—was the "final design of Providence." Enamored as he was with ancient Greece and Rome, their republics had been short lived, prone to corruption and outside attack; at no time had the ancients been able to capitalize on a "populous and extensive region, blessed with institutions securing enjoyment and transmission of regulated liberty," as Americans now could. An expanding population with access to limitless land was central to Everett's calculus, yet had North America's colonists been European, Providence's final design would have been unfulfilled. "One of the happiest features of the American character" was its "peculiarity" of population, for it was onto the "stock of English civilization" that time had "engrafted the languages, the arts, and the tastes of the other civilized nations." Had Americans been the "unmixed descendants of any one nation of Europe," then—even with perfect governance—they would have retained a "moral and intellectual dependency on that nation," and their experiment would have failed. One of the most "attractive and beautiful peculiarities" of Americans was that they had inherited from the English settlers all the "prominent qualities of the Anglo-Saxon," an "admixture of almost everything that is valuable" in the European states. This was why republicanism had failed in France, where the "former evil" of monarchical tyranny had existed in its most "inveterate form." So despite the "power of example" provided by the United States, the reaction was necessarily violent, with such "dreadful excesses" that the very name of liberty almost became odious. It remained for Americans alone to be "exemplars": they must never forget that because "the eyes of the world" were turned upon them, if they were to fail then they would "blast the hopes of the friends of liberty" throughout the world to eternity.[1]

---

1. Edward Everett, address at the Charlestown Lyceum, 28 June 1830, Fourth of July Oration in Charlestown, 1828, in *Orations and Speeches . . . by Edward Everett*, pp. 203–4, 143, 151, 157–58, 161, 157.

毁身为自由之友的期望",遍布全世界直至永远。[1]

如脚注所示,本段通过摘录爱德华·埃弗里特在美国独立日上长篇幅演说中的不同片段,综合出其对于美国例外论的信念的复杂画卷。我引用散落在丰富修辞中的简短引文,并以埃弗里特自己的行文风格和遣词造句进行了严密的转述。我远远没有以艾弗里特的身份表述这些言论,因为他把许多有关相似主题的段落挤到演讲里,所以反而轻描淡写了他的演讲对于1828年波士顿人的影响。

文本置入:迈克尔·E.查普曼,2009年

演讲进入高潮,也许在白兰地的催化下,他的声音随风飘向人群,旧时精英韦伯斯特的形象益发明显。正如旁观者后来回忆所言,韦伯斯特语速"缓慢而极其从容",自豪地宣称"邦克山纪念碑业已完工,它矗立在这里",建筑对象和目的无限崇高,耸立于地之间、海之滨,俯视着马萨诸塞三十万个居民的家。这不仅仅是纪念碑或艺术品。它自有目的,自有其赋予性格之目的,被冠以"崇高和道德庄严"之名义。事实上,在那一刻人们所听到的声音并非出自肉体之口唇,而是出于纪念碑的灵魂:它是"此一时刻的演说家"。它是一个单调的光轴。它没有碑文。"面对初升的太阳,未来的古物研究家将为其拂拭尘埃",它静静坐落在那里。但是,在清晨傍晚太阳起落之时,在正午日光炙烤之时,在"午夜月光更轻微的辉煌萦绕之刻;它在看,在说话,在活动,在每一个美国人的总体意会里"。韦伯斯特解释说,纪念碑教育性的意义,"它的沉默,但邪恶的话语",存在于它碑文的空白匿名之中。那天,它恰好借韦伯斯特之口说与众人,好似它将以未来的演讲与绵延的美国人后裔说话,当他们站立在碑前,围绕在碑前之时。因其独特的个性,韦伯斯特预言,它所传递的信息总是提倡"爱国主义和勇气的,有关公民和宗教自由的,有关自由政府的,有关人类道德进步和提升的"。因为他们的文明是建立于坚实的科学基础之上的,为自然和艺术知识广博的,道德精神所激发的文明。[2]

[原文]邦克山纪念碑业已完工。它矗立在这里。它矗立的自然位置幸运

---

1. Edward Everett, address at the Charlestown Lyceum, 28 June 1830, Fourth of July Oration in Charlestown, 1828, in *Orations and Speeches . . . by Edward Everett*, pp. 203–4, 143, 151, 157–58, 161, 157.
2. George Frisbie Hoar, *Autobiography of Seventy Years* (New York: Charles Scribner's Sons, 1903), I, p. 135; Daniel Webster, *An Address Delivered at the Completion of the Bunker Hill Monument, June 17, 1843* (Boston: Tappan and Dennet, 1843), pp. 5–6.

As the footnote indicates, this paragraph assembles a composite picture of Edward Everett's faith in American exceptionalism, drawn from different passages in a long, Fourth of July oration. I have interspersed short quotations of rich rhetoric with close paraphrasing in Everett's own style and vocabulary. Far from putting words into Everett's mouth, because he packed so many passages of a similar ilk into his delivery, I would argue that I have understated the impact his oration would have had on Bostonians in 1828.

Textual Immersion: Michael Chapman, 2009

Once into the meat of the speech, perhaps warmed by the brandy and with the wind backing around so his voice carried toward the crowd, Webster's old genius became apparent. Speaking "slowly and with great deliberation," as one spectator later recalled, Webster proudly exclaimed, "The Bunker Hill Monument is finished. Here it stands," infinitely high in its objects and purpose, rising over the land and the sea, visible from the homes of 300,000 citizens of Massachusetts. This was no mere memorial, or work of art. It had a purpose, a purpose that enrobed it with "dignity and moral grandeur," a purpose that gave it character. Indeed, the words they were hearing at that moment came not from mortal lips but from the very soul of the Monument: it was "the orator of this occasion." It was a plain shaft. It bore no inscriptions. "Fronting to the rising sun, from which the future antiquarian shall wipe the dust," it stood silent. And yet, at the sun's rising and setting, in the noonday blaze and the "milder effulgence of lunar light; it looks, it speaks, it acts, to the full comprehension of every American mind." In its blank anonymity—Webster was explaining—lay the Monument's oracle-like purpose, "Its silent, but awful utterance." On that day, it happened to be speaking to them through Webster, just as it would speak to them in future oratories through successive generations of Americans, as they rose up before it, and gathered around it. Because of its special character, its message, he predicted, would always be "of patriotism and courage; of civil and religious liberty; of free government; of the moral improvement and elevation of mankind." For theirs was a civilization founded on solid science, informed by knowledge of nature and the arts, stimulated by moral sentiment.[1]

[Original text:] The Bunker Hill Monument is finished. Here it stands. Fortunate in the high natural eminence on which it is placed, higher, infinite-

---

1. George Frisbie Hoar, *Autobiography of Seventy Years* (New York: Charles Scribner's Sons, 1903), I, p. 135; Daniel Webster, *An Address Delivered at the Completion of the Bunker Hill Monument, June 17, 1843* (Boston: Tappan and Dennet, 1843), pp. 5–6.

地显赫崇高，它的建立对象和目的却更为无限崇高，它耸立于地之间、海之滨，俯视着，马萨诸塞三十万居民的家。它承载着过去的记忆，观望着当下和以后的世代子孙。我刚提到了它建立的崇高意义。要是它不具有除了艺术品的创造外的任何其他设计，那么建造它的花岗岩宁愿沉睡在它的故居之中。它自有目的，意义赋予它个性。那个目的使它被冠以崇高和道德庄严之名。那众所周知的目的导致我们仰视它，带着敬畏。它本身即是此一时刻的演说家。它不是出自我之口唇，它不可能是出自任何人之口唇，那雄辩的口才今日力压群雄，鼓舞和激励着我周围的大众们。这有力的演说者不动如山矗立在我们面前。它是光轴。它没有碑文，面对初升的太阳，未来的古物研究家将为其拂拭尘埃。初升的朝阳也不会使得山顶奏出乐章。但是在清晨傍晚太阳起落之时；在正午日光炙烤的时候，在午夜月光更轻微的辉煌萦绕之刻；它在看，在说话，在活动，在每一个美国人的总体意会里，唤醒每一个美国人心中的热烈激情。它沉默而邪恶的话语，它深沉的哀伤，仿若把我们的视线聚焦到了1775年6月17日和随之而来的对于我们、我们国家，以及对于世界的结果，我们知道其结果会继续对人类命运施加影响直至世界末日的那一刻；它令我们日常生活的情感提升到崇高的高度——超越所有学科的藩篱，甚至先贤的典范作用，能够发挥的一切影响。今天，它有话对我们说。它未来的听众将是接下来的几代人，他们在它面前站立，围绕其周围。它的演说将是有关爱国主义和勇气的，有关公民和宗教自由的，有关自由政府的，有关人类道德进步和提升的，有关以英烈忠诚、为国牺牲的不朽回忆的……但是，只要目前的人类文明，是被建立在坚实的科学、自然的真正知识，和艺术的大量发现之上的，为道德情感所提升和净化的文明，只要地球上人类一息尚存，它就不会走向覆灭，那么此墓碑的建筑的对象和目的将会被传颂直到那一刻的到来。

本段描述了邦克山纪念碑社会历史的草图，基于丹尼尔·韦伯斯特最振奋人心的演讲之一。我的写作目的有如下三点。首先，重建该事件的重要性和戏剧冲突性；其次，证明韦伯斯特演讲的精彩性和感召力；最后，解释他认为墓碑沉默的天才在于一种通过诸如他自己和埃弗里特这样的精英来演讲的能力。比起完整句子或者引语段落来说，本文置入能更好地服务于那些目的。在韦伯斯特演讲中，以单数第三人称代词"它"开头的语

ly higher in its objects and purpose, it rises over the land and over the sea; and, visible, at their homes, to three hundred thousand of the people of Massachusetts, it stands a memorial of the last, and a monitor to the present, and to all succeeding generations. I have spoken of the loftiness of its purpose. If it had been without any other design than the creation of a work of art, the granite of which it is composed would have slept in its native bed. It has a purpose, and that purpose gives it its character. That purpose enrobes it with dignity and moral grandeur. That well-known purpose it is which causes us to look up to it with a feeling of awe. It is itself the orator of this occasion. It is not from my lips, it could not be from any human lips, that that strain of eloquence is this day to flow most competent to move and excite the vast multitudes around me. The powerful speaker stands motionless before us. It is a plain shaft. It bears no inscriptions, fronting to the rising sun, from which the future antiquarian shall wipe the dust. Nor does the rising sun cause tones of music to issue from its summit. But at the rising of the sun, and at the setting of the sun; in the blaze of noonday, and beneath the milder effulgence of lunar light; it looks, it speaks, it acts, to the full comprehension of every American mind, and the awakening of glowing enthusiasm in every American heart. Its silent, but awful utterance; its deep pathos, as it brings to our contemplation the 17th of June, 1775, and the consequences which have resulted to us, to our country, and to the world, from the events of that day, and which we know must continue to rain influence on the destinies of mankind to the end of time; the elevation with which it raises us high above the ordinary feelings of life,—surpass all that the study of the closet, or even the inspiration of genius, can produce. To-day it speaks to us. Its future auditories will be the successive generations of men, as they rise up before it and gather around it. Its speech will be of patriotism and courage; of civil and religious liberty; of free government; of the moral improvement and elevation of mankind; and of the immortal memory of those who, with heroic devotion, have sacrificed their lives for their country.... But if the civilization of the present race of men, founded, as it is, in solid science, the true knowledge of nature, and vast discoveries in art, and which is elevated and purified by moral sentiment, be not destined to destruction before the final termination of human existence on earth, the object and purpose of this edifice will be known till that hour shall come.

I have three aims for this paragraph, taken from a draft of a social history of the Bunker Hill Monument, and based on one of Daniel Webster's most inspired orations. First, to recreate the drama and importance of the event; second, to demonstrate Webster's oratorical brilliance and charisma, and

句数量显得过多，从而使得全篇文章太过直接和直观，所以我试图将其融入改写，并在引用中表示说明。

表示赞许（不抄袭）

因母亲严厉的加尔文教义在童年时受过心理创伤，伊克斯长大后更像他生活放纵的父亲一样世俗，天生不信任有组织的宗教，但是掩盖在"坚定不移地相信自身的道德正直感"之下，正如一本传记所言。

传记作者格兰海默·怀特和约翰·梅斯展示了因母亲严厉的加尔文教义在童年时受过的心理创伤，伊克斯长大后更像他生活放纵的父亲一样世俗，天生不信任有组织的宗教，但是掩盖在"坚定不移地相信自身的道德正直感"之下。[1]

———

引用其他学者和自身侵占其他学者的作品之间存在微妙的差别，这差别很容易被逾越，经常存在于无意之中。比较这两句话，第一句源于我的博士学位论文，第二句源于即将出版的书籍，两句都要说明一个观点，即内务部长哈罗德·伊克斯可能在道德上倾向于支持在西班牙内战中的忠诚派，正如他对支持与西班牙敌对的民族主义者的美国天主教高层抱有恶意一样。乍看之下，两句差不多相同，都引用了怀特和梅斯的传记。细看才会察觉实则不然。我很不好意思承认，但第一句暗示着这一观点要么是常识要么出于我的意见，想必是基于我的研究，伊克斯虔诚的母亲在心理上伤害过他，而他的父亲确是其楷模，诸如此类。但是这一观点既非常识也非我的研究成果，而是怀特和梅斯作品的结论，正如我在第二版中清晰指出的一样。当我写第一句的时候，我正寻找一个新的结构能够凸显伊克斯支持忠诚派的积极性；绝非有意抄袭，但我却心怀愧疚。

脚注

10. Justus D. Doenecke, *Storm on the Horizon: The Challenge to American Intervention, 1939–1941* (Lanham, MD: Rowman & Littlefield Publishers, 2003), pp. 170–71.

11. *Congressional Record, House Journal,* 75th Cong., 1st sess., 6 January 1937, p. 99.

———

1. 有关伊克斯成长的心理分析，参照 Graham White and John Maze, *Harold Ickes of the New Deal: His Private Life and Public Career* (Cambridge, MA: Harvard University Press, 1985), pp. 12–15, 25.

third, to explain his notion that the Monument's mute genius was its ability to speak through elites such as himself and Everett. Textual immersion facilitates those aims far better than would complete sentences or a block quotation. Webster's almost excessive opening of sentences with the third-person neuter pronoun *it* lends the passage a directness and an immediacy, which I have tried to mirror in the paraphrasing as well as illustrate in the quotations.

Giving Credit (Not Plagiarizing)

Traumatized as a child by his mother's strict Calvinism, Ickes grew up more like his loose-living father, secular with an ingrained distrust of organized religions, but capped by an "unwavering belief in his own moral rectitude," as one biography puts it.[1]

Biographers Graham White and John Maze show how Ickes, traumatized as a child by his mother's strict Calvinism, grew up more like his loose-living father, secular with an ingrained distrust of organized religions, but capped by an "unwavering belief in his own moral rectitude."[1]

There is a fine line between crediting other scholars and appropriating other scholars' work as your own, a line that is all too easy to cross, often inadvertently. Compare these two sentences, the first from my dissertation, the second from my forthcoming book, which I used to support an argument that Secretary of the Interior Harold Ickes may have been morally predisposed to support the Loyalists in the Spanish Civil War just as he was ill disposed toward America's Catholic hierarchy whose members backed Spain's rival Nationalists. At first sight, both sentences are virtually identical, with a citation to the White and Maze biography. A closer reading indicates otherwise. As I am embarrassed to admit, the first sentence implies that it is either common knowledge or my opinion, presumably based on research I conducted, that Ickes's pious mother traumatized him, his father was a role model, and so forth. But the assertions are neither common knowledge nor the fruits of my research, rather they are the result of the work of White and Maze, as I make explicit in the second version. When I wrote the original sentence, I sought a clear construction that fore-grounded the argument I was making about Ickes's pro-Loyalist activism; it was never my intention to plagiarize, yet I am guilty nonetheless.

Footnotes

10. Justus D. Doenecke, *Storm on the Horizon: The Challenge to American Intervention, 1939–1941* (Lanham, MD: Rowman & Littlefield

---

1. For a psychological profile of Ickes's upbringing, see Graham White and John Maze, *Harold Ickes of the New Deal: His Private Life and Public Career* (Cambridge, MA: Harvard University Press, 1985), pp. 12–15, 25.

12. F. Melder to the editor, *Catholic Worker*, 6:4 (September 1938), p. 5.

13. Doenecke, *Storm on the Horizon*, p. 174.

14. Ibid., p. 180.

15. Dorothea Liebmann Straus, telephone interview by author, 7 October 2005, digital recording and transcription, 25 min., author's collection.

16. Report of confidential informant Harold Neff, 6 May 1943, Federal Bureau of Investigation, file 65-1461, National Archives, College Park, MD, 10:420, emphasis in the original.

17. Charles E. Coughlin, "The Declaration of Independence," Sunday, 10 March 1935, in *A Series of Addresses on Social Justice, as Broadcast by Rev. Charles E. Coughlin Over a National Network, March 1935* (Royal Oak, MI: Radio League of the Little Flower, 1935), pp. 207–18.

18. Radiogram of 18 November, and memorandum from Howe to the mayor of 22 November 1938, in Mayor Fiorello La Guardia Papers, Municipal Archives of New York City, reel 530, documents 1376–80 (hereafter cited as 530:1376–80).

在此一系列典型脚注中，注意东安尼克所著书籍被第二次提及时的简化形式和在直接在此提之后的同上标示。引用的原文中包含何种强调形式（斜线或下画线）的时候，我都会在脚注中陈述出来；这确保了引用的清晰和连贯，因为有时我会在正文中去掉原文的强调形式。当偶尔需要在引文中增加强调形式时，你必须要在脚注中进行标示（"强调增加"或"强调是我的"），就像你需要陈述去掉强调形式一样。

复合脚注

存在一些材料汇编，特别是来源于前白宫时代的，强调罗斯福对于外交事务所持的态度。研究罗斯福政策制定的史学研究者经常提及他对旧世界的反感。"罗斯福对法国的态度"，托马斯·弗莱明评论说："几乎跟他对德国的态度一样消极的——并敌视的。"弗莱德里克·W.马克观察到他"对任何欧洲大国怀着些微的钦佩或尊敬"。约翰·来伯顿·哈珀强调罗斯福对欧洲的倒退和道德堕落的反感，这种与旧世界的"堕落"保持"距离"的态度被哈珀称之为"反欧洲半球主义"。可能因为罗斯福从未走访过伊比利亚半岛，史学研究者不评论过他对于堕落西班牙的认知印象或"精

Publishers, 2003), pp. 170–71.

11. *Congressional Record, House Journal,* 75th Cong., 1st sess., 6 January 1937, p. 99.

12. F. Melder to the editor, *Catholic Worker,* 6:4 (September 1938), p. 5.

13. Doenecke, *Storm on the Horizon,* p. 174.

14. Ibid., p. 180.

15. Dorothea Liebmann Straus, telephone interview by author, 7 October 2005, digital recording and transcription, 25 min., author's collection.

16. Report of confidential informant Harold Neff, 6 May 1943, Federal Bureau of Investigation, file 65-1461, National Archives, College Park, MD, 10:420, emphasis in the original.

17. Charles E. Coughlin, "The Declaration of Independence," Sunday, 10 March 1935, in *A Series of Addresses on Social Justice, as Broadcast by Rev. Charles E. Coughlin Over a National Network, March 1935* (Royal Oak, MI: Radio League of the Little Flower, 1935), pp. 207–18.

18. Radiogram of 18 November, and memorandum from Howe to the mayor of 22 November 1938, in Mayor Fiorello La Guardia Papers, Municipal Archives of New York City, reel 530, documents 1376–80 (hereafter cited as 530:1376–80).

In this series of typical footnotes, notice the short form of the Doenecke book at the second mention, and the substitution of ibid. in the note directly following. Whenever a quotation has emphasis (italics or underlining) in the original text, I always state in the footnote that it does so; this ensures clarity and consistency because sometimes I remove the emphasis. In the rare event that you add emphasis to a quotation you must always mention it in the footnote ("emphasis added" or "emphasis mine"), just as you should state when you have removed emphasis.

Compound Footnotes

There is a corpus of material, especially from the pre-White House years, that casts light on Roosevelt's disposition toward foreign affairs. Historians of Roosevelt's policymaking often refer to his dislike of the Old World. "Roosevelt's opinion of the French," comments Thomas Fleming, "was almost as low—and as hostile—as his opinion of the Germans." Frederick W. Marks observes that he "harbored little admiration or respect for any of the European powers." John Lamberton Harper stresses Roosevelt's aversion to the backwardness and moral turpitude of Europe, a "distancing" from Old

神地图"，但间接证据在总体评价中会表明它是负面的。

---

40. Thomas Fleming, *The New Dealers' War: FDR and the War Within World War II* (New York: Basic Books, 2001), p. 310; Frederick W. Marks III, *Winds Over Sand: The Diplomacy of Franklin Roosevelt* (Athens: University of Georgia Press, 1988), p. 124; John Lamberton Harper, *American Visions of Europe: Franklin D. Roosevelt, George F. Kennan, and Dean G. Acheson* (New York: Cambridge University Press, 1994), pp. 12–18, "distancing," p. 19, "decadence," p. 26, "Europhobic-hemispherism," p. 60. See Alan K. Henrikson, "The Geographical 'Mental Maps' of American Foreign Policy Makers," *International Political Science Review*, 1:3 (October 1980), pp. 495–530.

许多期刊和书籍出版商要求复合脚注，这意味着你需要把每一段落中的注释合并起来，以分号隔开，在段末形成一个单独的脚注。在本示例中，对于弗莱明和马克著书的引用标注是直截了当的，而且我可以简单地将哈珀著书的引用标注成pp. 19、26、60的形式。但是我需要引用在哈珀著书的引用中探讨罗斯福对于倒退的反感的页数，而且还要指明哪个引用在哪一页，故而才在脚注中包含了带有引号的单词。这样一来，这个脚注就已经含有76个单词，而且因为海里克森著书有关精神地图的引用区别于其他引用，属于一个单独的、方法论的领域，所以我决定将此引用单独成句。

参考文献示例

档案馆馆藏和未出版的文献

American Legion. National Convention Proceedings. American Legion Library, Indianapolis.

Cárdenas, Juan F. de. Correspondence. *America* Magazine Archive. Lauinger Library Special Collections, Georgetown University, Washington, DC.

Forbes, William Cameron. Papers [WCFP]. Houghton Library, Harvard College, Cambridge, MA.

———. "Journal of W. Cameron Forbes" [WCFP-J]. Series I, 5 vols.; series

World "decadence" that Harper terms "Europhobic-hemispherism." Perhaps because Roosevelt never visited the Iberian Peninsula, historians pass no comment on his cognitive image or "mental map" of decadent Spain, but circumstantial evidence when taken in sum indicates that it was negative.[40]

40. Thomas Fleming, *The New Dealers' War: FDR and the War Within World War II* (New York: Basic Books, 2001), p. 310; Frederick W. Marks III, *Winds Over Sand: The Diplomacy of Franklin Roosevelt* (Athens: University of Georgia Press, 1988), p. 124; John Lamberton Harper, *American Visions of Europe: Franklin D. Roosevelt, George F. Kennan, and Dean G. Acheson* (New York: Cambridge University Press, 1994), pp. 12–18, "distancing," p. 19, "decadence," p. 26, "Europhobic-hemispherism," p. 60. See Alan K. Henrikson, "The Geographical 'Mental Maps' of American Foreign Policy Makers," *International Political Science Review*, 1:3 (October 1980), pp. 495–530.

Many journal and book publishers require compound footnotes, meaning that you will need to combine the notes for each paragraph, separated by a semicolon, into a single footnote at the paragraph's end. In this example, the references for the Fleming and Marks books were straightforward, and I could have simply provided the Harper page references in the form, pp. 19, 26, 60. But I needed to cite the pages in Harper's study that discuss Roosevelt's aversion to backwardness, as well as make clear which quote was on which page, hence the inclusion in the footnote of the words in quotation marks. Because the footnote was already seventy-six words long at that point, and with Henrikson's work on mental mapping falling into a separate, methodological category from the other references, I decided to break into a new sentence.

Sample Bibliography

BIBLIOGRAPHY

Archival Sources and Unpublished Documents

American Legion. National Convention Proceedings. American Legion Library, Indianapolis.

Cárdenas, Juan F. de. Correspondence. *America* Magazine Archive. Lauinger Library Special Collections, Georgetown University, Washington, DC.

Forbes, William Cameron. Papers [WCFP]. Houghton Library, Harvard College, Cambridge, MA.

———. "Journal of W. Cameron Forbes" [WCFP-J]. Series I, 5 vols.; series

II, 5 vols. Compiled ca. 1946. Houghton Library, Harvard College, Cambridge, MA.

Harmon, Louise Benedict. Diaries, 1935–39. Private collection of Louise Meière Dunn, Stamford, CT.

Hart, Merwin K. Papers [MKHP]. Knight Library Special Collections, University of Oregon, Eugene.

———. Correspondence. *America* Magazine Archive. Lauinger Library Special Collections, Georgetown University.

Kelly, John Eoghan. Federal Bureau of Investigation, file 65-1461. National Archives, College Park, MD. Sections 1–11, serials 1–495.

La Guardia, Fiorello. Papers. Municipal Archives of New York City, New York.

Meière, Hildreth. Papers [HMP]. Archives of American Art, Smithsonian Institution, New York.

———. Untitled memoir, "Spain, August 1938," based on spiral-bound notebooks, "Diary—Spain, [August] 1938." 199 pp. (186 pp. plus pp. 24a–24m). In Hildreth Meière Papers.

Moffat, J. Pierrepont. Diary. Houghton Library, Harvard College, Cambridge, MA.

O'Reilly, Leonora. Papers. Microfilm edition of Papers of the Women's Trade Union League and Its Principal Leaders. Schlesinger Library, Radcliffe College, Cambridge, MA.

Roosevelt, Franklin D. Papers pertaining to family, business, and personal affairs, 1882–1945. Franklin D. Roosevelt Library, Hyde Park.

———. Papers as President, President's Secretary's File, 1933–45 [FDR-SF]. Franklin D. Roosevelt Library.

State Department. General Records, Central Decimal File, 1930–39, Record Group 59 [SD-CDF]. National Archives, College Park, MD.

Winchell, Walter. Federal Bureau of Investigation, file 62-31615. Available online, at http://foia.fbi.gov/foiaindex/winchell.htm.

已出版的文献

American Direct Investments in Foreign Countries–1936. Paul D. Dickens, ed. U.S. Department of Commerce, Bureau of Foreign and Domestic Commerce. Washington, D.C.: U.S. Government Printing Office (GPO), 1938.

Atheistic Communism (Divini Redemptoris): Encyclical Letter of His Holiness Pope Pius XI. New York: Paulist Press, 1937.

Confidential U.S. State Department Central Files: Spain; Foreign Affairs & Political, 1930–1939. Bethesda, MD: University Publications of

II, 5 vols. Compiled ca. 1946. Houghton Library, Harvard College, Cambridge, MA.

Harmon, Louise Benedict. Diaries, 1935–39. Private collection of Louise Meière Dunn, Stamford, CT.

Hart, Merwin K. Papers [MKHP]. Knight Library Special Collections, University of Oregon, Eugene.

———. Correspondence. *America* Magazine Archive. Lauinger Library Special Collections, Georgetown University.

Kelly, John Eoghan. Federal Bureau of Investigation, file 65-1461. National Archives, College Park, MD. Sections 1–11, serials 1–495.

La Guardia, Fiorello. Papers. Municipal Archives of New York City, New York.

Meière, Hildreth. Papers [HMP]. Archives of American Art, Smithsonian Institution, New York.

———. Untitled memoir, "Spain, August 1938," based on spiral-bound notebooks, "Diary—Spain, [August] 1938." 199 pp. (186 pp. plus pp. 24a–24m). In Hildreth Meière Papers.

Moffat, J. Pierrepont. Diary. Houghton Library, Harvard College, Cambridge, MA.

O'Reilly, Leonora. Papers. Microfilm edition of Papers of the Women's Trade Union League and Its Principal Leaders. Schlesinger Library, Radcliffe College, Cambridge, MA.

Roosevelt, Franklin D. Papers pertaining to family, business, and personal affairs, 1882–1945. Franklin D. Roosevelt Library, Hyde Park.

———. Papers as President, President's Secretary's File, 1933–45 [FDR-SF]. Franklin D. Roosevelt Library.

State Department. General Records, Central Decimal File, 1930–39, Record Group 59 [SD-CDF]. National Archives, College Park, MD.

Winchell, Walter. Federal Bureau of Investigation, file 62-31615. Available online, at http://foia.fbi.gov/foiaindex/winchell.htm.

Published Documents

American Direct Investments in Foreign Countries–1936. Paul D. Dickens, ed. U.S. Department of Commerce, Bureau of Foreign and Domestic Commerce. Washington, D.C.: U.S. Government Printing Office (GPO), 1938.

Atheistic Communism (Divini Redemptoris): Encyclical Letter of His Holiness Pope Pius XI. New York: Paulist Press, 1937.

Confidential U.S. State Department Central Files: Spain; Foreign Affairs & Political, 1930–1939. Bethesda, MD: University Publications of

America. Microfilm.

Congressional Record: Proceedings and Debates of the Third Session of the Seventy-fifth Congress of the United States of America. Vol. 83, pt. 6. Washington, D.C.: U.S. GPO, 1938.

Documents diplomatiques français, 1932–1939 [Diplomatic documents of France, 1932–39]. Series 2 (1936–39), 19 vols. Paris: Imprimerie nationale, 1974.

Documents on American Foreign Relations, January 1938–June 1939. S. Shepard Jones and Denys P. Myers, eds. Boston: World Peace Foundation, 1939.

FDR's Fireside Chats. Russell D. Buhite and David W. Levy, eds. Norman: University of Oklahoma Press, 1992.

Franklin D. Roosevelt and Foreign Affairs [FDR-FA]. Edgar B. Nixon, ed. First series. Vols. I–III. Cambridge, MA: Belknap Press, 1969.

Gallup, George H. *The Gallup Poll: Public Opinion, 1935–1971.* New York: Random House, 1972.

Germany and the Spanish Civil War, 1936–1939. Vol. 3 of *Documents on German Foreign Policy, 1918–1945: From the Archives of the German Foreign Ministry: Series D (1937–1945).* Washington, D.C.: U.S. GPO, 1950.

Investigation of Un-American Activities and Propaganda Activities in the United States: Report of the Special Committee on Un-American Activities. 4 vols., I, II. Washington, D.C.: U.S. GPO, 1938–39.

The Papers of Thomas Jefferson. Barbara B. Oberg, ed. Vol. 32. Princeton: Princeton University Press, 2005.

Proceedings of the 20th National Convention of The American Legion, Los Angeles, CA, 19–22 September 1938. 76th Cong., 1st sess., House Document no. 40, 53.

Public Papers and Addresses of Franklin D. Roosevelt: With a Special Introduction and Explanatory Notes by President Roosevelt. 1938 Volume: The Continuing Struggle for Liberalism. New York: Macmillan Company, 1941.

United States Foreign Policy (supplement). *The Reference Shelf,* 13:6. New York: H.W. Wilson Company, 1939.

日报

Periodicals are for the period of this study, unless otherwise stated.

Chicago Daily Tribune.

Jersey Journal (Jersey City, NJ). 1937–38.

America. Microfilm.

Congressional Record: Proceedings and Debates of the Third Session of the Seventy-fifth Congress of the United States of America. Vol. 83, pt. 6. Washington, D.C.: U.S. GPO, 1938.

Documents diplomatiques français, 1932–1939 [Diplomatic documents of France, 1932–39]. Series 2 (1936–39), 19 vols. Paris: Imprimerie nationale, 1974.

Documents on American Foreign Relations, January 1938–June 1939. S. Shepard Jones and Denys P. Myers, eds. Boston: World Peace Foundation, 1939.

FDR's Fireside Chats. Russell D. Buhite and David W. Levy, eds. Norman: University of Oklahoma Press, 1992.

Franklin D. Roosevelt and Foreign Affairs [FDR-FA]. Edgar B. Nixon, ed. First series. Vols. I–III. Cambridge, MA: Belknap Press, 1969.

Gallup, George H. *The Gallup Poll: Public Opinion, 1935–1971.* New York: Random House, 1972.

Germany and the Spanish Civil War, 1936–1939. Vol. 3 of *Documents on German Foreign Policy, 1918–1945: From the Archives of the German Foreign Ministry: Series D (1937–1945)*. Washington, D.C.: U.S. GPO, 1950.

Investigation of Un-American Activities and Propaganda Activities in the United States: Report of the Special Committee on Un-American Activities. 4 vols., I, II. Washington, D.C.: U.S. GPO, 1938–39.

The Papers of Thomas Jefferson. Barbara B. Oberg, ed. Vol. 32. Princeton: Princeton University Press, 2005.

Proceedings of the 20th National Convention of The American Legion, Los Angeles, CA, 19–22 September 1938. 76th Cong., 1st sess., House Document no. 40, 53.

Public Papers and Addresses of Franklin D. Roosevelt: With a Special Introduction and Explanatory Notes by President Roosevelt. 1938 Volume: The Continuing Struggle for Liberalism. New York: Macmillan Company, 1941.

United States Foreign Policy (supplement). *The Reference Shelf,* 13:6. New York: H.W. Wilson Company, 1939.

Daily Newspapers

Periodicals are for the period of this study, unless otherwise stated.

Chicago Daily Tribune.

Jersey Journal (Jersey City, NJ). 1937–38.

New York Times [*NYT*].
Philadelphia Inquirer. 1938–39.
PM (New York). Ralph Ingersoll, ed. June 1940–43.

周报和周刊

America: The National Catholic Weekly. Francis X. Talbot, SJ, ed.
Brooklyn Tablet (Brooklyn, NY). Patrick F. Scanlan, ed. Published every Saturday by the Tablet Publishing Company.
The Hour (New York). American Council Against Nazi Propaganda. Albert E. Kahn, ed. 30 April 1939–20 May 1943.
Ken (Chicago). Arnold Gingrich, ed. Biweekly. April 1938–March 1939.
New Masses (New York). Max Eastman, ed. 1936–37.
News of Spain (New York). Spanish Information Bureau. Biweekly. February 1938–February 1939.
Time: The Weekly Newsmagazine. November 1936–39.
Weekly Foreign Letter (New York). Lawrence Dennis, ed. June 1938–July 1942.

月刊

Catholic Action: A National Monthly (Washington, D.C.). National Catholic Welfare Conference.
Protestant Digest (New York). K. Leslie, ed. Monthly to May 1940, then bimonthly. December 1938–September 1941.
The Sign (Union City, NJ). "A National Catholic Magazine." Rev. Theophane Maquire, ed. 1936–41.
Spain: A Monthly Publication of Spanish Events (New York). Joseph M. Bayo, ed. Peninsular News Service. October 1937–January 1942.

电影

Blockade. Directed by William Dieterle. Starring: Madeleine Carroll and Henry Fonda. Producer: Walter Wanger. Script: John Howard Lawson. United Artists, 1938. DVD, 84 min. Chatsworth, CA: Image Entertainment, 1987.
"My Tour of Nationalist Spain, August 1938, by Hildreth Meière." Hildreth Meière. 16mm, 3 reels, Archives of American Art, Smithsonian Institution, New York. DVD, 33 min. Author's collection.

访谈

Dunn, Louise Meière. Interview by author, 29 October 2005. Stamford, CT. Digital recording and transcription. 120 min. Author's collection.

New York Times [*NYT*].
Philadelphia Inquirer. 1938–39.
PM (New York). Ralph Ingersoll, ed. June 1940–43.

Weekly Newspapers and Magazines
America: The National Catholic Weekly. Francis X. Talbot, SJ, ed.
Brooklyn Tablet (Brooklyn, NY). Patrick F. Scanlan, ed. Published every Saturday by the Tablet Publishing Company.
The Hour (New York). American Council Against Nazi Propaganda. Albert E. Kahn, ed. 30 April 1939–20 May 1943.
Ken (Chicago). Arnold Gingrich, ed. Biweekly. April 1938–March 1939.
New Masses (New York). Max Eastman, ed. 1936–37.
News of Spain (New York). Spanish Information Bureau. Biweekly. February 1938–February 1939.
Time: The Weekly Newsmagazine. November 1936–39.
Weekly Foreign Letter (New York). Lawrence Dennis, ed. June 1938–July 1942.

Monthly Magazines and Journals
Catholic Action: A National Monthly (Washington, D.C.). National Catholic Welfare Conference.
Protestant Digest (New York). K. Leslie, ed. Monthly to May 1940, then bimonthly. December 1938–September 1941.
The Sign (Union City, NJ). "A National Catholic Magazine." Rev. Theophane Maquire, ed. 1936–41.
Spain: A Monthly Publication of Spanish Events (New York). Joseph M. Bayo, ed. Peninsular News Service. October 1937–January 1942.

Films
Blockade. Directed by William Dieterle. Starring: Madeleine Carroll and Henry Fonda. Producer: Walter Wanger. Script: John Howard Lawson. United Artists, 1938. DVD, 84 min. Chatsworth, CA: Image Entertainment, 1987.
"My Tour of Nationalist Spain, August 1938, by Hildreth Meière." Hildreth Meière. 16mm, 3 reels, Archives of American Art, Smithsonian Institution, New York. DVD, 33 min. Author's collection.

Interviews
Dunn, Louise Meière. Interview by author, 29 October 2005. Stamford, CT. Digital recording and transcription. 120 min. Author's collection.

Sedgwick Jr., Ellery. Telephone interview by author, 10 May 2004. Longwood University, Farmville, VA.

回忆录、日记和当代作品

Acheson, Dean G. *Present at the Creation: My Years in the State Department.* New York: W.W. Norton & Company, 1969.

[Adams, John.] *Diary and Autobiography of John Adams.* L.H. Butterfield, ed. Vol. II. Cambridge: Belknap Press, 1962.

Browder, Earl. "The American Communist Party in the Thirties." In *As We Saw the Thirties: Essays on Social and Political Movements of a Decade.* Rita James Simon, ed. Urbana: University of Illinois Press, 1967.

Carlson, John Roy [(Arthur) Avedis Derounian]. *Under Cover: My Four Years in the Nazi Underworld of America—The Amazing Revelation of How Axis Agents and Our Enemies Within Are Now Plotting to Destroy the United States.* New York: E.P. Dutton & Company, 1943.

———. *The Plotters.* New York: E.P. Dutton & Company, 1946.

Dalton, Joseph Patrick. "Is Christian Corporatism Compatible with Democracy?" Master's thesis, Boston College, Chestnut Hill, MA, 1942.

Eberle, George T. "Portugal's Progress." WNAC radio address, 29 May 1938. *Catholic Mind*, 36:854 (22 July 1938), pp. 282–87.

Gomá y Tomás, Cardinal Isidro. *Por Dios y por España: Pastorales–Instrucciones pastorales y Artículos–Discursos–Mensajes–Apéndice, 1936–1939* [For God and for Spain: Collected pastoral letters, articles, sermons, and radio addresses, 1936–39]. Barcelona: R. Casulleras, Librero-Editor, 1940.

González Palencia, Angel. *The Flame of Hispanicism.* Lecture given at Stanford University, July 1938. New York: Peninsular News Service, 1938. Pamphlet, 14 pp.

Hart, Merwin Kimball. "America—Look at Spain: The Agony will be Repeated Here." Speech; broadcast from Málaga, 29 September 1938. Printed in *Spain*, 3:1 (15 October 1938), 5, 7, 20, and in *Vital Speeches of the Day*, 5:2 (1 November 1938), pp. 57–58.

Ickes, Harold L. *The Inside Struggle, 1936–1939.* Vol. 2 of *The Secret Diary of Harold L. Ickes.* New York: Simon and Schuster, 1954.

[Johnson, Hiram.] *The Diary Letters of Hiram Johnson, 1917–1945.* Robert E. Burke, ed. 7 vols. New York: Garland Publishing, 1983.

A Little Book for Immigrants in Boston. Boston: Committee for Americanism of the City of Boston, 1921.

St.-George, Maximilian J., and Lawrence Dennis. *A Trial on Trial: The Great*

Sedgwick Jr., Ellery. Telephone interview by author, 10 May 2004. Longwood University, Farmville, VA.

Memoirs, Diaries, Contemporary Works

Acheson, Dean G. *Present at the Creation: My Years in the State Department*. New York: W.W. Norton & Company, 1969.

[Adams, John.] *Diary and Autobiography of John Adams*. L.H. Butterfield, ed. Vol. II. Cambridge: Belknap Press, 1962.

Browder, Earl. "The American Communist Party in the Thirties." In *As We Saw the Thirties: Essays on Social and Political Movements of a Decade*. Rita James Simon, ed. Urbana: University of Illinois Press, 1967.

Carlson, John Roy [(Arthur) Avedis Derounian]. *Under Cover: My Four Years in the Nazi Underworld of America—The Amazing Revelation of How Axis Agents and Our Enemies Within Are Now Plotting to Destroy the United States*. New York: E.P. Dutton & Company, 1943.

———. *The Plotters*. New York: E.P. Dutton & Company, 1946.

Dalton, Joseph Patrick. "Is Christian Corporatism Compatible with Democracy?" Master's thesis, Boston College, Chestnut Hill, MA, 1942.

Eberle, George T. "Portugal's Progress." WNAC radio address, 29 May 1938. *Catholic Mind*, 36:854 (22 July 1938), pp. 282–87.

Gomá y Tomás, Cardinal Isidro. *Por Dios y por España: Pastorales–Instrucciones pastorales y Artículos–Discursos–Mensajes–Apéndice, 1936–1939* [For God and for Spain: Collected pastoral letters, articles, sermons, and radio addresses, 1936–39]. Barcelona: R. Casulleras, Librero-Editor, 1940.

González Palencia, Angel. *The Flame of Hispanicism*. Lecture given at Stanford University, July 1938. New York: Peninsular News Service, 1938. Pamphlet, 14 pp.

Hart, Merwin Kimball. "America—Look at Spain: The Agony will be Repeated Here." Speech; broadcast from Málaga, 29 September 1938. Printed in *Spain*, 3:1 (15 October 1938), 5, 7, 20, and in *Vital Speeches of the Day*, 5:2 (1 November 1938), pp. 57–58.

Ickes, Harold L. *The Inside Struggle, 1936–1939*. Vol. 2 of *The Secret Diary of Harold L. Ickes*. New York: Simon and Schuster, 1954.

[Johnson, Hiram.] *The Diary Letters of Hiram Johnson, 1917–1945*. Robert E. Burke, ed. 7 vols. New York: Garland Publishing, 1983.

A Little Book for Immigrants in Boston. Boston: Committee for mericanism of the City of Boston, 1921.

St.-George, Maximilian J., and Lawrence Dennis. *A Trial on Trial: The Great*

Sedition Trial of 1944. N.p: National Civil Rights Committee, 1945.

Writers Take Sides: Letters About the War in Spain, from 418 American Authors. New York: League of American Writers, 1938.

（出版物、期刊文章和学位论文）

ABC Blue Book, Publisher's Statements: Newspapers. Chicago: The Bureau, 1945.

Alpers, Benjamin L. *Dictators, Democracy, and American Public Culture: Envisioning the Totalitarian Enemy, 1920s–1950s.* Chapel Hill: University of North Carolina Press, 2003.

American Law Reports: Federal, Cases and Annotations. Vol. 67. Rochester, NY: Lawyers Co-Operative Publishing, 1984, pp. 774–96.

Balfour, Sebastian. "Spain from 1931 to the Present." In *Spain: A History.* Raymond Carr, ed. Oxford: Oxford University Press, 2000.

Brooks, Frank. "Egoist Theory and America's Individualist Anarchists: A Dilemma of Praxis." *History of Political Thought,* 15:3 (Autumn 1994), pp. 403–22.

Costello, Brian C. "The Voice of Government as an Abridgement of First Amendment Rights of Speakers: Rethinking *Meese v. Keene.*" *Duke Law Journal* (1989), pp. 654–58.

Costigliola, Frank. "Broken Circle: The Isolation of Franklin D. Roosevelt in World War II." *Diplomatic History,* 32:5 (November 2008), pp. 677–718.

Davis, Richard Akin. "Radio Priest: The Public Career of Father Charles Edward Coughlin." PhD diss., University of North Carolina, Chapel Hill, 1974.

Haber, William Haber. *Industrial Relations in the Building Industry.* 1930; repr., New York: Arno Press, 1971.

Lojendio, Luis María de. *Operaciones militares de la guerra de España, 1936–1939* [Military operations during the Spanish Civil War, 1936–39]. Barcelona: Montaner y Simon, 1940.

Martin, John. "In the Beginnings of 'Pacific Service': Early Stages of Hydro-Electric Development in North-Central California." *Pacific Service Magazine,* part I, 13:7 (December 1921), pp. 205–15, part II, 13:8 (January 1922), pp. 244–50.

McCarthy, Edward C. "The Christian Front Movement in New York City, 1938–1940." Master's thesis, Columbia University, 1965.

Moynihan, Daniel Patrick. *"Catholic Tradition and Social Change,"* Second Annual Seton-Neumann Lecture, May 7, 1984, Rayburn House. N.p.: United States Catholic Conference, 1984.

Sedition Trial of 1944. N.p: National Civil Rights Committee, 1945.
Writers Take Sides: Letters About the War in Spain, from 418 American Authors. New York: League of American Writers, 1938.

Published Works, Journal Articles, and Dissertations

ABC Blue Book, Publisher's Statements: Newspapers. Chicago: The Bureau, 1945.

Alpers, Benjamin L. *Dictators, Democracy, and American Public Culture: Envisioning the Totalitarian Enemy, 1920s–1950s.* Chapel Hill: University of North Carolina Press, 2003.

American Law Reports: Federal, Cases and Annotations. Vol. 67. Rochester, NY: Lawyers Co-Operative Publishing, 1984, pp. 774–96.

Balfour, Sebastian. "Spain from 1931 to the Present." In *Spain: A History.* Raymond Carr, ed. Oxford: Oxford University Press, 2000.

Brooks, Frank. "Egoist Theory and America's Individualist Anarchists: A Dilemma of Praxis." *History of Political Thought*, 15:3 (Autumn 1994), pp. 403–22.

Costello, Brian C. "The Voice of Government as an Abridgement of First Amendment Rights of Speakers: Rethinking *Meese v. Keene.*" *Duke Law Journal* (1989), pp. 654–58.

Costigliola, Frank. "Broken Circle: The Isolation of Franklin D. Roosevelt in World War II." *Diplomatic History*, 32:5 (November 2008), pp. 677–718.

Davis, Richard Akin. "Radio Priest: The Public Career of Father Charles Edward Coughlin." PhD diss., University of North Carolina, Chapel Hill, 1974.

Haber, William Haber. *Industrial Relations in the Building Industry.* 1930; repr., New York: Arno Press, 1971.

Lojendio, Luis María de. *Operaciones militares de la guerra de España, 1936–1939* [Military operations during the Spanish Civil War, 1936–39]. Barcelona: Montaner y Simon, 1940.

Martin, John. "In the Beginnings of 'Pacific Service': Early Stages of Hydro-Electric Development in North-Central California." *Pacific Service Magazine*, part I, 13:7 (December 1921), pp. 205–15, part II, 13:8 (January 1922), pp. 244–50.

McCarthy, Edward C. "The Christian Front Movement in New York City, 1938–1940." Master's thesis, Columbia University, 1965.

Moynihan, Daniel Patrick. *"Catholic Tradition and Social Change,"* Second Annual Seton-Neumann Lecture, May 7, 1984, Rayburn House. N.p.: United States Catholic Conference, 1984.

Payne, Stanley G. *Fascism in Spain, 1923–1977.* Madison: University of Wisconsin Press, 1999.

———. *The Spanish Civil War, The Soviet Union, and Communism.* New Haven: Yale University Press, 2004.

Sandeen, Eric J. "*Confessions of a Nazi Spy* and the German-American Bund." *American Studies,* 20:2 (Fall 1979), pp. 69–81.

Singleton, M.K. *H.L. Mencken and the* American Mercury *Adventure.* Durham, NC: Duke University Press, 1962.

Sterne, Evelyn Savidge. "Beyond the Boss: Immigration and American Political Culture from 1880 to 1940." In *E Pluribus Unum? Contemporary and Historical Perspectives on Immigrant Political Incorporation.* Gary Gerstle and John Mollenkopf, eds. New York: Russell Sage Foundation, 2001.

Wang Hongbin 王鴻賓, ed. *Zhang Zuolin he Fengxi junfa*《張作霖和奉系軍閥》[Zhang Zuolin and the Fengtian warlords]. N.p.: Hunan renmin chubanshe, 1989.

Zhao Xijun. "'Bu zhan er quren zhi bing' yu xiandai weishe zhanlue" ["Victory without war" and modern deterrence strategy]. *Zhongguo Junshi Kexue* [Chinese Military Science], 5 (2001).

———

副标题会按照每个项目不同而不同，尽管一般会按照出版、未出版第一手来源和第二手来源这三个范畴分开。以出版日期升序列出有同一个作者的两个以上作品。把标题的译文用罗马字体放在方括号，这是因为斜体字需要标注已出版的真实的、可搜到的标题（一个翻译过的标题就不可能搜到原文），就像最后几个例子所表示，存在着两个不同的格式，包括或不包括原来的字母。我倾向于把州名采用邮政缩写词；在州名属于出版社的名称时就没有必要单独提供，例如"北卡罗来纳出版社"。

Payne, Stanley G. *Fascism in Spain, 1923–1977.* Madison: University of Wisconsin Press, 1999.

———. *The Spanish Civil War, The Soviet Union, and Communism.* New Haven: Yale University Press, 2004.

Sandeen, Eric J. "*Confessions of a Nazi Spy* and the German-American Bund." *American Studies*, 20:2 (Fall 1979), pp. 69–81.

Singleton, M.K. *H.L. Mencken and the* American Mercury *Adventure.* Durham, NC: Duke University Press, 1962.

Sterne, Evelyn Savidge. "Beyond the Boss: Immigration and American Political Culture from 1880 to 1940." In *E Pluribus Unum? Contemporary and Historical Perspectives on Immigrant Political Incorporation.* Gary Gerstle and John Mollenkopf, eds. New York: Russell Sage Foundation, 2001.

Wang Hongbin 王鴻賓, ed. *Zhang Zuolin he Fengxi junfa*《張作霖和奉系軍閥》[Zhang Zuolin and the Fengtian warlords]. N.p.: Hunan renmin chubanshe, 1989.

Zhao Xijun. "'Bu zhan er quren zhi bing' yu xiandai weishe zhanlue" ["Victory without war" and modern deterrence strategy]. *Zhongguo Junshi Kexue* [Chinese Military Science], 5 (2001).

Subheads will vary according to the project, although there will usually be three main groupings for unpublished and published primary sources, and secondary sources. List two or more works by the same author in ascending order of publication. Set translations of titles inside square brackets and use roman; this is because italicization specifies the actual, text-searchable title of the publication (a given translation may not even be literal); as the last examples show, there are two styles, with or without the original characters. I prefer abbreviated postal acronyms for states; there is no need to give states when the state is part of the publisher's name (University of North Carolina Press).

中文的引用和引证

由于英式英语和美式英语标点格式和引证方法的应用和修改,以及各种标准,包括中国内地和不少顶尖学术出版社所处的中国香港因地域差异导致标点使用的差别,业已造成学者们写作时在标点应用上的混淆以及出版学术作品的不一致性。甚至出版于同一出版社的作品都往往存在着格式上的差异。源于香港的一个趋势值得我们关注,即在人文学科的写作中越来越倾向于采用国际美式标准,以求其简单化和平行化,即现今已发行到第十六版的《芝加哥论文格式手册》所倡导的格式系统。追随该动向,并考虑到中国的学术论文作者提交给国际期刊论文数量的与日俱增,我所推荐的中文书写、引用和引证的格式正是以英语写作为参照物的,或者在此种意义上来说,是以其他罗马系语言为参照物的。而且,当出现格式混淆问题时,我建议把《芝加哥论文格式手册》作为寻找答案的切实依据。我在下方总结了常用的标点疑难解决方案。

- 结束性的逗号和句号总要置于引号中,无论它们是否属于原文。
- 所有出版物名称,包括影片和期刊名称,皆置于书名号中;书名号部分以英语出版时会以斜体字方式出现。
- 省略号存在六个隔点。例如"我来了……我征服了"。位于句子结尾的省略号的标注方式为"……"。可以在MS-Word文档中用热键插入这个符号,按住Alt键,在数码键盘上输入"0133",然后放开Alt键。
- 若同一脚注中同时出现汉字和拉丁字母,在对汉字和其相关标点的编辑时使用标准中文字体——宋体/仿宋10号字——而对拉丁字母和出现的拉丁符号的编辑时使用Times New Roman 10号字,则显得至关重要,因为使用等宽宋体字会破坏拉丁字符的比例间距。为在编辑的时候提高精确度,可以放大脚注字号。
- 需要使用方括号标示出版作品的引文或译文中的添加内容时,使用等宽宋体方括号如"［托架］"比起使用黑体方括号"【托架】"在视觉上会显得轻灵许多。
- 破折号是由两个等宽对开破折号——构成的。输入时可以使用热键插入Alt+0151。
- 对开破折号是由稍短些的宋体字符显示出来的:1914—1918年。输入时可使用热键插入,方法是首先输入"2015",再按下Alt+x键。

QUOTING AND CITING IN CHINESE

Adoption from and adaptation of British- and American-English styles of punctuation and methods of citing sources, as well as different standards, including variations between mainland China and Hong Kong, the home of several leading academic presses, has created confusion among scholars and inconsistency in published academic work. Even recent works from the same press frequently exhibit stylistic discrepancies. As is most noticeable in Hong Kong, the trend is toward simplification and parallelism with the de facto American standard for writing in the humanities, the system advocated by the *Chicago Manual of Style*, now in its sixteenth edition. Following this trend, and cognizant of the rising numbers of Chinese theses writers who are submitting their work to international journals, the style I recommend here for writing, quoting, and citing in Chinese mirrors that for English, or the other romance languages for that matter. And when questions of style arise, I suggest that *Chicago* is a practical source of answers. I summarize, below, the most common difficulties.

- ending commas and closing periods always go inside the quotation marks, regardless of their presence or absence in the original text.
- titles of all published works, including films and the titles of journals, go inside double angle brackets; the brackets denote that were the title published in English it would be italicized.
- an ellipse has six dots. "我来了……我征服了。" Treat an ellipse at the end of a sentence like this: "……。" To insert this character in MS-Word with hot keys, hold down <Alt>, type 0133 on the numeric keypad, and release the <Alt> key.
- when mixing Chinese and Latin characters in the same footnote, it is critically important to use the standard Chinese font—Songti/SimSun 10-point—for the Chinese characters and related punctuation but switch to Times New Roman 10-point for the Latin characters and, where applicable, the Latin punctuation; using a monospaced Songti font will throw off Latin's proportional spacing. For added precision when editing, zoom in to increase the size of the footnote.
- when brackets are required, as when enclosing additions to quotations or translations of published works, the monospaced Songti ［托架］ looks less heavy-handed than the solid 【托架】.
- for an em-dash, use two monospaced —— characters. To insert with hot keys: <Alt> <0151>.
- for an en-dash, use the slightly shorter Songti character: 1914—1918年. To insert with hot keys, first type 2015 then <Alt> <x>.

外文资料的引证

引证外文资料的基本原则如下。每部出版作品皆存在其最初的出版语言。假设所引用书目的最初出版语言是法文。

脚注中：

Pierre Falloux, *L'histoire de la Révolution française* (Paris: Librairie plon, 2005).

书目中：

Falloux, Pierre. *L'histoire de la Révolution française*. Paris: Librairie plon, 2005.

注意：标题的斜体字化显示该引文源于一部出版作品。如果你是以英文撰写论文并希望在其中引用该作品，那么你需要以英语翻译其名称，即在方括号里标示其英文译文，并遵循大写字体、罗马字（非斜体字）的标准规范。

脚注中：

Pierre Falloux, *L'histoire de la Révolution française* [The history of the French Revolution] (Paris: Librairie plon, 2005).

书目中：

Falloux, Pierre. *L'histoire de la Révolution française* [The history of the French Revolution]. Paris: Librairie plon, 2005.

无论是哪两种语言的使用（中文—法文、西班牙文—意大利文、俄文—韩文、阿拉伯文—斯瓦西里文），此逻辑皆适用。在中文论文中引用此书的时候，如下所示。

脚注中：

皮埃尔·发卢，*L'histoire de la Révolution française*［法国大革命的历史］（巴黎：普龙书库，2005年）。

书目中：

皮埃尔·发卢。*L'histoire de la Révolution française*［法国大革命的历史］。巴黎：普龙书库，2005年。

假设王波用中文出版了一本有关法国大革命历史的书籍，则标示如下。

脚注中：

王波，《法国大革命的历史》（北京：和谐出版社，2007年）。

书目中：

王波。《法国大革命的历史》。北京：和谐出版社，2007年。

还有，如果你打算在一篇法文论文中引用此书，可以采取两种做法，前者更适合一部主要内容是有关中国历史的书籍，而后者则适用于主要内容是有关法国历史的书籍。

Citing Foreign Language Sources

Here are the basic principles for citing foreign language sources. Every published work has an original language of publication. Supposing the publication language of the book is French.

In a footnote:

Pierre Falloux, *L'histoire de la Révolution française* (Paris: Librairie plon, 2005).

And in a bibliography:

Falloux, Pierre. *L'histoire de la Révolution française.* Paris: Librairie plon, 2005.

Notice that the title is italicized to show that it is a published work. If you are writing a paper in English and want to cite from this work then you need to show its name in English, which you do inside square brackets, following the standard rules for uppercasing, and in roman (not italics):

In a footnote:

Pierre Falloux, *L'histoire de la Révolution française* [The history of the French Revolution] (Paris: Librairie plon, 2005).

And in a bibliography:

Falloux, Pierre. *L'histoire de la Révolution française* [The history of the French Revolution]. Paris: Librairie plon, 2005.

Whatever language pair you are using (Chinese–French, Spanish–Italian, Russian–Korean, Arabic–Swahili), the same logic applies. To cite this book in a Chinese language paper:

In a footnote:

皮埃尔·发卢, *L'histoire de la Révolution française*［法国大革命的历史］(巴黎：普龙书库，2005年)。

And in a bibliography:

皮埃尔·发卢。*L'histoire de la Révolution française*［法国大革命的历史］。巴黎：普龙书库，2005年。

Supposing Wang Bo had published a history of the French Revolution in Chinese:

In a footnote:

王波，《法国大革命的历史》（北京：和谐出版社，2007年）。

And in a bibliography:

王波。《法国大革命的历史》。北京：和谐出版社，2007年。

And again, if you wanted to cite this book in a French paper then you could use one of two methods, the first being more suitable to a work primarily on Chinese history and the second a work on French history.

中文和拼音，出现在脚注里：

Wang Bo 王波, *Faguo da geming de lishi*《法国大革命的历史》 [L'histoire de la Révolution française] (Beijing: Harmony Press, 2007).

中文和拼音，出现在书目里：

Wang Bo 王波. *Faguo da geming de lishi*《法国大革命的历史》 [L'histoire de la Révolution française]. Beijing: Harmony Press, 2007.

拼音，出现在脚注里：

Wang Bo, *Faguo da geming de lishi* [L'histoire de la Révolution française] (Beijing: Harmony Press, 2007).

拼音，出现在书目里：

Wang Bo. *Faguo da geming de lishi* [L'histoire de la Révolution française]. Beijing: Harmony Press, 2007.

Chinese and pinyin, in a footnote:

Wang Bo 王波, *Faguo da geming de lishi*《法国大革命的历史》[L'histoire de la Révolution française] (Beijing: Harmony Press, 2007).

Chinese and pinyin, in a bibliography:

Wang Bo 王波. *Faguo da geming de lishi*《法国大革命的历史》[L'histoire de la Révolution française]. Beijing: Harmony Press, 2007.

Pinyin, in a footnote:

Wang Bo, *Faguo da geming de lishi* [L'histoire de la Révolution française] (Beijing: Harmony Press, 2007).

Pinyin, in a bibliography:

Wang Bo. *Faguo da geming de lishi* [L'histoire de la Révolution française]. Beijing: Harmony Press, 2007.

如何进行历史研究

尽管本指南探讨的论题大部分能够适用于任何学科,但是历史学确实有其独特的思维方式。历史学是有关时代的变迁,往往更加关注重大历史事件和时代转折。虽然资料确实在历史研究中发挥着作用,但是历史学更是有关文本资料的解读。历史学是一门博大精深的学科——它所包含的研究领域甚至比三十年前地理学家所认为的研究范围还要广泛——包含了对绘画、音乐、思想、疾病,甚至战舰的历史研究,但是历史学研究的最终指向是人,研究人之难免有错的原因。不像数学或者物理学,历史研究很少,甚至根本没有可能得出一个绝对正确的答案,从而引起对经验主义或者客观性问题的探讨,也因此引起如何论证的问题,故而,我欲以对此问题的探讨作为本书的结语。

记得当我给我的中国学生上第一堂有关基于原始资料进行分析书写论文的课程时,当涉及评分标准是根据论点的冲击力和原创性来决定的时候,却遭到学生们的反对。他们认为"我们来到这所大学学习的目的是为了成为优秀的历史学家"。他们说:"假设能够完全正确地研究史实,我们绝对应该得出相同的结论。所以只有那些不同的论点才会得到不好的分数。"这确实是一个难以驳斥的逻辑,它使我想到了当我父亲推荐我读温斯顿·丘吉尔写的第二次世界大战史时曾经说过一句话:"我相信,你会同意它是一本好书,因为丘吉尔阐述了历史事实。"不过我的中国学生无疑会反对丘吉尔在书中所阐述的那些英帝国主义文明扩张的益处。学院派的历史学研究者确实应该追求历史研究的客观性,但是甚至连香格里拉中央档案馆的原始资料中都不包含绝对经验主义的真理。

一个国家的官方历史学研究成果绝大部分通过基础教育渗入本国的公民意识,民间历史学研究者撰写的新教材加深了此循环的全体公民意识。民间历史学研究者和官方历史学家都十分关注建立举国一致的全体公民意识,甚至在他们眼中,譬如只要呈现与爱国主义战争相反的史实就相当于对国家民族的背叛的程度。所以毫无疑问,一国编写的战争史,与其中所有相关的史实,绝对不同于另外一国的战争史。因此在我看来,历史的真实只能遵从于读者的判断,这就是为什么一位优秀的历史学研究者需要论证说服读者的论点,需要"以论证的形式提出论点"。衷心希望你们的论文写作过程一切顺利。而我所最期望的,乃是当你们读透这本指南之后,可以随心所欲地应用之。

DOING HISTORY

While most of the issues stressed in this guide are applicable to any discipline, history does have specific considerations. History is about change over time, and is often concerned with pivotal events and turning points. Although data has its uses, history is primarily involved with the interpretation of textual sources. History is a broad discipline—broader even than geographers considered their vast subject three decades ago—including the history of paintings, music, ideas, diseases, and warships, yet it should ultimately be a study of people and what makes them so fallibly human. Unlike the mathematical and physical sciences, when it comes to *doing history* there is rarely, if ever, only one correct answer, which raises the issue of empiricism or objectivity, and hence argumentation, that I would like to address here in a concluding remark.

When I assign my Chinese students their first analytical essay based on primary source material, with part of the grade dependent on the strength and originality of the argument, there are objections. "We have come to this university to learn how to be good historians," they say, "so providing we study the evidence correctly, we must all reach the same conclusion. Only those who make a different argument deserve a bad grade." It is hard to refute this logic, which reminds me of my father's recommendation to read Winston Churchill's history of World War II: "I'm sure you'll agree it's a thoroughly good job because Churchill presents the facts." Yet my Chinese students would no doubt disagree with the historical facts Churchill presented to support his argument for the civilizing benefits of British imperialism. Academic historians, for sure, should strive for objectivity, but not even in the state archives of Shangri-la did primary source texts embody empirical truth.

A nation-state's official history reaches its citizens in large part through their primary school education, becoming received wisdom that reinforces the cycle when citizen historians write new textbooks. Citizens and officials alike have such vested interests in establishing a national consensus that any challenge to the facts of, say, a patriotic war can be tantamount to treason. It is unsurprising, therefore, that one nation's wartime history, along with all the historiography necessary to support the edifice, sounds so different from another nation's. A given history, I therefore suggest, is only as true as those reading it judge it to be, which is why good historians are those who write convincing theses, who *advance a proposition as an argument*. Good luck with your thesis, only I hope that after reading this guide you do not need it.

词 汇 表

引语段落（节录） 长度为100个单词以上的引用方式，独立成段，没有引号，缩进排版，字体往往小于其余正文字体。

主体段落 位于序言段落与结论段落之间，大概250—350个单词。以主题句开始，以承上启下的结论性评述结束，以论据和论证为主要内容，并往往明示或者隐含了总论点的一个主要因素。

引证 从原文——无论是第一手还是第二手资料——中选取特定的部分进行正式的引证，可以引用原文中的语录、主张、论点、材料、事实（而非常识），[1] 在正文引用部分标示脚注符号，并在相对的脚注中精确标明资料来源的信息。首先，它告诉读者某些信息并非来源于你的原始思考或者亲身观察，而是来源于其他方式；其次，它可以引导读者亲自阅读引文资料来源以便证实你所引用的内容是正确的。

计量历史学 依靠数据，运算建模以及统计学进行历史研究的方法，往往应用于经济史或环境史领域。典型的作品是由经济学家罗伯特·福格尔和斯坦利·恩格尔曼合著的 *Time on the Cross*（《不公正时代：美国黑奴经济学》），该著作主张，使用自由劳动力进行劳动其实比使用种植园奴隶更加有利可图。

博士学位论文 一篇博士学位论文，往往由答辩委员会（导师与两到四名读者组成）进行审核，并举行公开答辩。博士学位论文是一篇学术性的多章学术专著，呈现基于档案研究的、原创的、有价值的论点，其容量通常为300—500页，双倍行距（80000—140000个单词）。

领域 你专业的主要分支之一。现列举一些历史学科的分支领域如：早期近代中国史、法国外交史、全球环境史、美国劳工史、古代军事史等。

检索工具 从卡片索引到在线文本搜索数据库，凡是能提供研究者评估档案馆藏情况的工具。

脚注参考 位于页末的、10号字体的注释，确切标明所引资料的来源以便其他研究者可以轻易找到它。

脚注参考号码 脚注位于句末（复合脚注位于段末）的上标阿拉伯数字注码，提供与脚注参考相对应的位置信息。

---

1. 再次强调，使用别人的总体观点也被看做引文，即引文不但包括逐字引用，也包括使用别人的不以逐字的方式引用的主张、论点、材料、数据。——译者注

GLOSSARY

block quotation (extract)   a lengthy quoted passage of 100 words or more, indented, as a paragraph, without quotation marks, and typically set in a smaller font size.

body paragraph   situated between introductory and concluding paragraphs, of around 250–350 words, beginning with a topic sentence and ending with a concluding remark, transitioning into the following paragraph, being of an evidentiary or interpretive nature, and typically containing or advancing a single main point that is a component part of the thesis.

citation   your formal acknowledgment of the source—primary or secondary—for a specific quotation, idea, argument, body of information, or factual data (other than common knowledge) that you have employed in your work, consisting of a footnote reference number and an accompanying footnote containing information that accurately references the source. First, it tells your reader that the information you are presenting derives not from your original thinking or first-hand observation but rather from another source; second, it enables the reader to visit the source in order to verify that the information you have provided is correct.

cliometrics   a historiographical method that relies on data, computational modeling, and/or statistics, typically in the fields of economic or environmental history. An archetype was *Time on the Cross* by economists Robert Fogel and Stanley Engerman, which argued that plantation slavery was less profitable than free labor would otherwise have been.

dissertation   a doctoral dissertation, typically adjudicated by a committee (advisor and two to four readers), presented at a public defense, comprising a scholarly, multi-chapter monograph based on archival research, of around 300–500 double-spaced pages (80,000–140,000 words), and which presents an original and significant thesis.

field   a major branch of your discipline; early-modern Chinese, French diplomatic, global environmental, U.S. labor, and ancient military history are all fields of the discipline of history.

finding aid   a device—from a card index to an online text-searchable database—that enables a researcher to evaluate the contents of an archival collection.

footnote reference   a note, set at the bottom of the page in 10-point type, identifying a source with sufficient accuracy for another researcher to

期刊文章 经过同行评鉴后，因其学术意义出版的大约6500个单词的研究性论文。

硕士论文 与博士学位论文构成相同，只是长度略短的作品，不像博士学位论文那么强调其论点（论证）的原创性和学术价值性，不一定需要通过公共答辩。

精练 删繁去冗——去芜存菁；précis是法语精确描述的意思，在英式英语中，意为缩写，通过删掉不必要的细节以呈现段落的主旨。

第一手资料 如日记、回忆录、信件、报告、演讲、新闻报道、采访、照片、漫画、影片或文化遗物等当时的或者与研究直接相关的原始资料。

路线图 一份著录、综述，或者目录，主要用于预告你的论文、论文章节或者整个研究计划的结构——即按出现的顺序写出文章中各部分的主旨——往往位于序言段落或者序言部分。

第二手资料 一篇基于原始资料而写成的期刊文章或者专著，或者一本合集收录了大量基于原始资料的第二手资料，在某些历史学研究和当代学术作品评论中，第二手资料也可能成为研究的第一手资料。

毕业研究论文（或者成为毕业学位论文、学年论文、毕业论文） 与硕士论文相似的本科论文，但是要求与研究生论文标准相比更为宽松。

副标题 设置为粗体字或者斜体字的标题，位于文章或章节部分的开头或者主要段落观点之间，通常副标题与下一个副标题之间会间隔1000—2000个单词。

论文 抽象地说，它是"以论证的形式提出论点"；具体地说，它是基于档案研究并提出独创性观点的学术作品，例如，研究性论文、硕士论文、博士学位论文等。

论题 选取你所研究领域的一个分支后所构成的你的研究对象。

主题句 在论文的语境中起到介绍相关段落，并暗示或描述其段落与该文章论点相关的功能的句子，没有主题句的段落就缺乏了目的和方向。

easily locate it.

footnote reference number a superscripted Arabic numeral placed at the end of a sentence (or paragraph for a compound footnote) that identifies a matching footnote reference located at the bottom of the page.

journal article a research paper generally of 6,500 words intended for a peer-reviewed scholarly publication.

master's thesis similar to a doctoral dissertation but typically of shorter length, with less emphasis on the originality and significance of the thesis (argument), and not always subject to a public defense.

précis cut the clutter—vanquish the verbiage; French (render with precision), in common usage in British English, meaning to shorten, to present the gist of a passage by discarding unnecessary detail.

primary source an original source such as a diary, memoir, letter, report, speech, newspaper article, interview, photograph, cartoon, film, or artifact created at the time of, or directly pertaining to, the period under study.

road map a description, overview, or list that maps out the structure—the main points in the order they appear—of your paper, chapter, or entire project, typically located at the end of an introductory paragraph or section.

secondary source a work such as a journal article or monograph that relies on original primary sources, or a synthesis that draws in large measure on other secondary sources that are themselves based on primary sources; in the case of a historiographical study or contemporary critique, secondary sources can become primary sources.

senior research paper (senior honors thesis, school year thesis, graduation thesis) similar to a master's thesis but conducted at the undergraduate level to less exacting standards.

subhead a heading set in distinctive bold or italicized type, at the start of a section or main-point break in an article or chapter, typically of between one and two thousand words.

thesis *a proposition advanced as an argument*; in its concrete form, a scholarly work of archival research that makes an original argument, such as a research paper, MA thesis, or doctoral dissertation.

topic a subset of your field that frames the subject of your research.

topic sentence introduces a paragraph and suggests or describes its function in the context of your thesis; a paragraph without a topic sentence will lack purpose and direction.

标示和编辑符号

✓	good thought or well phrased prose
awk	awkward expression
?	ambiguous, vague, or needs clarification
inf coll	informal language; colloquialism
p	passive voice used ineffectively, excessively
sp	spelling error
ww	wrong word
e.g.	provide example(s)
∽	transpose "I saw, I came, I conquered."
ℒ	delete "The dogs went too the park together."
∧	caret (insert) "The dog went to the park together."
⌃ ⌵	comma; apostrophe; quote mark; period "In 1930 Gomás dog said, Woof"
⌒ #	close up (one word); space "The board walk is way out over there."
◯	spell out "The US went to war 6 times during the 20th century."
≡	capitalize "Henry Kissinger and president Nixon boarded air force one."
/	lowercase "The President declared a State of Emergency."
=	smallcaps "Stonehenge was built in 5000AD." This looks better: "5000AD."
= ∧	hyphen "Short term margin-calls are retro active."
eN	en dash "The Great War (1914-1918)" should be "The Great War (1914–18)"
em	em dash "Next year--when I am older--I go to school." "Next year—when . . ."
¶	paragraph (wrap to a fresh, indented paragraph)
⌇	run in (close up line or paragraph break)
―	italics "The fin de siècle was characteristic of the end of the nineteenth century."

Marking and Editing Codes

✓	good thought or well phrased prose
awk	awkward expression
?	ambiguous, vague, or needs clarification
inf coll	informal language; colloquialism
P	passive voice used ineffectively, excessively
sp	spelling error
ww	wrong word
e.g.	provide example(s)
∩	transpose "I saw⌣I came,⌣I conquered."
⨍	delete "The dogs went to͟o͟ the park together."
∧	caret (insert) "The dog̭ went to the park together."
⌃ ⌄	comma; apostrophe; quote mark; period "In 1930 Gomás dog said, Woof."
⌒ #	close up (one word); space "The board⌣walk is way out over there."
○	spell out "The US went to war 6 times during the 20th century."
≡	capitalize "Henry Kissinger and president Nixon boarded air force one."
/	lowercase "The President declared a State of Emergency."
=	smallcaps "Stonehenge was built in 5000AD." This looks better: "5000ᴀᴅ."
≡⁄∧	hyphen "Shortterm margin-calls are retro⌢active."
eN	en dash "The Great War (1914-1918)" should be "The Great War (1914–18)"
em	em dash "Next year--when I am older--I go to school." "Next year—when . . ."
¶	paragraph (wrap to a fresh, indented paragraph)
⌒	run in (close up line or paragraph break)
—	italics "The fin de siècle was characteristic of the end of the nineteenth century."